THE

PUBLICATIONS

OF THE

Northamptonshire Record Society

FOUNDED IN DECEMBER, 1920

VOLUME XXIV

FOR THE TWO YEARS ENDED 31 DECEMBER 1971

DANIEL EATON. Painter Unknown.

THE LETTERS OF DANIEL EATON

TO THE

THIRD EARL OF CARDIGAN

1725 - 1732

EDITED BY

JOAN WAKE

AND

DEBORAH CHAMPION WEBSTER

Printed for
The Northamptonshire Record Society
by Dalkeith Press Limited
Kettering, Northamptonshire
1971

PRINTED IN GREAT BRITAIN

CONTENTS

ILLUSTRATIONS

PREFACE

THE letters here printed form part of the estate records of Edmund Brudenell Esq. of Deene Park, Northamptonshire, who has very kindly endorsed the permission formerly given by his father, the late George Brudenell Esq., for their publication by the Northamptonshire Record Society.

Daniel Eaton was land steward (hereinafter called steward) to the third Earl of Cardigan, on whose absences from Deene he was required to keep his master informed in writing of everything relating to the estate and household which was under his control. The reader will therefore find in Eaton's letters the picture of the running of a landed estate in the Northamptonshire and Leicestershire of the early eighteenth century, with its particular emphasis on Deene and Deenthorpe, and will also gain an impression of the recreations of the country gentry of the period. In them we are also introduced by name to some two hundred farmers, craftsmen and labourers who are seen actively at work in the woods and fields, and also to a number of professional men—stewards, clergy, lawyers, and surveyors in the neighbourhood of Deene or in London.

Those wishing to explore further any of the subjects dealt with in the letters will find much relevant material in the Brudenell MSS. and also in other private collections of records which have been so generously made available by their owners to students of history in the Northamptonshire Record Office at Delapre Abbey.

The letters were written on double sheets of foolscap paper imported from Holland, as is shewn by the "Pro Patria" watermarks. They were then folded into three, one section being tucked in between the other two and then sealed at the join. The direction (and postmark, if any) was added on the outside. This was before the days of envelopes. If a letter only occupied one sheet, the second sheet bearing the direction has since been torn off (paper was scarce in those days), thus destroying evidence of Lord Cardigan's itinerary. An account of the postal system of those days will be found in Appendix VII.

Apart from their subject matter the letters provide an interesting example of letter writing in the eighteenth century of a type which has rarely found its way into print. The three examples of which facsimiles are here given illustrate the handwriting and style of three different grades of English society.

Most readers of this book will realise that the dates used by Eaton were those normally current in England in the early eighteenth century, before the adoption of the Gregorian calendar, the "New Style", in 1751-2. Before 1752 the New Year began on 25 March; the editors have therefore given double dates (both old and new styles) for the letters written between 1 January and 24 March. All other dates in this book are in the "New Style".

J.W.

ACKNOWLEDGMENTS

So many people have helped in the preparation of this book during several years that we can hardly hope to mention them all by name. The letters were typed by Miss Monica Kirby, Miss Patricia Morris (now Mrs. Mather), and Mrs. Warren O. Ault. Dr. R. W. Hunt greatly facilitated the work of the editors by allowing the deposit of the letters in the Bodleian Library.

Sincere gratitude must be expressed by both editors to Mr. P. I. King, Chief Archivist of the Northamptonshire Record Office, and his staff at Delapré Abbey, and Miss Eleanor Charlton, for answering many queries; and to Miss Deborah Webster (now Mrs. Ivor Rogers) for research in the Brudenell MSS., and for other material help.

Mr. Edmund Brudenell has kindly allowed us to reproduce the portrait of Lord Cardigan and the letters of Daniel Eaton and William Wade; Mrs. Charles Eaton the portrait of Daniel Eaton; and the Duke of Buccleuch the letter of Lord Cardigan. To Mr. Bruce Bailey we are greatly indebted for the plan of the Deene estate in the third Earl's time, and to Mrs. G. D. Ramsay for the map of Deene and the surrounding parishes on p. xxii.

Our thanks are due to Dr. L. A. Parker for finding the third Duke of Rutland's hunting agreement at Belvoir Castle and for providing the transcript thereof, and to the present Duke of Rutland for permission to print it, as Appendix V; to Mrs. George Brudenell and the Hon. Mrs. Brudenell for information about the Deene estate; to Miss Margaret Crum for information on the watermarks of the paper on which the letters were written; and to Mr. G. F. Oxley for his account of the postal aspect of the letters (Appendix VII); to Mr. Paul Davenport of the *Oxford English Dictionary* staff, for material help with the Glossary; to Mrs. Anthony Pott, for copying Daniel Eaton's will in Somerset House (Appendix VI); to Dr. E. J. King and Professor C. N. L. Brooke for the assistance they have kindly given in the last stages of this book; and to our printers for all the care and attention they have devoted to their side of the work.

On her own behalf Mrs. Webster wishes to thank Mr. D. Allen Clewly and Mr. and Mrs. Clement Kendall for help with agricultural terms. And Miss Wake desires to thank Lord Spencer and Sir Gyles Isham for their help with the section on fox-hunting, Mrs. Penning-Rowsell for patiently typing many successive copies of the Introduction, Mrs. Green for much effective proof-reading and finally, to express her deep obligation and gratitude to Mrs. Howard Colvin who, in a very busy life, has given her countless hours of experienced, and to Miss Wake most enjoyable, editorial and research assistance, without which this edition of Dan Eaton's letters would never have been finished.

ABBREVIATIONS and SIGNS

A.S.R. 252 & 253
: Brudenell MSS., Accounts, Surveys and Rentals series, two volumes of estate accounts for 1727 to 1729 and 1729 to 1732.

B.D.
: Joan Wake, *The Brudenells of Deene* (1953).

Bridges
: John Bridges, *The History and Antiquities of Northamptonshire* (1791).

Finch
: Mary E. Finch, *The Wealth of Five Northamptonshire Families* (N.R.S., XIX, 1956).

H.M.C.
: Historical Manuscripts Commission.

I.Corr.
: The in and out letters of Sir Justinian Isham, 4th baronet of Lamport (1658-1730), at the N.R.O.

I(L).
: The Isham Collection of MSS., formerly at Lamport Hall, as above.

N.R.O.
: Northamptonshire Record Office.

N.R.S.
: Northamptonshire Record Society.

Nichols
: J. Nichols, *The History and Antiquities of the County of Leicester*, 4 vols (1795-1811).

Mont.Corr.
: Correspondence of the Montagu Family in the collection of the Duke of Buccleuch at Boughton House, Northants.

Pettit
: P. A. J. Pettit, *The Royal Forests of Northamptonshire. A Study in their Economy*, 1558-1714. (N.R.S., XXIII, 1968).

V.C.H.
: Victoria County History.

Wright
: T. Wright, *Dictionary of Archaic and Provincial Words* (1846).

SIGNS IN THE TEXT

[   ]   *Word(s) omitted in error by the author of the letter and supplied conjecturally by the editors*

[   ]   *Word(s) lost or illegible and supplied by the editors*

[ᵈ]   *Words written in error and subsequently deleted*

[ⁱ]   *Words inserted, either between the lines or in the margin*

CONCORDANCE

The first column gives the number of the letter in Bru. MSS., F. iii; the second refers to the present edition.

1	1	17 January 1724/5	57	69	7 August 1726			
2	2	22 ,, ,,	58	70	17 ,, ,,			
3	3	27 ,, ,,	59	72	7,8 September 1726			
4	4	1 February ,,	60	71	11 ,, ,,			
5	5	6 ,, ,,	61	82	13 October ,,			
6	7	13 ,, ,,	62	73	15 September ,,			
7	8	27 March 1725	63	74	18 ,, ,,			
8	9	10 April ,,	64	75	20 ,, ,,			
9	10	20 ,, ,,	65	76	25 ,, ,,			
10	11	25 ,, ,,	66	77	29 ,, ,,			
11	12	2 May ,,	67	78	2 October ,,			
12	13	4 ,, ,,	68	79	4 ,, ,,			
13	14	6 ,, ,,	69	80	6 ,, ,,			
14	15	9 ,, ,,	70	81	9 ,, ,,			
15	16	13 ,, ,,	71	83	16 ,, ,,			
16	17	15 ,, ,,	72	84	18 ,, ,,			
17	18	18 ,, ,,	73	85	19 ,, ,,			
18	19	20 ,, ,,	74	86	22-3 ,, ,,			
19	21	27 ,, ,,	75	87	26 ,, ,,			
20	22	30 ,, ,,	76	88	30 ,, ,,			
21	23	1 June ,,	77	89	31 ,, ,,			
22	24	3 ,, ,,	78	90	5 November ,,			
23	25	4,6 ,, ,,	79	91	8 ,, ,,			
24	26	8 ,, ,,	80	92	12 ,, ,,			
25	27	10 ,, ,,	81	93	12 ,, ,,			
26	28	12 ,, ,,	82	95	14 ,, ,,			
27	29	17 ,, ,,	83	94	16 ,, ,,			
28	31	22 ,, ,,	84	97	19 ,, ,,			
29	33	27 ,, ,,	85	98	21 ,, ,,			
30	34	1 July ,,	86	99	3 December ,,			
31	35	11 ,, ,,	87	100	6 ,, ,,			
32	36	13 ,, ,,	88	101	7 ,, ,,			
33	37	15 ,, ,,	89	102	18 ,, ,,			
34	38	18 ,, ,,	90	103	27 ,, ,,			
35	41	24 ,, ,,	91	104	29 ,, ,,			
36	42	27 ,, ,,	92	105	31 ,, ,,			
37	45	7-8 August ,,			{ 1 January 1726/7			
38	46	10 ,, ,,	93	96	16 November 1726			
39	47	12 ,, ,,	94	114	4 February 1726/7			
40	48	15 ,, ,,	95	106	4,5 January 1726/7			
41	49	11 November 1725	96	107	7 January 1726/7			
42	50	13 ,, ,,	97	108	12 ,, ,,			
43	51	16 ,, ,,	98	109	17 ,, ,,			
44	54	9-11 December 1725	99	110	21-2 ,, ,,			
45	40	22 July 1725	100	112	31 ,, ,,			
46	57	8 February 1725/6	101	113	1,2 February ,,			
47	58	11 ,, ,,	102	115	7 ,, ,,			
48	59	16 ,, ,,	103	116	9 ,, ,,			
49	60	22 ,, ,,	104	117	12 ,, ,,			
50	61	1-2 March ,,	105	118	19 ,, ,,			
51	62	4 ,, ,,	106	119	22-3 ,, ,,			
52	63	7 ,, ,,	107	120	26 ,, ,,			
53	64	19 April 1726	108	121	4 March ,,			
54	65	21 ,, ,,	109	122	8 ,, ,,			
55	66	24 ,, ,,	110	123	13 ,, ,,			
56	68	1 May ,,	111	124	18 ,, ,,			

112	125	25 March 1727	140	155	18 January 1728/9
113	126	29-30 March ,,	141	156	18 ,, ,, [sic]
114	127	9 April 1727	142	157	20 ,, ,,
115	128	13 ,, ,,	143	158	25 ,, ,,
116	129	18 ,, ,,	144	159	27 April 1731
117	130	20 ,, ,,	145	160	2 May ,,
118	131	23 ,, ,,	146	161	13 ,, ,,
119	132	25 ,, ,,	147	162	5 March 1731/2
120	133	26-7 ,, ,,	148	163	11 ,, ,,
121	134	30 ,, ,,	149	166	28 May 1732
122	136	4 May ,,	150	165	24 ,, ,,
123	137	7 ,, ,,	151	167	4 June ,,
124	142	18 ,, ,,	152	138	8 May 1727
125	139	11 ,, ,,	153	55	16 December 1725
126	140	14 ,, ,,	154	52	20 November 1725
127	141	16 ,, ,,	155	30	20 June 1725
128	143	21 ,, ,,	156	6	7 February 1724/5
129	144	25 ,, ,,	157	39	20 July 1725
130	145	28 ,, ,,	158	67	26 April 1726
131	146	30 ,, ,,	159	20	24 May 1725
132	147	1 June ,,	160	43	28-9 July 1725
133	148	6 July ,,	161	44	5 August 1725
134	149	3 October 1727	162	32	24 June 1725
135	150	9 ,, ,,	163	53	6 December 1725
136	151	11 ,, ,,	164	56	21 ,, ,,
137	152	27 November ,,	165	111	28 January 1726/7
138	153	30 ,, ,,	166	135	2 May 1727
139	154	15 January 1728/9	167	164	13 May 1732

GEORGE, THIRD EARL OF CARDIGAN. By Michael Dahl.

[Facing p. xv]

INTRODUCTION

LORD CARDIGAN[1]

Daniel Eaton's master, George Brudenell, third Earl of Cardigan, to whom these letters are addressed, was born on 29 September 1685, and was thirty-nine years of age in 1725, when these letters begin; he was some thirteen years older than Daniel Eaton. He was the elder surviving son of Francis, Lord Brudenell, and Frances Savile, his wife.[2] Lady Brudenell died in 1695, and Lord Brudenell in 1698 in the lifetime of his father, Robert, second Earl of Cardigan.

George Brudenell spent his early childhood in the Brudenell houses at Richmond and Twickenham. At the age of seventeen, with his younger and only surviving brother, James, he was sent to Rome with a tutor to complete his education under the general supervision of his first cousin the Duke of Shrewsbury, a leading Protestant and one of the outstanding and most highly esteemed characters of his age. Two months after their arrival in Rome, news came of old Lord Cardigan's death on 3 June 1703, and of George's consequent succession to the family honours and estates. In 1705 he was urged to return home by his uncle and guardian, Lord Dunbar, but he refused. He was then leading a life of dissipation in Venice, and the next we hear of him is his arrival in England on 29 April 1706, bringing with him a most undesirable woman who, according to a contemporary description, was "both old and ugly". However, he soon dropped her, reformed his ways and fell in love with Deene, where he spent the summer entertaining his friends with wild extravagance, culminating in a huge house party for the celebration of his coming-of-age on Michaelmas Day, 1706, when the festivities lasted for a week.[3]

Cardigan was still nominally a Roman Catholic, but on becoming engaged to Elizabeth Bruce, daughter of the Earl of Ailesbury, he gave his word that he would join the Church of England. The marriage was celebrated on 15 May 1707, at St. Martin's-in-the-Fields, by Dr. William Wake, Bishop of Lincoln, who wrote in his diary: "In the evening I married Lady Betty Bruce to Lord Cardigan".[4] There is still at Deene a large Bible which the Bishop gave to Cardigan, doubtless as a wedding present. On 12 January 1708, he took the oaths of Allegiance and Supremacy and his seat in the House of Lords, and was then in a position to take his full share in the life of the country. "From the time he married"—so wrote after his death his friend Lord Perceval—"he quitted all condemnable diversions, and made a very good husband, master, and father".[5]

---

[1] This account of Lord Cardigan is taken chiefly from Joan Wake, *The Brudenells of Deene*, (1953), ch. VII.
[2] The elder brothers had died in infancy.
[3] B.D., pp. 197-199.
[4] The diary is now in Lambeth Palace Library. Wake became Archbishop of Canterbury in 1716 and died in 1737.
[5] *H.M.C. Egmont MSS.*, i. 283, 284. Lord Perceval became Lord Egmont in 1733.

Lord Cardigan had inherited estates in Northamptonshire and four other counties, and also Cardigan House in Lincoln's Inn Fields in London, and the two houses mentioned above at Richmond and Twickenham. He rebuilt Cardigan House soon after his marriage, and there his eldest son was born in 1712, but it was destroyed by fire on 24 February 1725, with nearly all the contents including "several deeds of consequence". Cardigan's London residence thenceforth was in Clifford Street.

Queen Anne made Cardigan her Master of the Buck Hounds in 1712, but he only held the appointment for three years. Court life (and perhaps also George I, who came to the throne in 1714) was obviously not much to his taste. His principal interests were the management of his estates, farming, building, landscape gardening, and his deer park. His chief recreations were fox-hunting—including the breeding and maintenance of fox-hounds—shooting, racing, and cock-fighting. There is no mention in these letters of falconry. His favourite games were bowls and billiards. He was a man of some culture, and added to his library the works of Pope, Gay, Addison, Palladio, and Inigo Jones. Between 1720 and 1725 the learned scholar Joseph Sparke of Peterborough was employed to rearrange the library at Deene.[1] Cardigan had an easy flowing style in correspondence and a clear and graceful handwriting. (See Plate 2.)

He had four sons and two daughters, of whom the three younger sons, James, Robert, and Thomas, were born in the period of these letters and are frequently referred to by Dan. Cardigan was always on the best of terms with his brother James, whose country home was at Luffenham in Rutland, but who, as successively Master of the Jewel Office and a member of the Board of Trade and Plantations, was probably much in London. Dan used to help him with his estate affairs.

In Northamptonshire Cardigan was politically a leading Tory, and between 1714 and 1730 "his influence had been powerful in preserving the Tory representation of the County unbroken".[2] In the elections of 1714 and 1727 it was due to his efforts that Sir Justinian Isham was re-elected as a knight of the shire. His friendliness and hospitality to his country neighbours, discussed below, made this possible. He was a frequent attendant at the House of Lords[3] though, according to Lord Perceval, "he never distinguished himself there by speaking".[4]

Cardigan's country neighbours are naturally only mentioned incidentally in Dan's letters in connexion with estate affairs, but from the happy survival of the journals of Justinian Isham of Lamport[5] we have one or two intimate glimpses of him as the hospitable host at Deene, though before Dan's stewardship. On 22 June 1710, for example, Isham writes: "We set out for Lord Cardigan's whose day it was". He found there Mr. Kirkham (probably the squire of Fineshade), Lord Castlehaven,[6] "and some others, not very considerable. In the afternoon whilst they bowled", he continues, "I was to see the dog kennel which is paved with broad stones, and water in the middle, as also a handsome new pond".[7] On 7 September 1710, the

---

[1] For the interesting history of this library at Deene see B.D., pp. 238-9 and John Bridges, *History of Northamptonshire*, ii. 300.
[2] B.D., p. 204.
[3] He attended 23 times in 1725, 9 in 1726, 38 in 1727, 4 in 1728, 6 in 1729, 18 in 1730, and 8 times in 1731.
[4] *H.M.C. Egmont. MSS.*, i. 283, 284.
[5] Afterwards 5th Baronet (1687-1737).
[6] James Tuchet, 6th Earl of Castlehaven.
[7] I.L. 2686, pp. 22, 39. This kennel he had built for his pack of fox-hounds.

entry runs: "My Father and I went to Lord Cardigan's where was a pretty deal of company". Other local friends referred to in the letters are the Earl of Exeter, John, Duke of Montagu, of Boughton, Major Creed of Titchmarsh, Lord Griffin of Braybrooke and Dingley, Mr. Jackson, squire of Duddington, and another Mr. Jackson of Bulwick, Mr. Joye of Biggin, the Kirkhams of Fineshade, the O'Briens of Blatherwick, Mr. Robinson of Cransley, Lord Rockingham and his mother Lady Sondes of Rockingham Castle, Lady Strafford, Charles Tryon of Bulwick, John Tryon of Collyweston, and Lord Westmorland of Apethorpe.

Lord Cardigan was usually with his family at Deene for a few weeks over Christmas, and during the late summer and autumn. When Parliament was sitting in April and May the family were in London. He and Lady Cardigan spent a few weeks in Bath in 1730, 1731, and 1732, and the hunting season found him in Leicestershire, Lincolnshire, and Rutland enjoying his favourite sport with his special friends. When required by estate matters, but not often, he visited his Yorkshire property.

The first notification of a serious failure in Lord Cardigan's health is in the late summer of 1729, when Elmsall, his Yorkshire steward, wrote to him in some concern at his "congestion", which had prevented a visit to Yorkshire that year.[1] He was still hunting from Stroxton in November 1731, but when he went there again in February 1732, he found it too much for him and returned to Deene. By April he was seriously ill and in that month moved to Bath but became rapidly worse. "I am extremely grieved at your account of your own health, God Almighty send you better", wrote Dan to him in the last letter of this series (**167**). Cardigan was longing to get home, but only succeeded in reaching Tottenham Court in Wiltshire, the seat of his brother-in-law, Charles, Lord Bruce,[2] where he died on 5 July 1732, at the age of forty-six. His life had been short, but he had lived it to the full.

The impression of Lord Cardigan's character given by Dan's letters is perhaps of an exacting taskmaster, determined to get full value for every penny that he spent. But another series of letters written by Cardigan himself to John Booth, steward to the Duke of Montagu, shews him in a different light. In general he was on good terms with his country neighbours. A proposed exchange of land, however, with Lord Hatton (Cardigan's nearest neighbour at Kirby Hall) led to a long dispute and strained relations. But Hatton was a difficult man, and Cardigan by his own admission not always easy. In a letter to John Booth he described himself thus: "I am very tender of incroaching upon my neighbours, but I own I am very tenacious of my own rights and privileges".[3] But his letters to Booth also show him as ready to stand up for the rights of his tenants and indeed on occasion display a tender concern for the poor. For example in a letter of 10 April 1724,[4] he tells Booth of great complaints made by his Stanion tenants of damage caused by the Duke's carting across their meadow, hopes his Grace will compensate them, and points out that he himself always "hired ways out of my sales even of my own tenants".[5] On another occasion Cardigan wrote direct to the Duke of Montagu.[6] "My Lord", he said, "as I have had such frequent proofs of your Grace's goodness and charity, I take the liberty now to lay before you the unhappy circumstances of several poor labourers and

[1] Bru. MSS., F. iii. 210 (31 August 1729).
[2] Lord Bruce succeeded his father as 3rd Earl of Ailesbury in 1741.
[3] Mont. Corr., I, p. 118.
[4] *Ibid.*, p. 104.
[5] i.e. paid them for the right of carting wood across their land.
[6] Mont. Corr., I, p. 106.

cottagers of my town of Stanion, who, as I am inform'd, have incur'd your
Grace's displeasure by killing rabbetts in Geddington Chase" (a large wood
on the border of Stanion parish). These men were now being pressed by
the Duke to sign a bond which would have laid them open to prosecution
for infringing the laws of the forest, of which they had not been guilty, rabbits
being merely beasts of the warren and not of the chase, and in any case, as
Montagu pointed out, deleterious to the growth of timber. Cardigan stressed
the hardships that would result to everybody if "so many of them" were
sent to gaol, leaving their wives and children to be maintained at the expense
of the parish, and did not doubt but that the Duke would pity them.

To sum up, in these letters from Daniel Eaton his steward, we find Lord
Cardigan reflected as a typical country gentleman of most periods, the good
sportsman, the friendly neighbour, the keen and knowledgeable manager
of his estates, and seemingly, as a lively illustration of Miss Mary Finch's
thesis that successful landownership requires constant personal supervision
by the landowner of every branch of estate and household administration:
"it required hard work, a business sense, ingenuity and imagination".[1]

DANIEL EATON

Daniel Eaton was the eldest surviving son of Stephen Eaton of Deene,
a tanner by trade, by his second wife, Theophila Kettleby of Gaynes Park,
Hunts.[2] Stephen Eaton was born in 1670 and buried at Deene on 11 November
1719, so does not come within the scope of this book, but Theophila, who
lived at Deene during her widowhood and survived both Daniel and the
third Earl of Cardigan, is frequently mentioned. She was buried at Deene
on 22 June 1744.

Eatons swarmed in north and east Northamptonshire in the seventeenth
and eighteenth centuries, and are also to be found in the neighbouring shires
of Leicester and Rutland. Their names are frequently recorded in these
centuries in the parish registers and other parish records of the following
Northamptonshire villages: Irthlingborough, Great Harrowden, Stanion,
Weldon, Raunds, Woodford, Stanwick, Lowick, and both in the church
registers and borough records of Higham Ferrers,[3] and there are today many
Eaton entries in the Stamford, Peterborough, and Northampton telephone
directories.

Daniel was baptised on 26 July 1698, at Deene.[4] In addition to his half-
sister, Elizabeth Eaton (born in 1689) who "married a trooper" (**9, 130**), he
had an elder brother, Stephen, who died in infancy, and there was another
Stephen, born in 1701, who lived until 1736. Of his five own sisters, Mary,
the eldest, married William Bellamy of Deene, butcher, and Anne died in
1715 aged 12. Of Theophila, his third sister, who occurs in the letters, he
wrote "I think she has a far brighter genius than any of us" (**18**).

Class distinctions, which vary from age to age, seem certainly to have
been more fluid at this period than in the nineteenth century, and there
were many persons of independence and some education then living in the
villages who earned their livelihood as craftsmen, farmers, and tradespeople,
who could rise without much difficulty to a higher social status. Thus Dan,

[1] Finch, p. 170.
[2] Deene Parish Register, 26 December 1695.
[3] W. North's MS. extracts from parish registers.
[4] This and other particulars of baptisms, marriages and burials are from the Deene
Parish Register, unless otherwise stated.

son of a tanner and brother-in-law of the village butcher, is described as a gentleman in Deene parish register on his marriage (21 February 1731), in his farm leases towards the end of his life,[1] and in the copy of court roll of 1733 in which he appears as steward of the manor of Corby.[2] He had probably assumed this description on his enrolment as an attorney in 1727 (**137**). He appears as such in the entry of his burial in Deene parish register.

No records have survived about his early education. Whether there was a village school at Deene in Dan's boyhood is uncertain, though it is highly probable that one existed.[3] It is possible that he may have attended Oundle School, only 3 or 4 miles away, but there is a gap in the school register between 1699 and 1750. There were also grammar-schools at Kettering and Northampton at either of which he may have been a boarder. In April 1716, when Dan was 17, an item appears in the account book in the Brudenell MSS. at Deene: "Given to Daniel Eaton for his charges to London",[4] and in April the following year there are "Payments to Daniel for his master and for writing books, 6s. 6d.", and on 1 July, "Paid Daniel Eaton three months for his master, 30s.", and "10s. for his charges to Deene".[5] It seems beyond conjecture that he was sent to London for training in writing, the keeping of accounts, the handling of money, the collecting of rents, surveying, and a smattering of the law, which he probably received from Robert Webber, Lord Cardigan's principal steward, who lived at Cardigan House.[6] Dan no doubt learned much of the practical matters of the household, such as the purchase of linen and cloth, from his mother, and surely a great deal about estate affairs from his master. In the letting of farms and in keeping an eye on the tenants he had his own experience as copyhold tenant of a farm of his own to guide him.

Dan's writing first appears in the estate records on 23 February 1717, when he was 18 years of age, where we find him witnessing a receipt.[7] Robert Webber was getting old and was apparently not very active, though we find him still working in 1727 (**141**). At Deene Robert Lynwood was steward in the early years of the century and Dan probably started work as clerk or assistant steward under him. The Lynwoods had connexions with Duddington, where Robert Lynwood, described as "of Deene, gent.", acquired copyhold land in 1710. His two sons, Joseph and John, who occur frequently in the letters, were born in 1696 and 1702 respectively. John was the tenant of Winsal's Farm at Deene, living in the farm house in Deene subsequently reconstructed by Lord Cardigan as Little Deene. When Lord Cardigan took it over in 1725, Lynwood moved to Benefield (**25**). He was a Roman Catholic, but on 17 March 1726 his daughter "An" was baptised in Deene Church. He died in 1729.

Dan's duties as steward were manifold: "These included those of a present-day land agent . . . and major-domo of the household. Eaton was responsible at the age of twenty-six for . . . the supervision of the tenants in Northamptonshire, Lincolnshire, Leicestershire, and Rutland; the collection of the rents; the management of the woods; the building of cottages; alterations

---

[1] e.g. Bru. MSS., D. iv. 12, a lease from the 4th Earl of Cardigan to 'Daniel Eaton, gent.', of a farm at Deene (5 October 1736).
[2] N.R.O., YZ 4812.
[3] There are references in the Bru. MSS. to a schoolmaster at Deene in 1720, 1721 and 1722. There was a school there in the sixteenth century: B.D., pp. 82-83.
[4] A.S.R. 133.
[5] *Ibid.*
[6] B.D., p. 209. Cardigan House was in Lincoln's Inn Fields.
[7] A.S.R. 118.

and repairs to all buildings on the estate; the engagement of servants; and the payment of wages. The brewing, the brickmaking, the kitchen-garden, the stables, the kennels, the deer, the coal-supply, the purchase of cloth for the family and household, were all under his direction; accurate accounts of all incomings and outgoings had to be kept and submitted periodically for audit. His duties also comprised the annual perambulation of the parishes on the estate and attendance at the manor courts." He was also a competent surveyor and an expert valuer of standing timber.[1]

He obviously spent much of his life on horseback, chiefly riding round the Brudenell estates in Northamptonshire and Rutland. The Leicestershire manors were further afield, and his visits there often involved staying over-night. Business took him frequently to Kettering, Peterborough, and espec-ially, at least till 1727, to Stamford, where Mr. Denshire, Lord Cardigan's attorney, lived. When he got home again he had masses of accounts to write up, and during his master's frequent absences from home Dan wrote him the long and detailed reports here printed. He was busy on Sundays as well as on weekdays, and as he assures his master in letter **10**, he was never idle. He went occasionally to London and at least twice in our period to Yorkshire, to give a hand to William Elmsall, the Earl's steward on the Brudenell estates near Wakefield. He is found (from the estate accounts) holding rent audits in Lord Cardigan's outlying property at Hougham in Lincolnshire, and he occasionally attended Lord Cardigan at his hunting boxes at Hamby, Stroxton, and Cottesmore.

Dan's qualities and character shine through his letters. Of his diligence, his judgement, and intelligence, his devotion to his master's interests, his honesty, his kindness of heart and appreciation of the beautiful and his spirit when he felt he was being treated with injustice, each reader will find examples for himself as he reads these pages. Dan's attitude to his master was one of great respect, though he spoke up to him on occasion. In general, however, his letters strike a note of deference which is absent from those of William Elmsall, who was a much older man.

In the autumn of 1726 Dan had what was potentially a serious dispute with his master. After repeated complaints from the Earl, apparently annoyed at Dan's failure to write fully, and at his engagement of an assistant to transcribe the accounts for the Michaelmas audit, Dan, reduced to exasper-ation, wrote to the Earl (5 November 1726) as follows: ". . . I serve your Lordship in everything to the best of my capacity, and I wish that your Lordship was continual here, that you might take all the mony into your own hands and make what payments you thought proper. I am so far from getting anything by the payment of mony that, poor as I am, I would most willingly remit a part of my small sallary to be free from this plague" (**90**). This letter brought Cardigan to his senses. A fortnight later Dan wrote to him: "I shall most thankfully comply with any method your Lordship shall be pleased to take for reducing my accounts into a narrower compass"(**98**).

In late February or early March, 1727, at the age of 28 without informing Lord Cardigan beforehand of what he was about to do, Dan got himself enrolled in the Court of Common Pleas as an attorney ("an attorney of credit, making a certificate of my capacity"). About three months later he wrote to Cardigan and explained his reasons: ". . . whereas for these seven years past", he said, he had "disposed of a great deal of money upon mort-

---

[1] B.D., p. 211. For a closely comparable description of the duties of an eighteenth century steward see, Edward Hughes, 'Duties of an Eighteenth Century Agent', in *Essays in British and Irish History*, ed. H. A. Cronne and others (1949).

gages etc. to the general satisfaction and security of all my friends who have entrusted me as well as my own advantage, my just fees have sometimes been denied me, and I, having no authority to practise, could not redeem them by law. Now that case is altered, and I hope this may sometime or other be of conveniency to your Lordship. But I shall not endeavour to practise in any other way (**137**)." Before this date, Cardigan had employed Mr. Denshire of Stamford and his son, apparently both of them attorneys, for his local financial and legal business. But after 1 June 1727 (**147**) there are no further references in these letters to the Denshires.

Dan married at Deene on 21 February 1731, Elizabeth Sanderson, spinster, also of Deene. They had three sons, (1) Daniel, born 10 July 1732, who succeeded his father as steward to the 4th Earl of Cardigan, (2) William, who was gamekeeper to the 4th Earl, and died aged 24, and (3) Stephen, who took Holy Orders and became Archdeacon of Middlesex and a clergyman of distinction.[1]

After the third Earl's death Dan took over more land from the fourth Earl whom he continued to serve as steward. A manuscript inventory of his goods and chattels (including his farm stock but not his household goods), taken 3 February 1742, gives their value as £6025 0s. 6d.[2] Dan died on 15 January 1742 and was buried in the churchyard at Deene.

THE BRUDENELL ESTATES

On his grandfather's death in 1703 Lord Cardigan succeeded to estates in four counties and found himself the lord of the following manors: Deene, Stanion, Glapthorne, and Corby in Northamptonshire; Stonton Wyville, Slawston, Cranoe, and Glooston in Leicestershire; and Hougham and Marston in Lincolnshire. His Yorkshire estate, which had come to him through his mother, Lady Frances Savile, was in the neighbourhood of Wakefield, and, being under the supervision of William Elmsall, comes only incidentally into Dan's letters. All the manors above mentioned except Corby, Hougham, Marston, and Glooston, had been in the possession of the Brudenells since the days of Sir Robert Brudenell, Chief Justice of the Common Pleas to Henry VIII. The younger son of a Buckinghamshire landowner, he had purchased them with the profits he had made by the practice of the law. Hougham and Marston came into the family through the marriage of Sir Edmund Brudenell with Agnes Bussy, a Lincolnshire heiress, in 1539. Glooston had been acquired in 1632 and Corby was purchased towards the close of the seventeenth century from either the first or second Lord Hatton.[3]

Northamptonshire

Some explanatory remarks at this point about the civil and ecclesiastical divisions of Northamptonshire may be helpful to the reader. The County with the Soke of Peterborough contained some 330 parishes. The civil parishes did not always coincide with the ecclesiastical. Deene and Deen-

[1] H. I. Longden, *Northamptonshire and Rutland Clergy from 1500*, iv (1939), p. 191.
[2] A photocopy of this inventory, presented by Mrs. Baker, is in N.R.O.
[3] In some of these parishes there was more than one manor, e.g. a second manor in Glapthorne was acquired from Lord Cromwell in 1574. A detailed account of the descent of the Brudenell estates will be found in Finch, section VI. The population figures here given are an approximation between the Compton Census of 1676 and the first national census of 1801, except where a computation has been made from the number of families given by Bridges, which have been multiplied by five. The material for Bridges' *History* was collected between 1719 and 1724.

thorpe for example were two civil parishes until this century, but have always formed one ecclesiastical parish with the church at Deene. Neither did manors necessarily have the same boundaries as the parishes whose names they bore. In Northamptonshire there were frequently two or more manors in each parish, many of them having 'members' in adjoining parishes. Deene had members in Weldon, Corby, Gretton and Bulwick. The villages too frequently had hamlets (or 'innships' as Bridges often called them) at a distance, though usually in the same parish. The seignorial, ecclesiastical, and communal aspects of life interlocked and overlapped at every turn and were hardly sorted out until well into the nineteenth and twentieth centuries.

The position of DEENE and DEENTHORPE in relation to the situation of the Earl's other Northamptonshire manors is shewn by the plan here given. The two villages lie on either side of the main road about half way between Kettering and Stamford. The combined acreage is about 3,000 and the population in Dan's time was roughly 400.

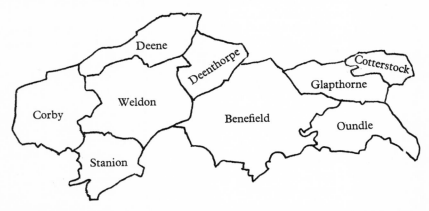

Within the limits of a manor, copyhold, freehold and leasehold land lay intermixed and the Brudenells, like other landowners, had for centuries been struggling to consolidate their estates by exchanges with their tenants. Consolidation was essential before inclosure could take place. By 1612 the whole of Deene had been inclosed (except for some pasture known as the Common), and most of it had been divided by the 1st Earl of Cardigan into consolidated farms, held under leaseholds, of from 30 to 50 acres apiece. The first Earl's efforts to inclose Deenthorpe had been defeated by Lord Hatton, then the lord of the manor there,[1] who after agreeing to inclose broke his agreement and sold his lands to his tenants and other purchasers. But by the time of the 3rd Earl these purchasers or most of them had been bought out, so that Deenthorpe as well as Deene was almost entirely in his ownership and had been completely inclosed.

The 3rd Earl had 22 farm tenants at Deene, of whom seven were paying rents of between £36 13s. 4d. and £23 5s. 6d.; six between £11 2s. 8d. and £3 10s. 0d., and nine between £2 12s. 6d. and 6s. 8d.[2] The lay-out of the farms had probably not varied much, if at all, since the time of the 1st Earl, who died in 1663. At Deenthorpe there were 27 tenants, of whom one (Mr. Conyers Peach) paid a rent of £69 15s. 5d. The rentals of eight others range

---

[1] Finch, p. 156. Cardigan probably acquired the manor with the land in the 1580s.
[2] A.S.R. 252 and 253.

from £28 19s. 6d. to £13 19s. 3d.; seven between £6 10s. 5d. and £3 3s. 0d., and thirteen between 10s. and 10d.[1] The Earl had in his own hands his home farm (or 'demesne') at Deene and Deenthorpe and also the park, which are discussed below. A half year's rents in 1729 brought in £265 7s. 1d. from the tenants of Deene and £268 3s. 2½d. from those of Deenthorpe.[2]

STANION village lies about three miles south-west of Deene, with the parish of Weldon in between. Before the present by-pass was constructed the main Northampton to Stamford road ran through the centre of the village. The acreage in 1849 was 1,850 a.[3] and according to Bridges, there were in his time "about fifty-six families there" (i.e. about 280 persons) and almost the whole parish was in the hands of George, Earl of Cardigan.[4] Cardigan had 34 farm tenants in Stanion, of whom three paid rents of £56 5s. 0d., £41 18s. 4d. and £20 12s. 6d. respectively. Ten paid between £11 17s. 6d. and £1 5s. 0d. and the rents of a further 21 were between 9s. and 9d.[5] The village lay in open-field husbandry and was not inclosed until 1805. A half year's rent in 1729 brought in £174 17s. 6d.

GLAPTHORNE is six miles from Deene, on the further side of parts of Benefield and Southwick. Whellan gives the acreage of the parish as 1,370 a. (1849), and Bridges describes it as "a village of about sixty families" (i.e. about 300 inhabitants). He also says that the whole parish, except two or three freeholds of small value, was in the possession of the Earl of Cardigan.[6] Cardigan had 14 farm and cottage tenants there, of whom 12 paid between £13 18s. 7d. and £2 17s. 6d. per annum; one paid 6s., and another 13s. 4d.[7] The arable fields of Glapthorne were very much intermixed with those of Cotterstock,[8] where Cardigan owned some land, probably appurtenant to the manor of Glapthorne. Glapthorne had been settled with other properties on Lady Cardigan at her marriage, and Dan used to ride over to collect her rent from her tenant Mrs. Steward, who lived at Cotterstock Hall (**32, 34**). In 1727 Lady Cardigan received nearly £225 as a half year's rent.[9]

CORBY is about 3 miles from Deene. In Cardigan's day, and down to the planting there of Messrs. Stewarts and Lloyd's steel-works in 1933 it was a large, long and straggling village of stone cottages. The parish contained 2,800 acres[10] and Bridges describes it as "a village of about 110 families" (about 550 inhabitants).[11] In Lord Cardigan's day about one third of the parish was covered with woods. It was in open-field cultivation until 1831. Lord Cardigan had 14 tenants there; 12 paid rents of between £13 18s. 7d. and £2 17s. 6d., one paid 6s. and one 3s. 4d. per annum. A half year's rents in 1729 brought in £69 1s. 0d.[12]

Leicestershire

The principal Brudenell manor in Leicestershire was always, and still is, STONTON WYVILLE, the rights of which had been acquired by Robert

[1] *Ibid.*
[2] A.S.R. 253.
[3] W. Whellan, *History, Gazeteer, and Directory of Northamptonshire* (1849), p. 815.
[4] Bridges, ii. 337-8.
[5] A.S.R. 252 and 253.
[6] Bridges, ii. 437.
[7] A.S.R. 252 and 253.
[8] Bridges' statement that 'the Earl of Cardigan is now lord of Cotterstock' is without foundation (ii. 438).
[9] A.S.R. 252.
[10] Whellan, *Directory of Northamptonshire*, p. 796.
[11] Bridges, ii. 295.
[12] A.S.R. 252 and 253.

Brudenell in 1499. With Stonton, the manors of Slawston and Othorpe, Cranoe and Glooston, all lying in one contiguous group, were acquired before 1512. Othorpe was only a farm and cottages and is not mentioned by Dan, but the tenants at Stonton, Slawston, Glooston and Cranoe were under his supervision and he rode over at regular intervals to collect the rents, holding his audits at Stonton Wyville. Stonton itself lies 10 miles from Deene. In the early eighteenth century there were 16 to 20 householders there (perhaps 100 people).[1] After the death of Sir Robert Brudenell the manor house was inhabited by the descendants of his younger son until the beginning of the eighteenth century and Nichols enumerates many Brudenell monuments in the church.[2] The manor had been completely inclosed before the end of the seventeenth century.[3] In 1729 a half year's rent brought in to Lord Cardigan £423 6s. 2d.[4]

Next to Stonton Wyville, SLAWSTON was the most important manor of the Brudenell estates in Leicestershire. In the early eighteenth century it had 43 households (about 215 people).[5] Writing in 1798, Nichols described the village as "long, narrow, and dirty".[6] Slawston was still in open-field in 1726, and in 1727 Cardigan, whose Northamptonshire property had benefited so much by inclosure in the previous century, decided to inclose the parish (**131**).[7] After several months of negotiation, including an interview with the commoners of the manor in the library at Deene, no progress had been made as a few freeholders, including the other chief landowner, Francis Edwards Esq., of Welham, were in opposition. Dan wrote to the Earl (**142**) "I believe an Act of Parliament will be the surest way to complete it". Lord Cardigan had 14 tenants in Slawston,[8] and in 1729 a half year's rent brought in £147 8s. 3d.[9] The parish was ultimately inclosed in 1793.[10]

GLOOSTON, close by, had in the early eighteenth century 25 households (a population of about 125).[11] About half the parish had been inclosed by the early seventeenth century but the remainder was open field until 1825.[12] In 1637 the Brudenells already owned nearly the whole parish and had then total rents of £340 a year.[13] In 1729 a half year's rents brought in £187 18s. 3d.[14]

CRANOE had 27 households in the early eighteenth century (c. 135 people).[15] The greater part of Cranoe belonged to the Brudenells and had been administered with Glooston since the late seventeenth century. There had been some inclosure before 1637 but the village, with Glooston, was not com-

---

[1] V.C.H. Leics, v. 309.
[2] Nichols, ii. 810 ff. Part of the hall still survived, then inhabited by a tenant.
[3] V.C.H. Leics, v. 310.
[4] A.S.R. 253.
[5] V.C.H. Leics, v. 297.
[6] Nichols, v. 797.
[7] The Inclosure Act was not obtained till 1793, when the Earl was allotted 810 a. In 1637 his predecessor had held 760 a., just over half the parish: V.C.H. Leics, v. 300. In 1793 the other chief freeholder and owner of three-quarters of the great tithes was Lady Jane Edwards: Nichols, v. 796. In 1731 there had been hopes that the Edwards family might sell their Slawston estate: Bru. MSS. F.iii. 243.
[8] Bru. MSS. F.iii. 269 (n.d. but c. 1731).
[9] A.S.R. 253.
[10] V.C.H. Leics, v. 297-303.
[11] Ibid., v. 113. There were 30 dwellings here in 1777: J. Throsby, The Memories of the Town and County of Leicester (1777), ii. 466.
[12] V.C.H. Leics, v. 114.
[13] Ibid.
[14] A.S.R. 253.
[15] V.C.H. Leics v. 81.

pletely inclosed until 1825.[1] In 1729 a half year's rent of Cardigan's Cranoe property brought in £168 15s. 4d.[2]

Lincolnshire

Though there are few references to it in Dan's letters, HOUGHAM was one of the most valuable of the Brudenell manors: in 1635 the rents amounted to £1,176 11s. 4d. and nearly 100 years later, in 1729, it brought in £1,014 16s. 2d. Like MARSTON, Lord Cardigan's other Lincolnshire manor, it had been inclosed in the first half of the seventeenth century. Babthorp's manor in Marston, however, produced only £405 11s. 10d. in 1635 and in 1729 Lord Cardigan's gross income from it was £362 10s. 4d.[3] The other two manors in Marston belonged to the Thorold family, to whom both Babthorp's manor and the far more valuable property at Hougham were sold in 1791.[4]

THE MANOR COURTS

One of Dan's duties was to attend the courts of Lord Cardigan's manors, and he mentions his attendances at Corby manor court in 1726 (**86, 87**) and in 1732 (**166**), and at those of Glapthorne in 1726 (**87**), and Weldon in 1729 (**154, 157**). Corby court dinner is mentioned incidentally in 1726 (**58**), and entries in the estate accounts kept by Dan of payments for manor court dinners on the Brudenell estates in Northamptonshire, and also at Slawston in Leicestershire, imply that courts continued to be held. At the end of the eighteenth century the 6th Earl was holding court baron and court leet for all his Leicestershire manors at Slawston, Slawston providing one jury and the remaining manors the other.[5]

A few references will be found in Dan's letters to "chief" or "hundred" rents. These were due to Cardigan as owner of the hundred of Corby, which as Bridges tells us had for centuries been in the possession of the lord of the manor of Corby. The hundreds were amongst the very earliest civil administrative and legal divisions in England. There were twenty in Northamptonshire, and most of them had passed from royal to private ownership by the thirteenth century. By the eighteenth century they were to all intents and purposes obsolete except for the collection of debts up to the amount of 40s. for the organisation of the militia, and for the annual collection of a few fixed fines and rents from the lords of the manors which constituted each hundred.[6]

The business at courts of manors was of a dual character. The view of frankpledge or court leet dealt mainly with matters concerning the village community as a whole and the management of the open fields, and the court baron chiefly with matters concerning the lord and his manorial tenants.

As, according to Miss Finch, the open fields of Deene were inclosed by the first Earl of Cardigan in 1612, and by 1628 most of the copyholds had been converted into leaseholds, there was no great necessity for frequent courts so far as this manor was concerned, though down to 1628 they seem to have been held with fair regularity. But for whatever cause, there is a gap

[1] *Ibid.*, v. 83; 6 George IV c. 12.
[2] A.S.R. 253.
[3] Finch, p. 200.
[4] B.D., pp. 82, 335.
[5] Nichols, v. 797.
[6] The Northamptonshire Record Office has a record of the Court of Orlingbury Hundred, held in 1850 for the appointment of a high constable: N.R.O., Young (Orlingbury) 1121.

in the surviving court rolls of this manor between 1629 and 1742, for which latter year the roll of a court for Deene and Deenthorpe, held at Deene on 26 October, has survived. There is no mention in the accounts of any court dinners at Deene in our period, so the evidence seems to show that the holding of the manor court there had fallen into abeyance. But this is not by any means conclusive, for as Stanion was still in open field cultivation, that reason alone would have made the holding of courts necessary, though again Dan is silent on the subject and in the Brudenell manuscripts there are no surviving court rolls of this manor between 1587 and 1742.

From the happy survival of a copy of court roll for the manor of Corby in the year 1733,[1] only a year after Lord Cardigan's death, we find that Dan was steward of this, as doubtless of all the Earl's Northamptonshire manors. In the Corby document, which is in his handwriting, he describes himself as "Daniel Eaton, gentleman, steward of this manor". For this office he was well qualified, both from his early training by Daniel Webber, attorney-at-law, as well as on account of his own status as a qualified attorney since early in 1727. It was not, however, essential for stewards of manors to be attorneys, though at our date it certainly seems to have been usual. Joshua Lantrow, Lord Hatton's attorney, was, for example, steward of his manors of Great and Little Weldon (both of them in open field cultivation), and this brings us to the consideration of three court rolls of these two manors for the year 1728[2] (the middle of our period), for the vivid light which they throw on the work of a manor as well as on the organisation of village life at this date, which was no doubt much the same in other manors of the neighbourhood before inclosure.

The first roll is of the court of Daniel, Earl of Nottingham[3] and William, Viscount Hatton for the manor of Little Weldon (adjoining that of Deene), held on 29 April 1728, Joshua Lantrow being steward. The business dealt with was nothing but a few presentments and fines for breach of the village by-laws, followed by the surrenders and admittances of seventeen tenants of the manor. The next roll, of 30 September 1728, is again of the court of the manor of Little Weldon. After the list of the officers of the manor, nothing but surrenders and admittances (twelve in number) are enrolled. The third roll, also dated 30 September 1728 is of the manor of Great Weldon. This deals almost entirely with the affairs of the village community and shews what an important and necessary part of rural life the manor courts played when the villages were still in open field cultivation (see Appendix IV).

On this roll are no surrenders and admittances. The record starts with the swearing-in and presentments of the officers of the manor, who, in addition to the steward and the bailiff, were the two tithing-men, the constable, the field-reeves, the ale-tasters, the overseers of the highways, and the pound-herd. Then follow the names of the fourteen men who formed the "homage or great inquest" of the manor, and the presentment of a few defaulters who had failed to attend the court. The roll then records that "the articles, pains, and orders", alias "the by-laws", of the manor, usually kept by the tithing-men, had been found to be torn and worn (they were probably on paper), and that at the request of the tenants of the manor the steward had inspected the rolls of the manor, and had read in open court the by-laws enrolled

---

[1] This copy of court roll (N.R.O., YZ 4812) was recently presented to the North-amptonshire Archives Committee by 'a gentleman of Corby'. The only business of this court was the admission of one tenant, Edward Munn.

[2] N.R.O., F.H. 991 (Great Weldon) and 4822 (Little Weldon).

[3] Daniel Finch, Earl of Nottingham and (1729) Earl of Winchelsea (1647-1730).

thereon, when certain of them had not been approved. It was then ordered, the roll goes on, by the whole homage and the free and customary tenants of the manor "that the orders and pains which follow [they had evidently been revised] shall in future be the orders and pains of this manor". Then follows the request of the court to the steward that he should enrol them on the rolls of the court, and give the tithing-men a true copy of them on parchment to be kept for the use of the tenants of the manor.

The roll then breaks out into English (all the previous business having been written in Latin) with the complete copy of the by-laws, thirty-one in number, with the amount of the fine payable for each written against it in the margin. They lay down, *inter alia*, the number of cattle and hogs which each man should keep; they provide that no man should plough up any baulk or meadow; that the hedges of the wheat field should be repaired; that the drains should be scoured; that every householder should send a stone-gatherer into the fields for six days in the year; that no person should glean peas or beans till harvest is done; that no person should keep geese except upon his own ground; that no mangy horses should be kept upon the common.

In addition to these purely agricultural regulations the laws contain some interesting orders shewing the manor at work, viz:— "That the jury [i.e. homage] shall meet every year on All Saints day at the usual place at the tolling of the bell"; "that the whole jury shall meet in the usual place to take all officers accounts when notice is given in the church"; "that every officer shall make and give up his accounts to the townsmen[1] at the church within forty days after he is off his office"; and finally "that the by-laws shall be read three times in every year, that is to say at the first parish meeting after Easter day, the first parish meeting after Lamas day, and the first parish meeting after All Saints day yearly in every year".

There are many points of interest in this roll, amongst which it may be noted that it deals with village matters generally and not solely with the manor of Great Weldon. Here in Weldon parish in 1728 were the following manors: those of Great and Little Weldon in the joint possession of Viscount Hatton and the Earl of Nottingham, also Hunter's manor and Griffin's manor,[2] belonging respectively to Lord Rockingham and to Lord Cardigan. Lord Cardigan's manor of Deene also, it will be remembered, had outlying members in Weldon. Here we find the business of the village community transacted at the court of the lord of the principal manor, that of Great Weldon. Daniel Eaton no doubt attended these courts to represent the interests of his master (**154, 157**).

The occurrence of village by-laws for the regulation of open field cultivation has been noted by Professor Ault in about five per cent of the court rolls of the Middle Ages for the midland area which he has examined in an extensive survey.[3] The similarity of those on our roll of 1728 to those of the fourteenth and fifteenth centuries is very striking.

The medieval by-laws were usually but not invariably in Latin.[4] The business of Weldon court concerning the appointment of officers, their pre-

[1] Here probably the leading men of the 'town', often the feoffees or trustees of the 'town estate'.
[2] Griffins manor was only 50 acres.
[3] W. O. Ault, 'Open-Field Husbandry and the Village Community', *Transactions of the American Philosophical Society*, N.S., vol. 55, pt. 7 (1965).
[4] The earliest of the English examples cited by Ault are one of Great Horwood, Bucks., of 1550 (no. 198, p. 85), and another of Weston-cum-Weedon, Northants, of 1564 (no. 206, p. 87).

sentments, and the surrenders and admittances of tenants of the manor is in Latin, as, until 1733, were the records of the central courts of the realm. Stewards of manors, therefore, must have had a modicum of Latin which was no doubt taught in all the town and country grammar schools of the period. The by-laws at Weldon, however, are in English. As they had to be read in open court, and a copy was required for inspection by the tenants, this was a practical convenience. Of the thirteen members of the homage by whom the orders of the court were signed on our Great Weldon roll of 1728, five were illiterate, signing by their marks.

Finally, the directions as to where the jury was to meet—"at the usual place"—are vague, but not so is the order that the officers shall give up their accounts "to the townsmen at the church". This order and the tolling of the bell to summon the jurors may mean that they also met there. For a general meeting of the villagers the church was probably the only building in the parish large enough to hold them.[1] In any event these orders shew the close connection of the church with secular affairs at this time, and indeed in the present century it is still customary for notices concerning secular government to be posted in the porches of parish churches.

Perambulations

In the Book of Homilies issued by royal authority in 1547, 1563 and 1572 and ordered to be read in churches will be found "An Exhortation to such parishes where they use their perambulation in Rogation Week for the oversight of their town", the perambulation being "the ceremony of walking officially round a forest, manor, parish or holding for the purpose of asserting and recording its boundaries". In this long exhortation are quoted texts from the Old Testament such as: "Thou shalt not remove the ancient bounds which thy fathers have laid" and others, reminding us of the malediction in the Commination Service in the Book of Common Prayer: "Cursed be he that removeth his neighbour's landmark", which originally read ". . . his neighbour's meer stones".[2] That the perambulation was regarded as a parish affair is also clearly shown in Dan's references to the subject in which he speaks of "the people of Deene" and "the people of Weldon". In his last letter Dan writes of "the meer which Weldon people made . . . upon the utmost verge of Weldon lordship", and how part of the boundary had no mark, but was traced by the Deene people at each perambulation, by agreement apparently between "the people" of each parish. In 1725 there had been trouble about the boundary between Church Langton and Stonton Wyville which was justly and amicably settled by Dan at a meeting with "Langton men" on the spot (**16**). Dan used on both occasions the word "meer" for the boundary stones or marks. He also mentions having attended the perambulation of Glapthorne in 1725, where none had been made for an interval of eight years.

Surveying

It is strange how in the days of scientific surveying with instruments these ancient customs should have survived. But in England old customs

[1] *Cf. Ibid.*, nos. 149 (p. 78), 211 (p. 89), and 223 (p. 96).
[2] Meer is derived from the Anglo-Saxon *maere*, boundary, and still survives in place names—for example, in the house known as the Mere at Little Houghton, Northants, which is next to the boundary between the parishes of Great and Little Houghton.

die hard and as Professor Galbraith has said: "New responsibilities and growing intelligence gave rise almost imperceptibly to new organizations, which for centuries might overlap and compete with the old before they finally superseded them".[1] It is interesting to find that in the eighteenth century these perambulations were taken seriously and that such dependence was still had "on the memory of mortal man". And surely a wonderful thing it is to be able, as it were, to watch the perambulators at work as we read the second paragraph of Dan's last letter of 4 June 1732 (**167**).

Dan in his letters refers to surveys which he has made of various fields, also to a plan of Little Deene and its surroundings (**123**), and to a draught of the alcove room at Deene Hall (which from its description would nowadays be called an elevation (**12**)). In letter **123** he refers to his surveying instruments and requests that Mr. Webber—who was in London with the Earl—should get him a new needle "from the person he bought my instruments of", so he was evidently among his other accomplishments a trained surveyor. This is not surprising, for land-surveying had been recognised as part of a steward's duties since the sixteenth century, and was certainly still regarded as such by some authorities in our period, though towards the end of the seventeenth century many whole time surveyors were at work.[2] Several maps of Deene survive which were made in the first half of the eighteenth century, the great era of estate map making.[3] A contemporary surveyor whom Dan mentions in connection with the proposed inclosure of Slawston was George Nunns, who was also working on several estates in Northamptonshire, including those of the Duke of Montagu, the Knightleys of Fawsley, the Thorntons of Brockhall and the Ishams of Lamport.[4]

WOODLAND

There was a large acreage of woodland on Lord Cardigan's Northamptonshire estates, all of which had been formerly part of Rockingham Forest. At Rockingham on the north-western edge of the forest William the Conqueror, as recorded in Domesday Book,[5] "ordered a castle to be made", and the site he chose, on a steep escarpment above the River Welland and domin-

[1] V. H. Galbraith, 'The Literacy of the Medieval English Kings', *Proceedings of the British Academy*, xxi (1935), p. 217.

[2] See John Fitzherbert's *Book of Husbandry* and *Book of Surveying* (both 1523). Edward Laurence, in his *The Duty of a Steward to his Lord* (1727) says that stewards should be 'full-time officials, with a good practical knowledge of agriculture' and 'a tolerable degree of Skill in Mathematics, Surveying, Mechanicks and Architecture' (pp. 22-3, 50). In this, and in the third edition of his book (retitled *The Duty and Office of a Land-Steward*, Dublin, 1731), Laurence recommended 'the improved theodolite, then recently perfected by the instrument maker, Jonathan Sisson of the Strand', quite possibly the man who supplied Dan with his instruments. Mrs. Davies has very kindly supplied me with a list of some twenty surveyors working on different estates in Northamptonshire, Buckinghamshire and Warwickshire between the mid-seventeenth century and *c.* 1710, none of whom she considers to have been land stewards, but of whom one was certainly an architect, William Talman.

[3] Other maps of the Hatton estate were made between 1582 and 1586 by Ralph Treswell. N.R.O., F.H. 272.

[4] A George Nunns in 1716 had made 'A Plan of Mannour House and adjacent places of Deene'. Mr. P. I. King informs me that there were two men of this name and that the Slawston survey was probably made by the younger (b. 1701). The Nunns were a Rushton family.

[5] *V.C.H. Northants*, i. 307. This volume contains a translation of the Northamptonshire Domesday with an interesting article thereon, both by J. H. Round.

ating the shires of Northampton, Leicester and Rutland, was certainly one of truly regal magnificence. From this castle William and his successors for the next four or five centuries hunted the deer in Rockingham Forest, for the very purpose of a forest from a monarch's point of view was the preservation of "the vert and the venison", but principally the venison.[1] A forest is "a certain territory of woody ground and fruitful pastures . . . privileged for wild beasts . . . in the safe protection of the King, for his princely delight and pleasure"—so wrote Manwood in 1592.[2] The forests therefore were subject to the laws of the forest, a highly elaborate judicial structure with a whole series of courts and a crowd of officials from justices to rangers and coppice-keepers.[3] The laws were revised from time to time and the forest boundaries altered by new perambulations, until in the nineteenth century the law of the forest was finally abolished and the portions of the old forest which remained in the possession of the Crown were handed over to the Commissioners of Woods and Forests. In our period Rockingham Forest, which had in pre-Conquest days extended from Stamford to Northampton, was reduced to an area of scattered woodland dotted with villages extending very roughly from Pipewell to Collyweston on the north, from Collyweston to Yarwell on the east, from Yarwell to Brigstock or Geddington on the south, and from Geddington to Pipewell on the west. Much even of this limited area had by the eighteenth century been granted or sold to private individuals, though even these parts remained to some extent subject to the forest law.[4]

Lord Cardigan's woods in Northamptonshire were as follows: in Deene were the large woods of Deepings and Prior's Haw, lying respectively on the south and west of the park. On the north-western edge of his estate adjoining the parish boundaries of Corby and Gretton and marching with Lord Hatton's lands and almost entirely surrounded by them, lay Deene Wood, also belonging to Cardigan, whereas the wood of Bangroves between Deepings and Prior's Haw was then the property of Lord Hatton. From 1725 until Cardigan's death in 1732 negotiations were carried on between Cardigan and Hatton for the exchange of Bangraves and Deene Wood (*see* p. xxxiii). Cardigan also owned a wood in Deenthorpe and another in Glapthorne. In the parish of Corby extensive woods had been acquired from Lord Hatton in 1686 by the second Earl of Cardigan. These woods covered about 1,200 acres,[5] and, with a large piece of waste next to them, adjoined the royal forest. In Stanion and Little Oakley both the Duke of Montagu and Cardigan owned woods which they had exchanged for others in the same parishes in 1723 (*see* p. xxxii). What woodland there was on the Brudenell estates elsewhere is uncertain.

Dan mentions "the accounts of the Leicester wood" (**88**) and woods at Glooston and Slawston are mentioned in the estate accounts. He also writes of timber in Howley Park and of valuing wood in Ardsley closes, New Park and Woodchurch (all in Yorkshire), but some of these references may concern only scattered trees and hedgerow timber.

There is no precise indication of the total acreage of the Brudenell woods in Northamptonshire in Cardigan's time, but they probably amounted to

---

[1] Pettit, p. 7.

[2] W. S. Holdsworth, *History of English Law* (7th edn., 1956), i. 94, quoting J. Manwood, *A brefe collection of the Lawes of the Forest* (1592).

[3] The forests were divided into coppices (copses) with grass ridings between them.

[4] For a full account see Pettit, *Royal Forests*. The private woods are clearly shown in the map accompanying his book.

[5] Pettit, p. 12. Bridges in his account of Corby says: 'Here are large woods the property of the Earl of Cardigan' (ii. 295).

something over 2,000 acres. The maps of the period, however, give a rough indication of their area relative to the extent of the whole estate.[1]

Owing to the growing shortage of wood for fuel, building, and the Navy in the eighteenth century, these woods were a valuable source of revenue. There are more references to the woods in Dan's letters than to any other subject, and their management was obviously one of the most important of his duties.

Lord Brudenell valued his timber at £255 15s. a year in 1635,[2] but though the wood accounts for the early eighteenth century do not survive, it is clear from the references in Dan's letters that the income in his day must have been much higher (See **1, 2, 58, 68, 112, 158, 163**).

The Purlieu Woods

Dan describes the woods in Little Oakley and Corby as purlieus or purlieu woods, and, as others have done since his day, found some difficulty in spelling this awkward word—'purlees', 'pour'lles' and 'purlue' are the forms he gives. The lawyers and the learned generally give many definitions of this word and the subject bristles with complications and difficulties. According to Holdsworth purlieus were 'certain land once forming part of the forest', still subject to the control of rangers as regarded offences against the vert and venison.[3] Cardigan's friend and neighbour, Charles Kirkham of Fineshade, defines purlieus as those portions of the royal forest which had been dis-afforested, 'excepting what related to the deer',[4] but Dr. Pettit tells us that 'the owners of purlieu land were exempt from the full burdens of forest law and were allowed to hunt the royal deer under specific conditions'. He contin-ues, 'in our later period (i.e. from 1641 to 1714) purlieu was used in this particular sense, *but was also applied hapazardly to any land or woods adjacent to the forest but outside its perambulation*'.[5]

Yet in the Rockingham Forest area the word still had a very definite legal meaning at the end of the eighteenth century, for James Donaldson, from Perthshire, who was commissioned in 1793 or 1794 by the Board of Agriculture to report on the agriculture of Northamptonshire, described the woods as consisting 'either of forests, chases or purlieu woods'.[6] The forests, he tells us, were subject to the depasturage of the deer and also at certain times of the year to the depasturage of the cattle of residents in the adjoining villages, but the purlieu woods, being private property, could be protected from the depredations of the deer and were therefore more profitable. His informant on this subject was Mr. Edmonds 'of Boughton house', the steward of the Duke of Buccleuch (descendant of the Dukes of Montagu). The underwood of the purlieus (and, no doubt, in all private woods in the district), he says, 'principally consists of hazle, ash, sallow, white and black thorn, and some

---

[1] In 1635, before the acquisition of the Corby woods, there were about 900 acres: Finch, p. 163 note 4.

[2] *Ibid.*, p. 200.

[3] Holdsworth, *History of English Law*, i. 97.

[4] C. Kirkham, *Two Letters to a Friend* (London and Stamford, 1726). The book is dedicated to an anonymous peer, 'a Pouralee-man and likewise a happy proprietor of numerous acres', a description which fits Cardigan better than any other of Kirkham's neighbours. Kirkham goes into much detail over early disafforestations, and claims that the statute of 6 Car. I c. 15 had finally settled the bounds of the forest and that all territories beyond them were free 'as if the same never had been forest' (pp. 10-11). (For further details of this work, including its full title, see below, p. xxxviii note).

[5] Pettit, p. 8 (my italics).

[6] J. Donaldson, *General View of the Agriculture of the County of Northampton* (Edinburgh, 1794), p. 32.

maple. It is generally cut from 11 to 14 years growth.' He then gives a detailed description, here summarised, of the method of the cutting, valuing and selling of the timber and underwood in the purlieus. After the fall of the leaf the woods were parcelled out into small lots or 'sales', of about a rood in extent, trenches being dug between each sale. The underwood was then valued and sold standing, for fuel, or hurdle-making. The standing timber in the sales was sold after the underwood, principally to 'carpenters, joiners, wheelwrights and other artificers'.[1] In the forest proper separate valuations were generally put upon the timber, the top and the bark respectively.[2] Donaldson's account, although written about sixty years after Lord Cardigan's death, seems to throw much light on Dan's incidental references to the procedure followed in our period, a procedure which had apparently changed very little in the intervening years.[3]

The reader of Dan's letters must bear in mind his terminology with regard to woodland. A 'sale' in these letters, when used in reference to woods, with one or two exceptions quite definitely means an *area* of woodland or park where the trees and underwood are to be offered for sale after much preparation in trenching, fencing and valuing.[4] As explained by Dr. Pettit, there can be no doubt that the fences of these areas were preserved for some years after felling and cutting, to protect the 'spring' (young growth) from depredations by the deer. That by 'viewing' Dan meant valuation is perfectly clear.[5] To take two examples out of many, on 18 May 1725 he wrote that the wood in Corby Sale had been 'view'd too dear' (**18**), and on 29 December 1726 he wrote, 'we view'd Stanion Sale yesterday, which, according to our valuation, comes to £80' (**104**).

Lord Cardigan's Negotiations with the Duke of Montagu and Lord Hatton

Both the Duke of Montagu and Lord Cardigan owned extensive woods in the parish of Stanion and Little Oakley, and the Duke's deer caused Cardigan great annoyance by escaping from Geddington Chase into his woods which adjoined the Chase. There they did great damage to the young saplings and, to the equal annoyance of the Duke, were killed by Cardigan's servants. But the two men were on good terms with each other, and also with each other's stewards, so that after negotiations, surveys, valuations and correspondence lasting for three years, an agreement for an exchange of woods was arrived at which was confirmed by Act of Parliament in 1723.[6]

Encouraged by the success of these exchanges with the Duke of Montagu, Cardigan hoped to settle his more complicated disputes with another neighbour in a similar manner. No fewer than twenty-three of Dan's letters refer to the long negotiations and disputes with Lord Hatton of Kirby Hall over their adjacent woods.[7] These differences were complicated by the fact that Hatton's lands, or some of them, lay in Rockingham Forest and were subject to the forest law, whereas Deene had been exempted from forest jurisdiction

[1] *Ibid.*, p. 38. Cardigan, however, sold much of his timber to chapmen.
[2] *Ibid.*, p. 35.
[3] Thomas Hardy, in *The Woodlanders*, gives vivid descriptions both of an auction sale of wood and of the process of barking trees for the tanners. I am indebted to Mrs. H. M. Colvin for this reference.
[4] Wright's *Dialect Dictionary* gives the definition: 'a division or "quarter" of a wood, of which the underwood is cut down and sold'.
[5] This usage is given by Wright.
[6] 9 George I, c.14. In Bru. MSS., I. vii, there is a large number of documents about this exchange.
[7] There had been a little trouble early in 1725 about a boundary fence between their two estates but this had been smoothed over by Dan at a meeting with Mr. Lantro (**7**).

in the middle ages when it was a grange of Westminster Abbey. Cardigan was of the opinion that the simplest way to solve the problem would again be by an exchange of woods, and in 1725 he started negotiations to this end. Owing to the fortunate survival of two series of his own letters on the subject, one to Lord Hatton,[1] the other to John Booth, the Duke of Montagu's steward,[2] it is possible to give an outline of Cardigan's side of the story partly in his own words.

On 8 February 1731 he wrote to Mr. Booth: 'My wood is call'd Deene Wood, and lyes in the heart of my Lord Hatton's Forest, and my Lord's wood is call'd Bangraves and lyes upon my park pale' (i.e. between the two other woods of Deepings and Prior's Haw, both belonging to Cardigan). On the exchange being proposed Hatton at first seemed willing to negotiate, and each chose three men to meet and value the woods, 'which they all did, and sign'd both valuations (i.e. one for Hatton, one for Cardigan). But for what reason I never could hear, this affair was drop't by his Lordship, who at first was much more earnest for the exchange than I was, for my wood can destroy most of his forest . . . but since we have lived in a state of war. I have kill'd great numbers of his deer and this unneighbourly way is likely to continue, unless such a person as the Duke of Montagu wou'd undertake to be a mediator.'[3] From the next letter we learn that the Duke has offered his mediation, and that Mr. Booth is 'to be the sollicitor who is not only conversant in these affairs, but seems to shew a friendly zeal to settle harmony and good neighbourhood'.[4] On 22 February Cardigan wrote that Deene Wood was 'full 45 acres' with good timber and fine saplings; Bangraves was 'near 75 acres', and no timber, or very large top saplings, so that there was no very great difference in value. 'Deene Wood lyes actually in the heart of the forest, and I have kill'd within these twelve months upwards of 50 brace of deer'.[5] On 29 May Cardigan sent to Booth particulars of the lands which he proposed to give to Hatton with Deene Wood in exchange for Bangraves, pointing out that these lands were all inclosed and therefore proportionately of greater value than land subject to common rights. He added that so long as Deene Wood belonged to him he had the power of killing any of Hatton's deer, which power was worth a consideration additional to the value of the lands.[6] Cardigan thought Hatton's proposals impracticable, and was convinced that he was not in earnest about the exchange. Cardigan was also sure that Parson Goode, the rector of Weldon, (who had rights in part of the lands to be exchanged) was stirring up trouble between him and Hatton—"that incendiary" as he described him more than once in the course of the correspondence.

Lord Cardigan also had disagreements with Lord Hatton over free hay,[7] i.e. over hunting rights in those parts of the Brudenell estate which had once been royal forest, and over the rights of the commoners of Weldon and Corby to depasture their cattle in the purlieu woods of Rockingham Forest and in an area of waste land adjoining Deene Wood. Cardigan wrote to Booth on 10 July 1731: 'I claim free hay through the whole Lordship of Deene

---

[1] B.M., Add. MS. 29569.
[2] Mont. Corr., I, pp. 101-5, 108-119.
[3] Ibid., p. 109.
[4] Ibid., p. 110.
[5] Ibid., p. 111.
[6] Ibid., p. 115.
[7] 'The suffix "hay" ("gehaeg"), originally meaning an "inclosure", was used in medieval English to denote "part of a forest fenced off for hunting": Stenton and Mawer, Chief Elements in English Place-Names, pt. 2, p. 30.

originally granted to the Abbots of Westminster, under whom I claim. There is a piece of waste ground, out of all dispute in my opinion, in Deene Lordship, it joins upon Deene Wood. Peach Lord Hatton's keeper hangs sewels,[1] not only upon the waste, but even upon the hedge of Deene Wood . . . this is a manifest infringement upon my rights . . . This waste is the place where my tenants turn their cattle upon, which from thence escape into the Forest, in which place Deene tenants have right of common . . . Tho' this thing in dispute is of no value, yet the subjecting of any part of Deene Lordship to the Forest rules, is what I can't comply with upon no terms, knowing that I have an undoubted right from the Abbotts to enjoy all libertys and priviledges they formerly enjoy'd, and I am sure no subsequent grant or preambulation can prejudice what was originally granted by the Crown to the said Abbotts.'[2] 'We have', he continued in another letter, 'enjoy'd the Deene estate ever since Harry the Seventh, we bought it of Ivo de Deene, who bought it of the Abbotts of Westminster, . . . and we pay to the Dean and Chapter of Westminster for ever 18 (pounds) a year.'[3] Cardigan was evidently able to convince Hatton that he was in the right, for three weeks later he wrote to Booth the letter which is illustrated on the opposite page and of which a text appears below.

Early in 1732 further trouble arose, referred to at length in Dan's last two letters (**166, 167**). Cardigan claimed a right of way leading out of Prior's Haw across Hatton's land to Weldon village. As Cardigan wrote to Booth from Stroxton on 21 February 1731: 'Since Prior's Haw was a wood, noone can disprove but the timber and underwood was ever brought down one particular road to Weldon and no other.'[4] In another letter Cardigan told Booth what had occurred: 'Peach, keeper to my Lord Hatton, did in company with others, enter into an agreement to meet the next morning at Prior's Haw

[1] Sewell, a line of feathers fastened on twine and placed a foot or two from the ground in the open parts of a forest, to keep the deer within bounds: A. E. Baker, *Northants Glossary*, ii. 216.

[2] Mont. Corr., I, p. 117.

[3] *Ibid.*, p. 118. Cardigan's history is not impeccable here: the Brudenells had owned Deene since the reign of Henry VIII, and Ivo de Deene had been the Westminster tenant in the time of King John (Bridges, ii. 300-1). The Brudenell family still pay £18 a year to the Ecclesiastical Commissioners.

[4] Mont. Corr., I, p. 114. A road in a wood meant a grass road or riding. Cross country 'roads' were then as often as not 'green lanes', i.e. covered with grass. Weldon village was about two-thirds of a mile from the edge of Prior's Haw.

Mr Booth   Deene.   August 2 :   1731

I send you tomorrow an Haunch of venison, which I hope will be with you on Wednesday morning, & come sweet.

I am for Yorkshire on Friday next in order to settle some of my affairs there, from thence I shall wait on the Duke of Montagu at Naresborough.

I am glad Ld Hatton is made sensible of the errors of his keeper Peach. That fellow has been at the bottom of all disputes, and if he continues in my Lords service, his forest will be ruin'd, for I & many more destroy the deer, because they lye upon his walk, & for a punishment to him, we do it, that my Lord may know he has a bad servant.   In haste

Yr wellwishing friend & servant
Cardigan[5]

[5] Mont. Corr., I, p. 119.

Mr Booth   Deene. Aug't 2'th 1731

I send you to morrow an Haunch of
Venison, which I hope will be with you on
wednesday morning, & come sweet. ⎯

I am for yorkshire on friday next in order to
settle some of my Affairs there, from thence
shall wait on the Duke of Montagu at
Naresborough. ⎯

I am glad L.d Hatton is made sensible of
the Errors of his Keeper Peach. That fellow
has been at the bottom of all disputes, and if he
continues in my lords service, his Forest will be
ruin'd, for I & many more destroy the Deer, because
they lye upon his walk, & for a punishment to
him we do it, that my Lord may know he has
a bad servant. In haste   yo.r wellwishing
                           friend & servant
                             Cardigan

LETTER OF LORD CARDIGAN TO JOHN BOOTH.
(about ¾ original size)

[Facing p. xxxiv]

bridge in order to make ditches and trenches against my wood way, to prevent anyone coming out of the wood, or to break my coach whenever I attempted to pass that way. This was agree'd upon under a penalty of money. Yesterday morning Neal Hodgkin, Wells and Lincet all of Weldon met to fulfill their wicked scheme, but Peach who had contrived this, took care not to appear, but the other three had begun when D. Eaton came to them, and advis'd them to forbear, they went no further, but return'd home with their spades.'[1] By the following June Dan had evidently consulted counsel in the persons of a Mr. Cutbeard or Cuthbert and a Mr. Rose, whose advice was that if Hatton remained adamant the cause would stand a good chance in the House of Lords, but Lord Cardigan died a month later.

Charles Kirkham was probably referring to this sort of dispute when he wrote of the feuds which might sometimes arise between "pour-allee men" owing to the uncertainty of the law as to how many deer found wandering to an alternate property may be killed, and offered a few words of friendly advice: 'Let the law of nature be the judge, and all will be well, which is, to do as you would be done by . . . Let every man that is possess'd of this right, follow but that Golden Rule before recited, then shall they enjoy the profit with a just satisfaction, and the sport and pastime with true pleasure and delight.'[2] But how it all ended the records do not relate. No Act of Parliament for the proposed exchanges was passed in the third Earl's lifetime, and the probability is that it was all left in the air when he died.[3]

THE PARK

In addition to all the land leased to farm and cottage tenants on his various manors and to the large woods on all his estates, Lord Cardigan was the owner of an immense park adjoining his family mansion of Deene Hall. So important indeed was the park that the mansion itself became known eventually as Deene Park.[4]

Parks in England were probably from the beginning, and have certainly been for the last four or five centuries, an "amenity", a status symbol, a graceful and appropriate setting for the principal residence of the family when manor houses no longer stood, as they did in earlier times, near their neighbours in or close to the village street. Twenty-seven parks were marked in Speed's map of Northamptonshire in 1610, and Morton records that over twenty were stocked with deer in 1700.[5] The possession of a herd of deer was, indeed, one of the principal reasons for having a park, but the parks themselves were and still are an outstanding part of the beauty of England.

Deene Park, one of the half a dozen largest in the County,[6] was in existence in the first half of the sixteenth century, and was enlarged by the Brudenells

---

[1] *Ibid.*, p. 113. Cardigan there described Peach as a 'notorious rogue, the man that has rais'd such an implacable dispute between the two familys of Kirby and Deene'.

[2] *Two Letters to a Friend*, pp. 14-15.

[3] Both Bangraves and Deene Wood are now part of the Brudenell estate, but Bangraves still belonged to the Finch-Hatton estate in 1878. Bangrave was also the name of a stretch of land on the north of Bangraves wood, along the S.E. border of Deene parish. This is clearly shown on Henry Paxton's map.

[4] This was probably not until the nineteenth century. Neither Morton nor Bridges call Lord Cardigan's house, Deene Park. It appears, however, as such in Britton's *Beauties of England and Wales* (1810), vol. XI, and in *Paterson's Roads*, (1829).

[5] Pettit, p. 4.

[6] The others being Fawsley, Althorp, Castle Ashby, Rockingham and Milton.

more than once in the reign of Queen Elizabeth I.[1] In 1612 the first Earl of Cardigan increased it from 183 to 240 acres, and once more in the reign of Charles I, so that by 1642 it was 350 acres in extent. This magnificent stretch of fine rolling turf studded with elm, oak, ash, thorn and other timber trees and well stocked with sheep and deer was not likely to have been reduced in size during the eighteenth century. Sections of it were occasionally fenced off and laid for hay, as indeed in the third Earl's time (9). As the architecture of the family dwelling was designed to please the eye, so was the park laid out and planted as "a prospect of inland scenery" (NED) for the recreation and aesthetic satisfaction of the owner and his friends and neighbours, a satisfaction fully shared by Dan Eaton, who wrote to Cardigan enthusiastically about the beauty of the park on more than one occasion.[2]

The park gave Lord Cardigan a splendid opportunity to emulate on a smaller scale the landscape gardening which had been a few years before carried out at Boughton with the gardens of Versailles in mind by Ralph, Duke of Montagu. As at Boughton a convenient brook (a tributary of the Willibrook) flowed the length of Deene Park from the Corby boundary, disappearing underground at intervals and re-appearing again through "swallow" or "swallet holes" as they are called.[3] This brook was diverted near the Hall, where a cascade and a canal were constructed, and beyond them a large pond, the outflow of which now runs down to the lake under a very pretty stone bridge, still one of the beauties of Deene.

The deer with which the park was stocked were a matter of great concern to the Earl, not only for their ornamental value, for they are indeed one of the most graceful of quadrupeds, but as providing a welcome variety in diet, a change from the everlasting beef and mutton. This herd, partly of red and partly of fallow deer, was no doubt descended from the wild deer of Rockingham Forest.[4] It was in the care of the park-keeper, John Peak, who lived in the lodge in the Park. He was responsible for the health of the herd (a difficult matter in the wet seasons of 1725-6 and 1726-7), for feeding them in the winter, and for killing them when venison was required. He kept a park book, namely, a record of the deer, of venison sent to London to the Earl for his household, and as presents to his friends there, as well as to many of his country neighbours and on occasion to the villages round about for a venison feast.[5] Unfortunately this book has not survived.

Venison was as much a status symbol as was a park, a much prized monopoly of the landowners. The forest villagers however also had a taste for venison, deer-stealing was rife at this and probably at every other period and Northampton gaol in the third earl's day was full of deer-stealers.[6]

Before leaving the subject of the park mention must be made of the deer leap on the boundary between Lord Cardigan's and Lord Hatton's estates, to which Dan refers in his last letter—and more especially because the term is not well defined in the NED. There is to this day a deer leap in the wall of Boughton Park which the writer was shown with pride by the late owner some 30 to 40 years ago as having been given to his ancester, Sir Edward Montagu, by Queen Elizabeth I. It is a depression in the outside of the wall

---

[1] Finch, p. 147: in 1586 'the Brudenells were seeking to enhance their prestige by extending Deene Park'.
[2] See **10, 111, 161**.
[3] See Beeby Thompson, *The Brooks and Rivers of Northamptonshire*, pt. II of *The River System of Northamptonshire* (Northampton, 1929), pp. 69-71. See also **76** for Dan's account of a fox going to ground in a swallow-hole.
[4] *V.C.H. Northants*, i. 133.
[5] e.g. to the labourers of Stanion: B.D., p. 233.   [6] *Ibid.*, pp. 232-3.

or fence of a deer-park low enough to enable deer to jump with ease into the park, but with a steep drop on the further side to prevent them from jumping out again. It may be suggested that Her Majesty gave Edmund Brudenell the deer-leap into Deene Park on the occasion of her visit there in 1566. The deer acquired in this way came of course from the royal forest of Rockingham.

THE HOME FARM

Crops

It is evident from the many references in these letters to crops of various kinds as well as to livestock, that Cardigan kept some of his land at Deene, and it seems also at Deenthorpe, in his own occupation.[1] In the nineteenth century and after this would have been called the home farm, but the term is nowhere used by Dan. From this farm came the supplies of beef, mutton, poultry, dairy produce, flour and the rest for the consumption of his household (and probably also for that of certain of his employees), as well as corn and milk for the stables and kennels. This land, together with the park and gardens, represented the demesne of the manor in pre-inclosure days when the lord's arable was originally intermixed with that of his tenants in the innumerable strips of the open fields, and their flocks and herds were depastured together on the common waste. On most manors, however, consolidation by exchange, followed by piecemeal inclosure by lords of manors, had been gradually progressing since the middle ages, for in spite of certain advantages the system had great practical drawbacks.

From the sixteenth century at least the process of inclosure had made possible those farming innovations and experiments which by the eighteenth century had become very much the fashion both with enterprising landowners and the larger tenant farmers.[2] In Northamptonshire as well as in the neighbouring counties of Rutland, Leicestershire and Warwickshire mixed farming had been general from the sixteenth or seventeenth centuries.[3] John Norden, in his description of our county (1591), says: 'This Northamptonshire is a most pleasant shire', with 'manie and notable sheep pastures, rich feedings for cattle, firtile corn grounds and large fields greatly inrichinge the industrious husbandman.'[4] And so it remained in the reigns of George I and George II. It was then still very largely in open fields for, as Mrs. Thirsk says, 'the villages of Leicestershire, Northamptonshire and Warwickshire waged the fiercest struggle of all to defend their common fields against enclosure in the sixteenth and seventeenth centuries'.[5] This may truly be said also of the greater part of the eighteenth century.

Lord Cardigan was not a leading innovator but was quite up-to-date with his farming. Some grass land was ploughed in 1731 for growing turnips (**161**). Dan refers to wheat in several of his letters but also on many occasions to

---

[1] This is suggested by the following two entries under 'Discharge 1728' in the estate accounts under 24 June 1728: 'to half a year's rent of land in Deene in your Lordship's hands due at Michaelmas 1727, £24 19s. 9d.', followed by 'to half a year's land in Deenthorpe in your Lordship's hands, £28 19s. 6d.' (A.S.R. 252). This was evidently a book transaction.

[2] See G. E. Mingay, *English Landed Society in the Eighteenth Century* (London, 1963), pp. 163-188.

[3] J. Thirsk, in *The Agrarian History of England and Wales, Vol. IV. 1500-1640*, ed. J. Thirsk (Cambridge, 1967), pp. 89-99.

[4] Quoted in Joan Wake, *The Montagu Musters Book, 1602-1623* (N.R.S., vii, 1935), p. xv; see also Harold Whitaker, *A Descriptive List of the Printed Maps of Northamptonshire, A.D. 1576-1900* (N.R.S., xiv, 1949), p. xii.

[5] *Agrarian History*, iv. 89.

'grain', using this word as the generic term for other kinds of corn crops as well as for wheat.[1] Other crops specifically mentioned are barley, oats, beans, clover, cinquefoil, rye-grass, trefoil and sainfoin. These five green crops were of comparatively recent introduction into the country.[2] Morton says that '*Rye-Grass* is with us accounted the best thing in the world for woodland in enclosures, (I say enclosures, because there is no practising this or any other improvement in the open fields.) 'Tis now our usual way to sow it together with *Trefoil*.' Sainfoin, he says, was grown for mowing; 'the cows and sheep are turned in upon the aftermart'.[3] Dan's opinion of trefoil was very high; he said that it could increase the value of some land from 13s. 4d. to £1 an acre the first year after its sowing (**5**). Of these green crops, says E. L. Jones, 'by far the most important was sainfoin'.[4] And so thought Charles Kirkham of Fineshade, who devoted half his little book to the cultivation of this crop. 'This grass', he says, 'has got the preference of all other grass in England'. He concludes with the story of its introduction from France by a M. Fleury in the reign of Charles I, as related to him by the second Lord Hatton.[5]

All these home-grown crops, however, were not enough for Cardigan's requirements, and in addition to seed and seed-corn he bought quantities of barley, wheat, beans, oats and straw from his neighbours, as shewn in the estate account books, as well as in Dan's letters. On 20 June 1725 Dan mentions the high prices of grain, which, he says, 'I think must be from the late great transportation, which has so exhausted the old stock that it will hardly last while new comes' (**30**). Many of these purchases were probably to supply the needs of Cardigan's hunting stable. He also bought a great deal of malt for brewing, and in 1726 the purchase of a small quantity of hops is mentioned (**82**).

Cardigan kept cattle, horses, sheep and pigs, using the word hogs for the last-named. Livestock was probably as a general rule bought and sold privately or at the local fairs, of which there were many, but in 1728 he bought 108 Scotch sheep at 9s. 6d. apiece and in 1726 23 Scotch cattle.[6] He also on occasion sent sheep and cattle for sale as far afield as the Grantham or London markets, London being about 70 miles distant. Ploughing at Deene was still done, perhaps not exclusively, by oxen, as is shown by several entries in the accounts: 'for four drawing oxen at £3. 15s. 0d. apiece' (5 February 1728), 'for two chains, two yoaks and a plough for the oxen £1. 2s. 6d.' (23 March 1728).[7] There was also a special plough for destroying ant-hills, an implement of which the present editor has never heard before,

---

[1] e.g. 'We have a most fine spring, and all sorts of grain very prosperous' (**137**).

[2] Trefoil (alias lucerne), rye-grass and sainfoin were first introduced into England in the mid-seventeenth century. Clover made its way slowly, and in 1750 was still unknown in many counties: E. L. Jones, *Agriculture and Economic Growth in England, 1650-1815* (London, 1967), pp. 153-8. In 1727 Cardigan bought twelve strike of rye-grass seed, to sow a new road in New Wood, and in 1728 another entry in the accounts runs, 'to 12 lbs of clover seed to sow upon the common, £2 17s. 9d.' (A.S.R. 252).

[3] J. Morton, *The Natural History of Northamptonshire* (1712), p. 482.

[4] *Agriculture and Economic Growth*, p. 69.

[5] C. Kirkham, *Two Letters to a Friend. The First shewing and demonstrating by law, the rights and privileges of Pouralles, or Free-Hay. The Other directing the management of that profitable grass call'd Saint-Foyn, upon barren land, from the Author's own experience, and the best collections of all those who are thought to write well on that subject. With a remarkable and particular account when and how, and by what accidental means it first came and was brought over from Normandy into this Kingdom* (London and Stamford, 1726). The Northamptonshire Record Society owns a copy of this very rare work, from the library of Mr. J. A. Gotch (N.R.S. pamphlet, no. 556).

[6] 5 October 1728; A.S.R. 252.

[7] A.S.R. 252.

[Facing p. xxxix]

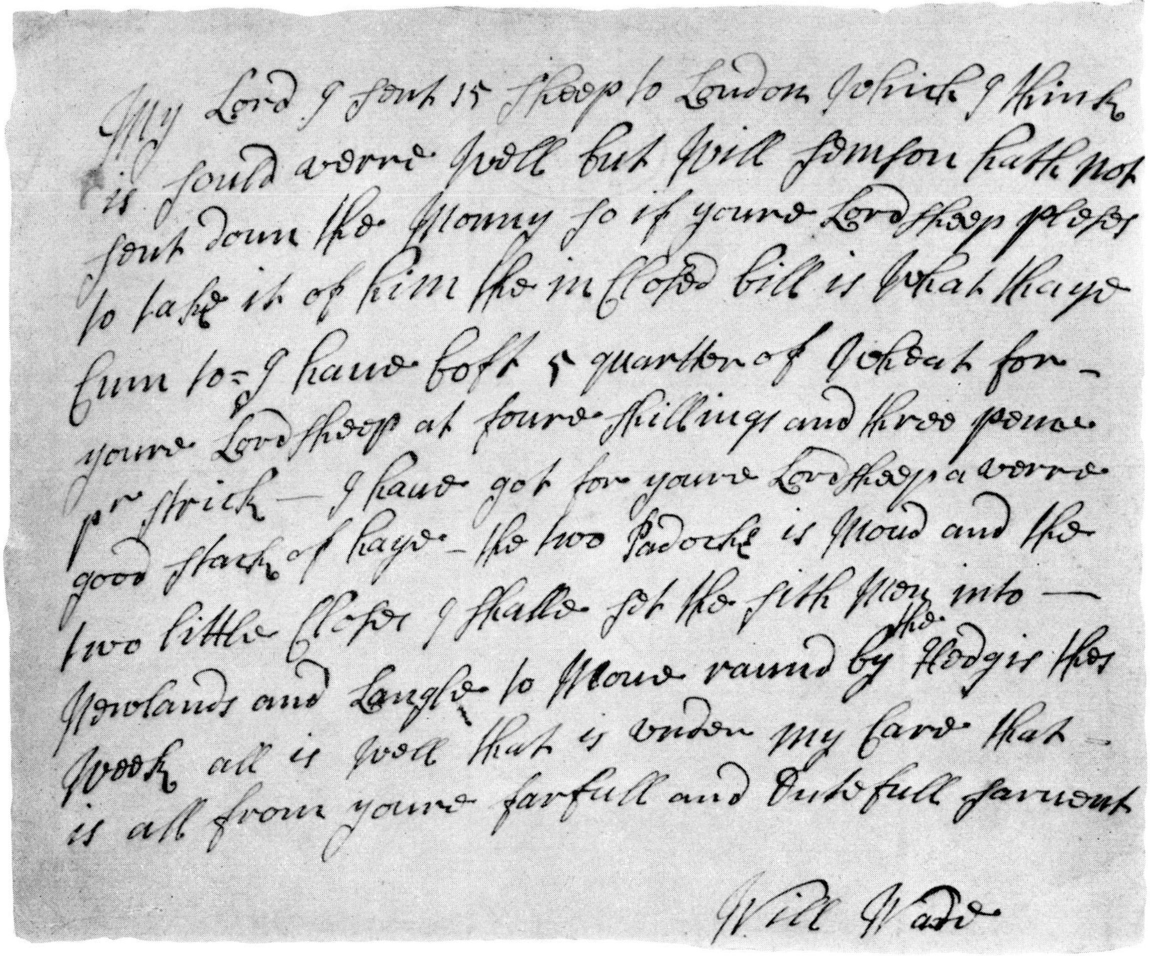

My Lord I sent 15 Sheep to London which I think
is sould verre well but Will Samson hath not
sent down the Monny so if youre Lordshep pleses
to take it of him the in closed bill is what thaye
cum to — I have bot 5 quarter of Wheat for —
youre Lordshep at foure shillings and three pence
pr strick — I have got for youre Lordshep a verre
good stack of haye — the two Padocks is Mowd and the
two little Closes I shalle set the sith Mow into —
Mowlands and Langside to Mowe raind by the Hodgis thes
week all is well that is under my care that —
is all from youre farfull and dutefull sarvent

Will Wade

Letter of William Wade to Lord Cardigan.

though the pest of ant-hills in grass fields was well enough known in Northamptonshire in her day—i.e. before the First World War.

Management

The day-to-day management of the home farm could not have been other than a whole-time job, and from Dan's frequent references to him and the happy survival of one of his letters, it is obvious that Will Wade was the man in charge at Deene. In the nineteenth century he would have been known as the farm bailiff, but the term does not occur in either the letters or the estate accounts. Though apparently under Dan's general supervision, Wade was clearly responsible for the purchase and sale of cattle, sheep and pigs at local fairs and in the London and Grantham markets, and for the purchase of grain and malt, though some transactions were carried through at Dan's specific orders (**137, 152**). Even seeing to the bottling of beer was at least on one occasion one of Wade's duties (**12**). Although he was barely literate he had to keep exact accounts, for much money passed through his hands, and these accounts had to be submitted to and 'stated' by Dan at regular intervals before they were sent on to the Earl. Wade was able to assist Dan in valuing timber and farm buildings, and together they decided what land was to be laid for hay. Wade was the tenant of one or two small closes at Deene. By the end of 1727 his name has dropped out of the letters so far as references to farming are concerned,[1] and he may have retired or died in that year, unless he had taken to communicating with Lord Cardigan direct. There are certainly fewer and fewer references to the home farm in Dan's own letters after this date. In earlier ones he conveys many messages to the Earl from Wade, all couched in his own favourite phrase or a variant thereof: 'all things under his care are well'. One letter in Wade's own hand very fortunately survives, and is illustrated opposite; it gives a vivid picture of two or three days' hard work, and brings to life a conscientious and reliable servant.

WORKMEN AND LABOURERS

Work by the great

Lord Cardigan employed very few regular whole-time labourers on his home farm and estate generally. Nearly all the work such as ploughing, reaping, mowing, hay-making, carting, fencing, hedging and ditching, and apparently all the work in the woods, was done 'by the great', as it was called. This term meant at a fixed price for the job, by contract, either with individuals or with gangs of men from Deene and Deenthorpe, supplemented

---

[1] 'Wade's land' referred to in 1729 as untenanted (**154, 155**) may mean the land formerly in the occupation of Will, or that of another person of the same name.

My Lord I sent 15 sheep to London which I think is sould verre well but Will Semson hath not sent doun the monny so if youre Lordsheep pleses to take it of him the inclosed bill is what thaye cum to—I have boft 5 quartter of wheat for youre Lordsheep at foure shillings and threepence pr strick—I have got for youre Lordsheep a verre good stack of haye—the two padocks is moud and the two little closes I shalle set the sith men into Newlands and Langle to moue raund by the Hedgis thes week all is well that is under my care that is all from youre farfull and dutefull sarvent

Will Wade[2]

[2] Bru. MSS. F. iii. 281.

when necessary by gangs from Stanion, Glapthorne, Weldon and Corby. That this system was in use is evident not only from the letters but from the estate accounts, from which the following examples are given: 'to Deene and Deenthorpe labourers for mowing £7 2s. 2d.' (17 October 1728); 'to John Wells in full of his bill for work with his teame £10 5s..' (22 April 1728); 'to the labourers for mowing and carrying the hay in Sheep Close and in the Paddock £2 16s.' (26 August 1727); 'to the labourers for carrying the oats upon the common £3 12s.'; 'to the labourers for reaping the oats at 3s. per acre and pecking the stubble at 1s. per acre and earnest £8 14s.'; 'to the people that bound up the oats as per particular and shock'd and rak'd the barley upon the Common £6 7s. 6d.'; 'to the labourers for carrying the hay and making the haycocks in Newlands and Langley £6 2s. 4d.'; 'to the garden labourers for mowing weeds in the park last summer as appears by the Park Book £1 18s. 4d.' (23 February 1728).

It is clear that women were employed on the farm, but not very frequently. In 1728 thirty-two haymakers, nearly all of them women, were paid for work in Hall Banks, and another entry records a payment of £2 12s. 6d. 'to the women that shock'd and rak'd the stuble' (26 August 1727).[1] None of the payments indicate the rate of pay for each worker.

That working 'by the great' on landed estates in Northamptonshire was no new custom in the third Earl's day is clear from a volume, from the south of the county about 40 miles from Deene, in the Cartwright of Aynhoe collection, entitled 'Agreements with Workmen' and covering the period between 1665 and 1692.[2] The volume consists of *copies* of agreements which have been formally executed between Richard Cartwright, lord of the manor of Aynhoe, and the 'workmen' concerned. The work to be done and the amount to be paid for it is clearly specified in each instance. A great many of these contracts were for building or for hedging and ditching. Some were for mowing or other jobs, and one even for covering Mr. William Cartwright's coffin with lead and putting his name and the date of his death on it. But they differ from those on the Deene estate in that in general they were made with one or two persons, and only on one occasion with as many as three. This leads one to suspect that the contractors, or some of them, may have employed other workmen on the various jobs, whereas Lord Cardigan's contracts seem to have been with all the members of each particular gang.

Lord Cardigan's reason for using this method of getting his work done is explained very well in Dan's letter to him of 3 October 1727 about alterations and additions to Little Deene (**149**). There was of course a contract with the masons for the stone and brick work,[3] but when it came to the woodwork inside the house Dan wrote: 'I think it will be the best way to bargain with the joiners to make the staircase by the great. This is indeed an uncommon way of proceeding but as I can compute what the workmanship will come to when the manner of finishing is laid down, it will certainly prevent uneasiness in your Lordship, when you are sure the workmen can't wrong you by being idle. And it will save me a great deal of trouble in looking after them, for I shall take care to describe the method in which they are to proceed in such a manner in the contract, if I make one, that they shall want no further instructions till the work is finish'd.'

In the same year (1727) that Dan was writing thus to Lord Cardigan Edward Lawrence's book, *The Duty of a Steward to his Lord*, was published, in which the author wrote that a steward should "endeavour to make himself

---

[1] All these references come from A.S.R. 252 and 253.
[2] N.R.O., C(A) 4611.   [3] Printed below, Appendix 1.

master of the true prices of all sorts of work relating to husbandry, that he be not impos'd upon, or obliged to watch the day workmen, which commonly prove the most chargeable method".

There may have been advantages, too, on the labourers' side of this system, which probably put them in a stronger position than if they had been working for a regular wage, for Dan had to bargain with the gangs for each job, paying them a small sum in 'earnest' money when the bargain was concluded as security that it would be honoured.[1] On the other hand our records are silent as to probable periods of unemployment, especially in the winter. On two occasions there were disputes between employer and employed, of which there is an interesting example in letters **57** and **63**, when in February 1726 a gang of five Deenthorpe men refused to work at Deene, and received an ultimatum from the Earl. As they were living rent free in his cottages, no doubt he felt he had some claim on their services. A more serious dispute ending in a strike occurred at Deene in November 1726, with the gang of labourers who had been engaged to fence a sale in Deepings Wood (**90**). Lord Cardigan was trying to get them to commute their customary perquisite in the shape of 'bottles' (i.e. an allowance of faggots) for a money payment, but when the men met Dan at the wood and discovered the Earl's intention they refused to work 'at any price'. So Dan went off to Stanion and engaged twenty labourers to do the job. A week later they appeared, but in the meanwhile had evidently heard what was in the wind, for they also refused to work without their bottles. 'I could do nothing with them', wrote Dan, 'but call'd them fools for their pains and sent them back again . . . There has been some snake in the grass amongst Stanion men' (**92**). On 21 November Dan wrote again that the labourers were adamant, and had declared that Lord Cardigan had 'promis'd them possitively that when they agreed to work without wood in the Park sale last year, that you would never hinder them of their wood for the future' (**98**). Corby labourers now come into the picture. By 21 November Dan had persuaded them and the Stanion gang to work at the Deene sales without wood (bottles), but only on condition that both Deene and Deenthorpe labourers 'may work with them and have their wood'. Dan added that it would be 'almost impossible to subvert their resolution', and in effect advised Cardigan to give way over such a trifling advantage (**98**). By 1 December Dan had another letter from his master, refuting the men's accusation, and in another interview with Dan they submitted (**99**).

Before leaving the subject of labourers mention should be made of the boon teams which carted coal to Deene for Lord Cardigan free of charge, either from the nearest pits or from wharves on the river Nene.[2] The teams were those of his farm tenants, and this service is mentioned in some of the farm leases of the period. The amount of carting done was computed in money values and entered in the estate accounts as part of the farm rents. 'As soon as the roads are better', wrote Dan, 'I shall order the sea coal to be brought in by the boon teams' (**12**; 2 May 1725), and again 'the roads here are so very bad that I fear we shall not get pit coal at any rate' (**19**; 20 May 1725). Boon teams are reminiscent of medieval labour services.

The 'pit coal' was brought overland from pits in Leicestershire and

---

[1] e.g. 'To Deen and Deenthorpe labourers for earnest when I bargain'd with them for fencing Deen Wood, 15s. 11d.' (A.S.R. 252; 21 February 1728).

[2] Boon teams are frequently mentioned in the estate accounts of our period, and the term 'boon days' also occurs (A.S.R. 252 and 253). The custom of labour services in part payment of rent was still common in Ireland in the second half of the eighteenth century, and is referred to by the novelist Maria Edgeworth in *Castle Rackrent* (Oxford English Novels edn., 1964, pp. 14-15, 104).

Warwickshire some thirty to forty miles from Deene; the 'sea coal' was that which was shipped round by sea from Northumberland and up the river Nene as far as it was navigable. The roads at this time were so bad as often in winter or wet weather to be impassable, so much so that sea coal was easier to obtain than that from the pits, and a great impetus was thus given to river navigation. Acts were passed in 1714 and 1724 to make the Nene navigable from Peterborough to Northampton, and the gradual advance of the work can be followed in the Brudenell accounts. In January 1728 the boon teams were fetching the Earl's coal from Wansford, and in August of that year from Perio mills in Southwick parish. In 1729 Cardigan started to build his own private wharf at Cotterstock, which was completed in 1731 or 1732.[1]

Wage earners

There is evidence from the accounts that on the Deene estate in our period some men were employed at a regular wage. The lowest paid received from 3s. to 4s. a week. This sounds to us a starvation rate, but in the 1830s and 1840s labourers were expected to keep a wife and family on 9s. a week, and the present writer can remember seeing one such man wielding a besom in his old age about the year 1889.[2] In considering these wage rates allowance must be made for inflation. Moreover the cottage rents at this time on Cardigan's estates were little more than nominal, and many employees may have been living rent-free—as were the rebellious labourers of Deenthorpe. There were also perquisites such as free milk, fuel, etc., which varied from estate to estate and from farm to farm.

The following extracts from the account books shed some light on the situation at Deene in Dan's time: 'To James Perry, 2 years wages, £9 18s.' (14 November 1727); 'To Will Rowell for a fortnight's labourer's work, 15s., . . . to the same for three week's board wages, 15s.' (23 February 1728); 'To John Upson, a month's wages, 12s.' (i.e. 3s. a week; 1 December 1728); 'To John Peak, ½ years wages, £10' (18 December 1728); 'To Richard Harrison, ½ a years shepherds wages due Michaelmas last, £4' (21 October 1728).[3]

It must be noted that the Earl was scandalously slow in paying his bills, and he was even worse about paying his employees of whatever degree. For example, Dan had to make the following entries in the account books: 'To Will Brown the carter in full for 2 years wages due to him August 25th 1725, £14' (23 December 1727); 'To Richard Harper, one years wages, £25, due 20th October 1720' (10 September 1728). His accountant and bailiff, though no doubt for the time well paid, only received their salaries at half-year intervals. The amount of Dan's salary is nowhere mentioned.

BUILDING

One of Lord Cardigan's principal interests at Deene was the reconstruction of a farm house to serve as an alternative residence for himself and his family, or perhaps as a dower house for the Cardigan widows. The subject is referred to in no fewer than seventy of these letters. "The house looks extreamly

---

[1] A.S.R. 253. From inquiries kindly made for the present writer by Mrs. S. P. G. Ward the site of this wharf has been identified as being next to Cotterstock mill. The final traces of it only disappeared within the last few years.
[2] Information given c. 1912 by Mr. William Surridge of Courteenhall, then 78 years of age. 'His neighbours were very good to him', he added.
[3] See also **10**. He also had 'the keeping of one cow constantly'.

beautifull upon the park", wrote Dan (**19**). It was lived in by Mr. John Lynwood until 1725, when the Earl took it over and Lynwood moved to Benefield. An unfinished draft of the agreement for the completion of the alterations, between Christopher Dexter, carpenter, of Gretton, and John Winsall of Great Weldon, mason, of the one part and Daniel Eaton on behalf of the Earl of Cardigan on the other part, dated 31 July 1725,[1] gives full particulars of the work. It was apparently finished, or nearly so, by the end of October 1727.[2] In Dan's opinion, when completed it would be "one of the prittiest little houses in England" (**41**).

Unlike many of his contemporaries who rebuilt their homes, Cardigan was in the main satisfied with Deene Hall as he found it, but Dan's letters record the taking down of a tower there and alterations or repairs to the chapel, dining-room, library, blue room, the alcove room, and staircases. He added a billiard room, however, for by this date the game was becoming fashionable in gentlemen's houses.[3] Outside the house he built a dog-kennel, a summer house, a bowling green house, a dairy and a barn, and made alterations to his stables.

The Earl's conversion to the Protestant faith gave him an interest in the parish church deeper than could have been felt by his Roman Catholic ancestors since the sixteenth century. The church was evidently in very bad condition, for in these seven years he spent considerable sums on its repair, renewing the roof, re-paving the floor, and erecting pews for his family and servants.

For all these various operations good stone was needed, and for this two neighbouring quarries were available. Several entries are to be found in the estate accounts for 1728 for the carriage of loads of stone to Deene from the quarry at Stanion which belonged to the Earl as lord of the manor.[4] The statement in the *Victoria County History* that Stanion stone had been worked out "long before the eighteenth century" is incorrect.[5] As late as 1906 these extensive now disused quarries to the east of the village were known as "Lord Cardigan's pits".[6] The other quarry which belonged to Lord Hatton was at Weldon and was therefore close to Deene, but Weldon stone is only mentioned by Dan in one letter (**45**), in which he recommended its use for a mantelpiece at Little Deene. It is likely, however, that the stone supplied to Lord Cardigan by the masons who were working by the great was from this famous quarry which is still being worked today.[7] For paving Deene church Ketton stone from Rutland was used. For his roofs the Earl had no need to go outside his own parish, for there was a slate pit at Deene, and the present writer saw those great slabs leaning against a wall there in the 1920s ready to be watered when a hard night frost was expected, in order that they might be split the more easily to the right thickness before being cut into the sizes needed for use as slates. The barns and hovels were roofed with thatch.

A considerable amount of building in brick—probably the kitchen garden walls among other things—was also done in Cardigan's time, the bricks being made from clay dug on the estate. Brick makers in Northamptonshire were few in comparison with stone-masons. The first mentioned in the letters is

---

[1] Printed below, Appendix 1.
[2] The progress of the work can be followed in the entry in the Subject Index under Building, Little Deene.
[3] It is mentioned by Shakespeare but was then only played in inns and taverns: *Encyclopaedia Britannica* (11th edn., 1910), iii. 934-5.
[4] A.S.R. 252.   [5] *V.C.H. Northants*, ii. 295.   [6] *Ibid.*, p. 301.
[7] For articles and notes on Northants stone and slate quarries, see *Northamptonshire Past and Present*, ii. 46 and iv, 71.

Horn who was evidently working at Deene in or before 1726 (**92**). In November of that year Thomas Newson of Towcester was engaged (**92**), and his name appears several times in the estate accounts for 1728. Jonathan Lewtener, recommended by Lord Gower, came from Staffordshire, but after a few months "thought fit to march off " in April 1727, after causing scandal in the village by "keeping a whore at Bulwick" (**130**), and leaving debts behind him (**132**). He was replaced by Will Newdall, who occurs in the letters only as "the poor fellow" or "the poor laborious fellow".[1]

In May 1727 Cardigan engaged two brickmakers from Derby who "came to inquire for work". Newdall was paid 5s. a thousand for making bricks, but was to have 6s. if he dug the clay himself (**140**). In July 1727 he had £4 4s. 0d. for "making and burning 16,800 bricks". In 1728 the amount paid had risen to 6s. 6d. per thousand.

It is interesting to learn that clay suitable for making tiles was dug in Deene Park.[2] Indications of where the brick clay came from are given in the names of the following closes "in the manor of Deene" which occur in the lease of a farm from the fourth Earl of Cardigan to Daniel Eaton, viz: Pingle Brick Leys, Brick Meadow, and Brick Close.[3]

Large quantities of lime for making mortar were of course needed for all these building operations, and possibly also for agricultural use, though this is not mentioned in the letters. In 1725 Cardigan was buying lime from his tenant John Lummis who had a lime-kiln, but in 1726 the Earl built his own kiln, and burnt a great deal of lime there in that and the following year.

ACCOUNTS AND FINANCE

Dan's most responsible task was the collection of rents in Northampton-shire, Leicestershire and Rutland, which amounted in the course of a year to over £2,000. The income from sales of wood also went through his hands, and he paid all the bills, wages, and sums owing for work by the great. Lord Cardigan was nothing if not a business man, and every halfpenny of the money for which Dan was responsible had to be accounted for. Not only had half-yearly statements to be submitted to the Earl but he also required interim abstracts. For this work of accountancy Dan had, of course, been properly trained as a young man.

Separate accounts, therefore, in different books, were kept: for the estates (and many of the household expenses such as coal, and including the farm and cottage rents); for the Park; for timber sales (known as 'wood money'); the dog kennels (fox hounds and spaniels); James Ashley's (the huntsman's account for stable expenses); and the home farm (known as 'Will Wade's account'). Separate accounts were also kept for Cardigan's joint hunting establishment with Lord Gower, and for his share in the Duke of Rutland's hunting confederacy.[4] All the receipts for the domestic servants' wages at Deene were at this time carefully pasted into a book. No wonder that Dan so often had to sit up half the night, and finally was obliged to hire the services of a professional writer and accountant to help him to get through all his work.

How did Dan convey to Lord Cardigan, who was so much away from

---

[1] **132**n., etc.
[2] **144**.
[3] Bru. MSS. D.iv.12; E.xvii.9; D.iv.11a.
[4] Most of these accounts have now disappeared. For those surviving, see Catalogue of Brudenell MSS.

home, the money he needed for his day-to-day expenditure? Highway robbery was not infrequent in the eighteenth century. The letters shew that Dan took quite large sums over to Mr. Denshire, Lord Cardigan's attorney, at Stamford, as on 18 December 1726, when the twelve miles of road were covered with ice (**102**), and in March 1727, when Dan paid £70 'into his hands' (**125**). He may also have sent bags of golden sovereigns to London by the wagon which took provisions to Lord Cardigan. By this date, however, other means had been invented for transferring money values from one place to another, which were already in use by Mr. Denshire in 1726. In December of that year Dan wrote to Cardigan: 'I came to Stamford on Thursday, where I got returns for £500, to be paid in London in a fortnight, viz: by Mr. Denshire to Mr. Child, £400, and by another person, who will have money in town for hogs, etc., to Mr. Gibson, £100, which money I shall lodge in Mr. Denshire's hands till Mr. Gibson's bill comes down. The two inclosed bills I got in Grantham, for I could not hear of any other . . . I was forced to pay the usual price for returns, viz: 10s. in the hundred, but that at Stamford cost me nothing.' (**105**) On 13 March 1727 Dan again wrote of sending money to Cardigan by bills, and hoped to send more by returns (**123**). He enclosed at the same time 'Mr. Child's note for £400', and wrote to Cardigan: 'I sent your Lordship by the last post three bills for £98 17s., and I believe I may venture to promise your Lordship to send by next Saturday's post bills to make that sum up (to?) £200. I shall go to Stamford Fair on Thursday, and if I can't meet with returns there I don't much fear but that I shall meet with success amongst my acquaintance at Kettering on Friday. I will get the bills payable as soon after that date as I can.'

These bills by which Dan sent money to Lord Cardigan were bills of exchange, which had been in use from the high middle ages for the international transfer of money. They had been used in England for purely internal purposes from at least the second quarter of the seventeenth century.[1] Among the advantages of the bill of exchange used for inland purposes was the elimination of the various expensive legal processes which had previously been necessary for the transfer of money. The word "return" used by Dan can occasionally also signify a bill of exchange, but more usually means an arrangement by which a claim to money payable in London, e.g. the price of cattle sent up from the country to Smithfield Market, was transferred to a representative of some local landowner visiting London.[2]

FOX-HUNTING

Hunting, so frequently mentioned in these letters, has been one of the chief attractions of Northamptonshire at least since the reign of William the Conqueror, who built Rockingham Castle and hunted from there in his royal forest. The quarry was chiefly the deer, but for many centuries the otter, the badger, and the hare were also victims of the sport.

Lord Cardigan had been Master of the Royal Buck-hounds to Queen Anne, and for the first year of his reign to George I, but there is only one reference to this sport in Dan's letters when James Brudenell declared his intention

---

[1] L. Stone, *The Crisis of the Aristocracy 1558-1641* (Oxford, 1965), p. 512.
[2] See Mrs. Margaret Gay Davies's article, "Country Gentry and Payments to London, 1650-1714", *Economic History Review*, XXIV (1971), pp. 15-36. Mrs. Davies found references to returns in the 1650s, the beginning of the period for which she used the archives of three midland counties, including Northamptonshire, for her present study.

of hunting a deer in Shortwood.[1] Harriers (hare-hounds) were kept by many of the gentry of Northamptonshire in the seventeenth century, and Lord Sunderland's hounds at Althorp in 1635 are considered by T. Guy Paget as more likely to have been harriers than fox hounds.[2] Hare hunting on horseback is frequently mentioned by Thomas Isham in his diary between 1671 and 1673.[3]

Foxes became so numerous in the early seventeenth century that James I issued an order permitting hounds and huntsmen to pursue them on to anyone's land.[4] The earliest reference to fox-hunting in our county that we have come across is in a letter to Sir Justinian Isham of Lamport of 1 December 1657, from Nicholas Carew of Pytchley.[5] The purpose of the hunt on this occasion, however, was to get rid of an animal which was doing Carew's warrener "much iniurie amonxt his cunnyes". Foxes, in fact, were looked upon as vermin and rewards for their destruction (usually a shilling a head) were paid by village constables in our county until towards the end of the eighteenth century,[6] when in the shires it had evidently become a crime to trap or shoot a fox—as later satirised by W. S. Gilbert in *Ruddigore*.

Fox-hunting as a sport, however, had certainly started in our county in the reign of Charles II. On a map of Hardwick of 1684 a fox hunt in progress is clearly depicted.[7] James II, as Duke of York, had stayed at Dingley with James Griffin to hunt the fox, as recorded later by one of the Griffin family in the parish register there.[8] There are many references to fox-hunting in the reigns of James II and William III to be found in the Isham correspondence; e.g. in 1693 James Griffin excused himself for not seeing Isham on the score that he "must make his first compliment to fox-hunting".[9] From the diaries of Sir Justinian Isham (1687-1737)[10] we learn that from 1710 it was the practice among many Northamptonshire squires to keep a few hounds and to unite them with those of their neighbours into a pack to hunt over their estates, occasionally the hare no doubt, but more often the fox, which does not run in rings in a limited area like the hare, but goes for much longer points and therefore gives far better sport. The fields were small, but surprisingly often included a few ladies. Bagged foxes were not uncommon. By this time Squire Andrew of Harleston kept a whole pack of fox hounds, which on 24 October 1710, had a record run.[11] In fact by this date fox-hunting generally was well established, as the popularity of Nicholas Cox's book on the subject entitled *The Gentleman's Recreation*, and published in 1674, bears witness. By 1721 it had run into six editions. Oddly

[1] Letters **34** and **35**. Dan reported later that Lord Hatton's servants had been hunting and killing deer on Cardigan's land (**90**), but this was merely poaching.
[2] T. Guy Paget, *The History of the Althorp and Pytchley Hunt, 1634-1920* (1937), p. 2.
[3] I (L) 5271. *The Diary of Sir Thomas Isham of Lamport*, ed. Gyles Isham (1971).
[4] E. W. Bovill, *English Country Life 1780-1830* (1962), p. 222. I am indebted to Lord Spencer for this and other references, as well as for useful criticism of this section in draft.
[5] I.Corr. 443.
[6] In the following parishes the last payments for a dead fox occur in the years stated: Old, 1786; Marston Trussel, 1769; Boddington, Crick and Wicken, 1777; Stanion, 1782. This gives a good coverage of Northamptonshire. I am indebted to Mr. C. E. C. Burch for these references to the relevant parish constable's account.
[7] Paget, *History of the Althorp and Pytchley Hunt*, facing p. 32.
[8] F. Hall, *The Registers of Dingley* (1926), p. 153, quoting notes by Edward Griffin, rector there 1777-1840.
[9] I.Corr. 1506.
[10] I (L) 2686.
[11] From Blewbury Covert to Gumley Wood in Leicestershire, a ten-mile point (*V.C.H. Northants*, ii. 355).

enough a book with the same title about the other contemporary, and may we say more civilized, craze of landscape gardening was published at about the same time.

How soon Lord Cardigan took to hunting after he settled down at Deene in 1703 is uncertain, but in 1708 he bought some hounds which for two or three seasons his brother James kept for him at his home at Luffenham in Rutland.[1] It is possible that he was hunting from there with the Noels, whose pack had been hunting the country, later to be known as the Cottesmore, since the end of the seventeenth century. By 1710 some kennels had been built at Deene, which Cardigan proudly shewed on one of his "days" in the summer of that year to his neighbour Sir Justinian Isham.[2] The first mention of hounds and fox-hunting in Dan's letters is on 1 June 1725 (23) and in the following year he sent Lord Cardigan a list of hounds (96), by which time there was a hunters' stable as well as a coach-horse stable at Deene.

Fox hounds had been bred sometimes perhaps from deer hounds, but more often it is supposed from hare hounds (usually known as harriers) into a distinct, taller and more stalwart race than the latter. Lord Cardigan bred his hounds at Deene, where they were trained by his huntsman Jack Kingston and his head kennel-man in the surrounding country and sometimes as far afield as Cottesmore. Many are the reports which Dan gives in these letters of their condition and the progress of their training which included teaching them not to chase sheep, deer or rabbits. Accounts of runs are also given, such as the one on 25 September 1726, when they found in Jenkinson's spinney, ran through Collyweston Park, crossed the Welland, and killed in the open near Tinwell (76). On another day Kingston took a gun with him, and shot a fox before the hounds in Laxton Wood to give them a taste of blood (47). A two hour hunt from Laxton in September 1726 ended in the fox going to ground in a swallow hole. As a rule, of course, the foxes tried to get back to their earths, which, from the fox hunters' viewpoint, made earth-stoppers necessary. They are, however, only once mentioned (68), but the payments to labourers on hunting days which occur frequently in the estate accounts of our period,[3] evidently refer to this practice, which entailed going out before dawn when the foxes return to their lairs—a cold and unpleasant job in mid-winter. One of John Wootton's hunting pictures at Althorp dated 1733 depicts an old earth-stopper.

The economics of hunting may be studied in detail in these letters and in the Brudenell estate accounts. The hounds were fed mainly on horse flesh varied by an occasional old cow. For example, Cardigan paid Matthew Wade of Harringworth £4 15s. 9d. for thirty-eight loads of horseflesh on 20 May 1729, and £1 17s. 6d. for fifteen loads for the spaniels.[4] In 1730 a payment of £40 10s. 0d. was made for oatmeal and milk for the hounds. In August 1730 Thomas Thompson was paid 24 weeks' wages (in arrear) for "making" the dogs' meat at Cottesmore and elsewhere at 3s. a week, for which he was kept waiting for six months.[5] Old Mrs. Eaton received payment on 8 October 1728, for 25 gallons of milk "the dog-doctor had for the hounds in May 1727". But this delay in payment of wages and for goods was a characteristic of the age, even the pay of soldiers and sailors being as a rule in scandalously heavy arrears.

[1] A.S.R. 133.
[2] I (L) 2686.
[3] e.g. 21:2:1728, 'To Stanion labourers in full of their bill for hunting days in the last two seasons, £1 5s. 3d.', and another bill for the same amount in 1729 (A.S.R. 252).
[4] Ibid.
[5] A.S.R. 253.

Straw for bedding down the hounds was bought in 1728 at the rate of 10*d*. the load.[1] To the cost of the hounds must be added the cost of the horses, their keep and that of the hunt servants, the wages of the latter, and the saddlers' bills. In fact the expenses of fox hunting must have accounted for a large proportion of Lord Cardigan's income.

Cardigan used to quarter his hounds (long after puppy-hood) on his farm tenants, which did not make for his popularity, though farmers in Northamptonshire and elsewhere have seldom objected to "walking" a fox-hound puppy as it is called, during the summer months. "The hounds have done a great deal of damage among the lambs. . . . they are so troublesome they [the tenants] don't know what to do with them", wrote Dan after a visit to Cranoe (**125**), and again "Those people that have hounds in Leicestershire beg your Lordship would let them be brought home. They are two years old, but very troublesome" (**60**). The hounds were taken on foot from county to county, even from Yorkshire, and sometimes arrived at Deene so lame and footsore that they took weeks to recover. But in 1727 an entry in the accounts records a payment of £5 11*s*. 3*d*. "for carriage of hound whelps to Yorkshire".[2]

The health of the hounds and horses was always a matter of concern, as is evident from Dan's reports in so many of his letters; distemper among the hounds is referred to and a case of suspected poisoning. A "dog-doctor", John Fardell, is twice mentioned. The most serious complaint to be reported was an outbreak of madness (possibly rabies, but perhaps the milder complaint now called hysteria) which gave a lot of trouble in 1726 and 1727. The hounds affected were drenched and chained up in isolation, and at length, at Lord Gower's behest, they were "ordered to the salt water". "The hounds are return'd from the sea", wrote Dan, "but they drounded two and lost a third" (**107**). This cure by dipping in sea water for madness in dogs was recommended in *The Sportsman's Dictionary* for 1735. But prevention is better than cure, and care was always taken by Dan after this outbreak to keep the hounds in kennels "three days before the full and change of the moon and three days afterwards" (**125**; 25 March 1727). This action is explained by the definition of lunacy in the Oxford English Dictionary as "intermittent insanity as formerly attributed to the changes of the moon".

The records of pedigrees of the Fitzwilliam hounds exist at Milton without a break from about 1760,[3] but it is doubtful if any surviving lists of hounds in Northamptonshire go back as far as the one that Dan sent to Lord Cardigan in 1726 (**96**). The names of these hounds—Bluecap, Lovely, Peeler, Diamond and the rest—sound like music to the ear, and those of us who used at the turn of the century to end every hunt ball by singing John Peel at the tops of our voices as we galloped round with our partners in red tail coats to this rousing tune will be delighted to find those of Ranter and Ringwood amongst them. Descendants of the original pack at Deene without any manner of doubt are chasing the fox over many parts of England today.

The social and perhaps also the political implications of fox-hunting in these early days are interesting. Sir Gyles Isham suggests that the Tory squires of Northamptonshire hunted together. Certainly no evidence seems to have survived that Cardigan, a consistent Tory, ever hunted with the Althorp pack, but there is no doubt that some of his later hunting associates were Whigs. Distinctions of rank, however, definitely asserted themselves, for when Cardigan and his aristocratic friends took seriously to the sport

[1] A.S.R. 252.
[2] *Ibid.*
[3] Information from Lord Fitzwilliam.

they formed their own confederacy apart from the squirearchy, even though it obliged some of them to desert their homes and their counties for months together during the hunting season.

Thus between 1709 and 1732 Cardigan had hunting establishments at Cottesmore in Rutland, at Stroxton in Lincolnshire, and also at Hanby Grange in the same county, which he and his friend Lord Gower rented jointly from Sir Charles Buck. There can be little doubt that the main attraction to this part of the country was the near neighbourhood of the third Duke of Rutland, whose enthusiasm for the chase was such that he had migrated from Haddon Hall, the cradle of his race in Derbyshire, to Belvoir Castle on the boundary of Leicestershire and Lincolnshire, that he might devote himself to the joys of fox-hunting.[1] He was soon joined during the hunting season in an informal association with Lord Cardigan, Lord Gainsborough, Lord Howe and Lord Gower, all of whom had estates in one or more of these counties. The area hunted roughly corresponded to the area now covered by the Belvoir, Cottesmore, Pytchley and Woodland Pytchley Hunts. They moved their horses and hounds from one centre to another as occasion required, uniting their packs on hunting days, but each probably, as Cardigan did, employing his own huntsman and certainly numbers of whippers-in, kennel-men, grooms and stable-helpers at considerable expense. Many a glorious gallop across country with a southerly wind and a cloudy sky —a burning scent, and the music of the pack in front of them, must these boon companions have had together, as with the gradual progress of inclosure the thrill of jumping and the greater demands on courage and skill in riding added enormously to the pleasures of the chase—a manly exercise indeed.

It must be mentioned that in 1726 Cardigan moved his hounds and hunt servants for a short time to Wothorpe, Lord Exeter's large house two miles from Burghley and three from Stamford, presumably to hunt that district with his friend Lord Exeter, who, though sympathetic to the sport, is never referred to in these letters as a fox-hunting man.

These hunting arrangements of the Duke of Rutland and his friends became so complicated that in 1730 by joint consent a formal and legally binding agreement, dated 6 May 1730, was drawn up, signed, sealed and delivered by all five parties in the presence of witnesses. The Duke's copy is still at Belvoir Castle, and it is by the kindness of the present Duke that we have been allowed to print it as Appendix No. 5. Guy Paget has drawn attention to the fact that other such confederacies existed at this date.[2] The Belvoir agreement was not the first of its kind to illustrate the tendency of the nobility to "keep themselves to themselves" in the matter of fox-hunting, and in 1729 a formal agreement on similar lines had been executed by the Duke of Richmond and the Earl of Tankerville for hunting in the Goodwood-Midhurst-Chichester area of Sussex, which was the origin of the Old Charlton Hunt,[3] the Melton of the early eighteenth century. This deed was witnessed by the Dukes of Grafton, St. Albans, Bolton, and Montrose. Charlton is a hamlet in the parish of Singleton, and in Singleton church is a monument

---

[1] T. F. Dale, *The History of the Belvoir Hunt* (1899).

[2] e.g. in 1713 a hunting agreement was executed between Sir John Tyrwhitt, Robert Vyner and Charles Pelham for hunting the country now represented by the Cottesmore Hunt.

[3] Lord Bathurst considered that the hunt thus set up was known as 'The Confederate Hunt' (*The Charlton and Raby Hunt*, 1938, pp. 32-3). I am greatly obliged to Dr. L. A. Parker, Archivist to the Leicestershire County Council, for finding this document among the muniments at Belvoir, and for making me a transcript thereof.

to Thomas Johnson,[1] huntsman to the Duke of Richmond, whose "knowledge in his profession . . . gain'd him the approbation of several of the nobility and gentry" among whom in the list which follows were the (third) Earl of Cardigan, his friend Lord Gower, and the Honourable Mr. Spencer.[2] The inscription ends with the following verse:

> "Here Johnson lies, what Hunter can deny
> Old honest Tom the Tribute of a Sigh,
> Deaf is that Ear, which caught the op'ning Sound,
> Dumb is that Tongue, which chear'd the hills around.
> Unpleasing Truth, Death hunts us from our Birth
> In view; and Men, like Foxes, take to Earth."[3]

Sad to say, Cardigan did not enjoy his new sporting association for very long. We find him hunting from Stroxton in November 1731, but by the spring of 1732 he had found it "too much for him" and wrote to the Duke of Rutland resigning his partnership.[4] On 4 June, Dan wrote to his master then at Bath, expressing serious concern for his health. He died in the following July, and was buried at Deene, his pall-bearers being six of his old Northamptonshire fox-hunting friends.

J.W.

---

[1] The Earl of March, *Records of the Old Charlton Hunt*, p. 9. The Charlton Hunt was formed in 1737/8 (*Ibid.*, p. 40).
[2] This was John Spencer of Althorp (1708-1746), fourth son of the third Earl of Sunderland, and father of the first Earl Spencer.
[3] *Records of the Old Charlton Hunt*, p. 90.
[4] Bru. MSS. F. iii. 282, 283.

THE LANGUAGE
OF THE LETTERS

We may orient Dan Eaton's language by a handful of near-contemporaries. He was two when Dryden died. Pope was ten years Dan's senior, Gay eleven. Dan's London schooling may have overlapped with Swift's letters to Stella, 1710-13. *The Spectator* appeared in 1711-13, *The Rape of the Lock* in 1712; *Robinson Crusoe* in 1719, six years before these letters begin; *Gulliver* in 1726, while Dan was having chambers and garrets plastered at Little Deen. *The Beggar's Opera* appeared in 1728, during a year-long gap in the letters. *Pamela* came out in 1740, eight years after Lord Cardigan's death, two before Dan's.

Technically, Dan's language seems about what we might expect: most of its "variants" from our later-established "norms" appear also in writers like Steele or Swift, whose language would have been termed "perfectly well-bred". He has also his own variants, which to the town-bred ear would have sounded countrified, or specifically local. The to us "old-fashioned" ring of his English comes partly from his actual vocabulary; partly from certain now outmoded turns of phrase; from occasional grammatical forms; and of course from the flourishes of courtesy in an age when a gentleman in bowing might still sweep his hat to his breast. "I have receiv'd the honour of your Lordship's letter." "I am your Lordship's most humble and most faithfull servant." "His Honour has got sixteen teeth." Really they are rather simple, even compared for instance with the greater formality of Dan's older opposite number, William Elmsall, Lord Cardigan's steward in Yorkshire. (*Cf.* **162-3**).

Vocabulary

A little browsing in the Glossary and Subject Index will introduce the reader to the comprehensive technical and semi-technical vocabulary of Dan's estate management, involving everything from legal and administrative terms like *chief rent, perambulation, right of common, meer,* and *boon teams,* down to the *"gudeons"* for a mill-wheel. Household affairs appear in the *copper* for *"breewing"* (they *"tear'd"* it), *sea-coals,* a *weather-glass,* and measures like *chalder* or *chaldron, scoe, strike, tod.* The accounting which sometimes palled fills his letters with financial terms. For our "extra" he writes *extraordinary* in full. He dates his rent-collections and other affairs by the Church calendar (*Lady-day, Michaelmas,* etc.); by folk festivals (May-day, Midsummer); by the natural seasons (*this grass,* "spring").

When he writes of building, especially Little Deen, can we now and then detect a little relish for a word newly-acquired—*architrave, cove, floated ceiling, stucco impost?*

Dan uses many land, water, farm and forest terms: *hovel, close, waste, warren, foddering, paddock, lay-ground, fallow* and (as a field-name) *Lammas; cold land; in good heart; laid high, laid for grass; eddishes* for the *quick-stock.* Under Little Deen cellar they find "a *surly* solid dry rock". They plant *treyfoil, cinqfoil, saintfoyn, ray-grass,* and *quick.* They must *cock-hedge* or *plash* their hedges.[1] They *cast* ant-hills; *grub* or *stub* (up) roots. In that wet land "the waters are *out*" in all the brooks (cf. *overflown* below)[2], and a fox escapes down a *swallow-hole*. (See Glossary). Forestry involves *spinneys*, *spring* "young growth", *treys*, a *deer-leap*. *Chapmen* buy bark when it *runs* or *is pill'd* and *timber*, *dodderels*, "*saplins*", *coppice-wood*. Labourers demand their *bottles—faggots*.

Dan describes an occasional *most fine chase* after the fox with enthusiasm but with few technicalities. He uses many about hounds, horses, and especially farriery, some of which, like *stifled* and *rowell'd*, may surprise the uninitiated. Many of the hounds' names became traditional. (*cf.* letter **96** and "John Peel".) Horses he identifies variously: *your Lordship's pad mare, the cropt guelding, Old Ball* or *the Ball'd horse; the Kirkham mare*, bought from the neighbours at Fineshade; *the Hornby colt*, after his sire; *the Beeson mare* (**106, 108**), probably from Beeston in Yorkshire, close to Leeds.[3]

Or a word may represent eighteenth though not twentieth century usage. Here we enter the important field of "semantic drift", the gradual and sometimes subtle change of meaning or use. His *intrepidity*, with its ironic overtone, amounts to "brashness". *Genius* is "native intelligence or mother-wit", and correspondingly *ingenious* and *ingenuity* refer to this quality rather than to "skill in contrivance or invention".[4]

Some words were then more specific. If Dan has *not agreed*, he has not negotiated a formal bargain. If he promises to be *more particular*, he will furnish more precise particulars later. Especially, his *I hope* is much stronger than ours: he "looks forward confidently".[5] Thus there is real confidence in his hope about his sister's qualifications, Lady Frances's recovery from the small-pox, the new carpenters' working well, and the kennel's now being safe from infection (**18, 140, 126-7**). For our weakened sense he would probably say "I desire" or "I wish it may". Similarly, *want* means only "lack, need", not "desire". Misreading can give a slightly comic effect, as in "Why we shall send for malt is because we shall *want* it" (**85**). *Perfectly* had not then taken on our grudging condescension: *perfectly well* may be honest praise.

The "ingenious reader" may enjoy considering Dan's use of *apt to* ("ready to"), *family* (often "household" or "servants"), *regular*, *perfect*, "*possitively*", *husband*, *thief*; *resolve*, *resolutions*; *proceed*—in **139** are *proceedings* "goings-on"?

Spelling

Few of Dan's abbreviations call for comment. Several times he uses y^e for "the" (**23, 68, 105; 55** y^e *Iron*). In dates it seems he did not mentally pronounce while writing: for "21st, 22nd, 23rd" he automatically writes *21th, 22th, 23th* by unconscious analogy with "24th" etc. For proper names he regularly uses a colon (*Walt:, Will:, Dan:*), suggesting perhaps a conscious abbreviation rather than a nickname.[6] Therefore though we (perhaps over-

---

[1] In Leicestershire now they say "splash". Could this be a "portmanteau" of *plash* and *slash*? See Glossary.

[2] Still current. Cf. "When the river is *out* of its banks . . ." (*Appalachia*, XXXVI, 1, 47, June, 1966).

[3] Therefore near Haigh Hall and Thornhill, where William Elmsall lived; see **162-3**. Possibly she was one of those bought by Elmsall about which he wrote numerous letters to Lord Cardigan. (Bru.F.iii. 169 ff.)

[4] See **18; 150, 164; 40**. *Cf.* C. S. Lewis, *Studies in Words*, s.v. WIT.

[5] *NED*: "To expect with desire, or to desire with expectation"; Mod., often in weakened sense, expressing little more than a desire.

[6] On the other hand, F.iii.281 (plate 3) is signed "Will Wade". Dan's colons may have been mere habit.

familiarly) call him "Dan", in intention he may have been subscribing himself "Daniel". Crumbs of evidence are letter **1** signed (unsayably) *Da:*, and **10** endorsed *Daniel Eaton's letters.*

Most of his "variant" spellings signify only that the norm had not yet hardened. *To morrow, bycause, atall, a way, a sunder* might be one word or two. *Munday, grainary,* even *wave* "waive" and *sword* "sward" were still in use. *Glassier* and *kenell* were old-fashioned or bygone. Others look like Dan's own rationalizations: *columnade, courseway* "causeway" (from earlier "causey"), *cistiron.* This last he later conforms, possibly after Lord Cardigan, to *cistern.*

Dan's interesting spellings are those which indicate his pronunciation. His *sign'd, pay'd, return'd,* etc., show that he did not sound a final *-ed.* Though this use even in prose was far from new (see e.g. Milton's *Areopagitica,* 1644), it is worth mentioning, since in the Augustan quest for a standard, Swift had lately objected to such "clipped" words.[1] Apostrophes may help Dan manage dubious plurals like *chimny's, grainary's.* Comically, they become automatic before many final *d*'s even where no letter is omitted: *forwar'd, Stamfor'd, understan'd, billiar'd, shoul'd.*

Pronunciation is probably revealed by *fullin mills, saplins, Uppinham; ne'er; Old* "Wold"; *joice* "joists"; by *canell, tarrier, jaums* "jambs"; and perhaps by *glassier* "glazier", *grainary, rabots, whither* "whether", and *wast* "waste": does he, like an Elizabethan, rhyme it to *hast?* Like Pope, Dan would certainly have rhymed "tea" to "obey": cf. *dales* "deals", *lay-ground* (cf. "lea"), "land under a cover-crop"; and probably his ubiquitous *extreamly. Man(n)or* "manure" probably represents "manoor" such as any barnyard still provides, or "manore"—the difference could be slight. For "kiln" he writes both *kill* and *kiln.* He has also both *kitchin* and *kitching; venture* and *venter*—both forms were carried to New England. Do his *carabines* and *cistiron* suggest a heavy country *r* like that exported to America?[2]

One forest word appears variously as *Hall, Hole,* and (from a different source) *Haw.* Another he writes twice *purlue woods* (**3, 54**), apparently saying it like today's (standard) "purlieu". But later his *Purlees* (**166**) and perhaps *Pour'lles* (**130**) seem to indicate something closer to the original Anglo-Norman *purale* "perambulation". Was he first living up to a citified acquired standard and later reverting to the familiar form?

Grammar and Idiom

A number of Dan's phrases are those comfortable non-conformities still familiar on both sides of the Atlantic: "Twenty of *them* labourers" (**90**); "*who* we met" (**3**); "L., W., and *myself* view'd . . ."(**3**); "The person . . . is *him* that will bring it" (**45**); "I *see* but one buck, which was a pollard" (**130**); "the man who *run* away" (**144**; so did Tom the piper's son!—at about this time?); "better than you *was*" (**94**); "was *wrote* upon the 10th Inst." (**94**); "they *drounded* two (hounds) and lost a third" (**107**); "the ant-hills are *laying* on heaps" (**5**); "the meadows . . . were *overflown*" (**87**).[3]

Most of Dan's grammar and idiom are normal for his time. Rarely he uses a verb like *followeth* (**5**), though once (**154**) the old form *hath* rescues him from a choice between *has* and *have.* Regularly the hounds *are come* (not

[1] Letter to *The Tatler*, no. 230 (1710); *Proposal for Correcting . . . the English Tongue* (1712). See A. C. Baugh, *Hist. of the Eng. Lang.*, 1957, p. 313. Yet Swift used them himself in writing to Stella.
[2] Several of Lord Cardigan's country correspondents spelled with multiple *r*'s. See F.iii.281 (Wade), 263-4 (Yorkshire tenants).
[3] A Nova Scotia farmer of my acquaintance says they are "flowed".

"have"). His *is* may be quite strong, with the force of "has already been done", as in (**38**) "the timber of the roof *is rais'd*". Other auxiliaries may be stronger than ours or have a different shading. (**7**) "Mr. Lynwood *must build*" is more strongly future, "*will* be obliged to". *Should* can be merely the past of *shall*, with no obligation: (**26**) *should have paid* is not "ought to have paid" but merely "was to pay"; (**25**) "where the sundial *should be*" means "was to have been"—they superseded it by a window. *Would* can keep its sense of "desire", and with some strength: (**3**) "what he *would have left*" is "what he wished them to leave". Dan piles up his auxiliaries fearlessly to get the right level of tense: (**7**) "you *would not have sufferd* the backing *to have been cut* down". Another form we have lost is (**34**) "they *would have had us din'd* with them", and (**132**) "Your Lordship would have had me gone to Wellom".

Prepositions, often unstable, readily give an antiquated flavour, as in *at spring* (**99**). *On* seems logical in "to lay Mr. Lynwood's goods *on* heaps" (**7**), and is reduced to *a* in *a shooting* and *ahunting* (both in **82**), *a sunder* (**88**). Dan freely ends with a preposition, ". . . comply *with*". He also uses the old substitution, then still current, (**4**) ". . . that he was apprenticed *withall*".

Dan's construction (**141, 145**), *made him he did* (or *could*) *not thrive*, seems unusual.[1]

His *wish*, corresponding to our *hope*, may take different auxiliaries, but apparently not conveying degree of doubt: (**84**) "I *wish* Pywell *may* pay his rent"; (**139**) "I *wish* the intrepidity of his (Lummis's) continual proceedings *does* not . . . prove his overthrow". (*Cf.* the less-than-acceptable modern "I *hope* he *does*".) Again, he writes (**128**), "They have not fol'd yet, but I *expect* every day *when* they will". The *when* seems to emphasize the futurity which *expect* implies.[2]

Odder than this *when* is Dan's *while* meaning "until": (**60**) "He would gladly stay at Deen *while grass comes*, that he may keep his horse without charge"; (**151**) "He will stay *while he has finished*". This, I am told, "is still current usage in Lincolnshire and the north of England. When automatic level crossings were introduced there a couple of years ago, signs which read 'Do not cross while red lights flash' led to some accidents. They were amended to say 'when'."[3]

Dan's usual introductory phrase with *Here* (corresponding to our "There is . . ." etc.) is common in *The Spectator* and Swift. "*Here has been* Eberill the joiner" (**124**); "*Here is* an estray Pricket come into the Park" (**85**). His "*Here was* snow fell *here*" is no more repetitive than our "*There was* snow *there*", and more logical than our "*There* has been snow *here*".

In general his idioms belong to his time. Some, since lost in England but not in America, therefore sound like Americanisms. His *sick* and *ill* are synonymous. A phrase like "The sash window which (you) *would have made*" now, I am informed, distresses some English hearers when Yankees say it. *Off of*, still common in Northamptonshire, is equally at home in New England. As for "I dare not let *teams* fetch the gravil bycause they will *rut the Park*" (**74**), perhaps Dan is writing loosely. Yet it sounds intriguingly as if here

---

[1] See *NED*, Make, IV, 52. Its handful of archaic examples all include ". . . that . . .", thus are not perfect parallels.

[2] Dan and his era would have no truck, one surmises, with the illogical modern Anglicism "I *expect* it *is*", "I *expect* he *did*", which amuses visitors from the U.S.A. Surely their localisms of *guess, reckon, calc'late* are more accurate synonyms for "think", "suppose", "imagine", "estimate"?

[3] Information from the General Editor. The *NED* gives this sense as dialect, with numerous earlier examples. Miss Wake reports it as current among country folk in Northants., *c.* 1900.

(though not elsewhere) he might be equating *team* with *wagon*. Yankees too sometimes "hitch up the hoss and team", and may even have a "single team" —a wagon for one horse.[1]

The style is the man

Our delight in Dan Eaton's language comes not from any "quaintness" but from his naturally good style, and perhaps even more from our sense of the person behind it.

Writing under pressure and in hard-wrested bits of time, Dan cannot plan his sentences ahead but must pour off his ideas as they rise, in long eager sentences rushing on from one subject to another, often doubling back to an earlier one. But they are merely non-stop, not rambling. He goes to his point without diffusion. His sentences may end with (if anything) a full stop or a dash or two. His paragraphs are long, often most of a letter. Sometimes he solidifies his page even more by filling out a short line with dots or little flourishes.[2]

Excitement or anxiety may upset his style and show in words crossed out or interlined, and even in the handwriting. See **35** about Tom Hutchinson; the explanation in **37**; chagrined bulletins on Pywell (**36, 38**); and the Battle of the Bottles (**80 ff.**). In **48**, fearing to sound familiar, he alters *call at* to *wait upon* (Mr. Brudenell). An unjust rebuke or implication stings him to asperity: see his protests about wheat, vouchers, hours of writing, and minding his tongue (**34, 81, 86; 54** and **167**). The sententious aphorisms dear to his period, which he uses only a couple of times, seem to represent not ornament but embarrassment, as a person suddenly struck self-conscious may stiffen in what looks like a pose. See **6**, where he fears to sound grasping —and how the reasons pile up!—and **40**.

Dan's language is refreshingly simple and concrete. He is concerned not with abstractions but with ray-grass, a leaking copper, a drench for steers and horses, a tiny boy's new *little bed*. Many comfortable turns of phrase seem Dan-like: "I made matters easy between S. and B. (**9**)" (Dan the peacemaker!); "I think it is *a great deal of pitty* . . ." (**135**). He has the countryman's homely, sometimes ironic humour that is as characteristic of New England as of old. The bad bricklayer *thought fit to march off* (**132**). At Blatherwick he *could not be honour'd with an audience* (**90**). When John Lynwood is revealed a rogue (**130**), "Poor unfortunate man, he has been forc'd to remove from Benefield *incog. for better air*".

As Miss Wake observes in her Introduction, "Dan's qualities and character shine through his letters". For such objective letters, these notably show the writer's feelings. He tends to words of emphasis, often optimistic or exuberant: (**133**) *most fine*; (**145**) *highly delighted*; (**131**) *with the greatest joy imaginable*. Favourites are *extreamly*; (*very*) *possitively*; *fast* ("vigorously": it snows and rains and the deer thrive *very fast*).

His language constantly shows Dan's tender heart. "For he, poor man, when we came to seiz for six pound . . . had but one poor cow of his own, which I could not bear to take away" (**9**). Another matter he leaves "intirely in your Lordship's breast" (**68**)—the loaded word pleads. "Little Master

---

[1] I do not think that American colloquial use observes the *NED* distinction between a cart with two wheels and one horse, and a wagon with four wheels and two horses. A New Englander reading Miss Baker's *Northants Glossary* may be surprised that she thought many items worth including, since he himself takes them for granted as what "everybody" says.

[2] The full length and consequently full structure of Dan's sentences is probably the only important feature which the reader cannot discover from our text.

Brudenell" is "as merry as possible" and "goes alone very strongly". (For Dan's feelings for his black horse see **45**.) *Per contra*, a few people he really dislikes, with apparent reason, such as Mr. Roberts of Wardley and Mr. Ward of Stoke, as his succinct phrases let us know. Humour often tempers his exasperation with others, like his bumbling friend Lummis (e.g. in **139**).

And then this plain-spoken man cares so much for beauty that once in a while it flowers in something very like poetry. Even the date may be eloquent. In **161**, in mid-May, when Dan has been but three months married, "The Park is now in perfect beauty".

D.C.W.

THE LETTERS OF DANIEL EATON

[1]   [*Sunday, 17 January, 1724/5.*]

My Lord,

    I receiv'd the honour of your Lordships letter and according to your command have sent the inclosed to Mr. Allam; I have given orders to the people your Lordship mentioned to dispose of their cocks. My Lord Albemarl's groom is not yet come.

    Wee have receiv'd 120£. of Corby wood mony for this year & I hope we shall receive the rest on Tuesday, which is the day appointed. To morrow I intend to examine into the wood affair at Glapthorne, and I will be at Upingham on Wednesday, & on Thursday wee shall sell Leicestershire coppice wood, when I will use my endeavour to make Worth clear the last years wood account.

    All the rest of your Lordships commands shall be carefully obey'd by

> Your Lordship's
> most humble
> and most faithful servant,

Deen, January 17th, 1724.   DA: EATON

[2]   [*Friday, 22 January, 1724/5.*]

My Lord,

    On Munday last John Lummis & I were at Glapthorne and examined into every article of the labourers bill, and we found nothing in it false. The measure of the hedge was right, and what they had said concerning a great part of it not being plash'd last time this part of the wood was sale we found to be true. Therefore since they had done justice I paid them, and we have sold most of the coppice wood that was left, to be paid at Midsummer next.

    On Tuesday last we receiv'd 130£. more of Corby coppice wood mony, and that which is not yet paid for is sold into such hands that I don't think there will be ten pounds unpaid when I leave this country. I believe we have chapmen enough to buy more wood than wee shall have to sell in the park; the labourers will have finished it and I believe we shall sell it on Wednesday next.

    On Tuesday night I receiv'd the honour of your Lordships letter, and on Wednesday according to your command I went to Uppingham, where I met Mr. Denshire & Mr. Allam. Mr. Denshire deliver'd up your Lordships bond to Mr. John Lynwood so soon as the assignment was executed, but he did not deliver it to me; he desir'd me to present his humble duty to your Lordship and begs that he may have a proper discharge from Mr. Wilcox's bond, which when he has got he will very readily resign the other. So I have your Lordships receipts still in my custody.

I endeavour'd to perswade Mr. Allam to take Mantons farm, and told him that there would certainly be more land to be laid to it in a very short time; but he says he is very sure it cannot be worth the rent your Lordship has fix'd upon it. He says that this week he will examine particularly into it & will let me know his resolutions on Munday next. If he will not take it there is a great many people ready for it. Mr. Hull, whom I saw at Uppinham, says he will take it if your Lordship and he can agree about the price. I told him what it was to be let at, and he seem'd to think that it was worth the mony, or near it, for he knows some of the land; but I did not give him any encouragement to go to see it, for I told him I thought it was promis'd. There was several other people with me to enquire about it; so that I am sure (notwithstanding what Mr. Roberts may attempt to the contrary), so soon as your Lordship is determined about it, it will not want a tenant. But I shall proceed no further in it, except with Mr. Allam, untill I receive your Lordships further commands.

Yesterday we were in Leicestershire and have sold the coppice wood. It comes to 29£., and but 16 parcells, and I think it is rather better sold than it was last year. The mony is to be paid at May Day. Edward Worths wood account was not ready, but I have made him promise me to come to Deen on this day se'night and clear it. I have been today in Deenthorpe closes & have discharg'd the tenants from plowing, but they beg they may plow a little longer, there land not being in order to lay down. Nevertheless I have forbid them till your Lordship comes to Deen. I have like wise been at Kirby to day to talk with Mr. Langtro about the park, but he was not at home.

My Lord Albemarls servant came on Munday, & Loxly & the grey mare went with him on Tuesday. On Wednesday my Lord Exeter sent six cocks, and I sent strict orders, in writing, with them to there quarters, & they are taken care of. Mr. Jones has sent your Lordships paper, and two quire for me when I come to Hamby.

I am,
      my Lord, Your Lordships
         most humble and
            most faithful servant,

Deen, January 22th, 1724.   DAN: EATON

[3]   [*Wednesday, 27 January*, 1724/5.]

My Lord,

On Satu[r]day last John Lummis & Will Wade & my selfe view'd and valued all the hovells & barn floors Mr. Lynwood has in Deen, and Ward was with us, but did not resolve what he would have left; he comes again today, when he is to give his final answer. I can not perceive that Pywell has abus'd the fences by cutting them, but he has neglected that part which is next to Weldon field, which I think he ought to repair before he quits the land. I deliver'd your Lordships orders to Reddyhoofe, which he promises to comply with.

On Sunday I receiv'd the honour of your Lordships letters, and on Munday I went with Mr. John Lynwood to Benefield to see the houses, one of which I must own is a wretched place. It stands in one of the worst places in the town, and there is now only two bays of building which can stand, and they are very low. Nevertheless the addition of two other bays, as Mr. Worly proposes (who we accidentally met as he was going into Warwickshire), will make the house habitable. But the great barn & stable, which are all the out houses there are, I am sure can stand but a very few years, for both the walls & timber are extreamly decay'd, & Mr. Worly does not propose altering them; and when they fall Mr. Lynwood must build them at his own charge.

The other is a very convenient and agreeable house, and I think not too big, with all manner of convenient outhouses, and no superfluous ones, except that half the great stable is sufficient, & if Mr. John Lynwood might have it, I really think it would be more for his advantage than the other. But this I believe is impossible, for I see very clearly thro' Mr. Worley's design, tho' he is very close & subtle. I am much mistaken if Mr. Worley does not intend this house for himself. For Mr. Joy has had a mind a long time to buy his lease of Biggin, and I know that he has been endeavouring to perswade Mr. Joy to build him an house elsewhere, but I don't yet see the foundation of it laid; and since he has had the cream of Biggin Grounds, he is certainly the more willing to part with them for better (which he has cast an eye upon). And by what I have heard of Mr. Joy, he knows his business better than to lay out 500£. upon an house for his steward, when 50£. will repair & make one convenient that is already built; and the less charge Mr. Worley puts Mr. Joy to, the more he can afford to give him for his lease.

I wonder that Mr. Jones, Mr. Joseph & Mr. John Lynwood have not discovered this, who have been so frequently in Mr. Worleys company. I found that he rais'd difficulties where there really was none, for it is contrary to reason to think that Mr. Grey, who has only three of family, and himself & wife in years, would not quit that house where he lives, and has only two years certain, for a third part of the mony that must be laid out in altering the other. What I have said may perhaps be wrong, for it is only my conjecture, but I believe your Lordship will think it probable; and I have some other reasons for what I have said, two [sic] tedious to mention now.

I have advis'd Mr. Lynwood to make a fast bargain for the land so soon as Mr. Worley returns, for I don't think it too dear; I was round it with him on Munday. I likewise advis'd him to be rul'd by Mr. Worley, who certainly has power to do him very great service.   Mr. Allam was here on Munday, but he has not taken the land; he has sent your Lordship a letter wherein he has express'd his thoughts upon it. He bid me let it if I could to any body else.

I was yesterday at Stanion and receivd some more arrears of chief rent, and Will Rowlat, who owes more than all the rest, will be with me on Fryday next. I find that there is a piece of his land containing about 40 square yards enclos'd by the Duke of Montagu into Winshaw. Most of it was freebord in Winshaw before; and whereas he was not excepted in the Act of Parliament as Thomas Kilbourn was, Mr. Booth & Mr. Walter say that your Lordship ought to make him satisfaction for it, his Grace being freed from it by the Act. Now since Rowlats demands are reasonable, for he only d[e]sires an allowance for it out of his arrears of chief rent, I shall allow it him on Fryday if I hear nothing from your

Lordship to the contrary, for Mr. Denshire told me that if these people were resolute, we could not redeem the chief rent by law.

I paid the labourers their bill & told the cottagers what they were to trust to as to their rent. We have cry'd the sale in the park for Munday next. Mr. John Lynwood tells me that he has wrote to your Lordship to desire Manton's farm, and beggs that I would not let it till I have your Lordships further commands. I shall examine particularly into Deenthorpe affairs to day, & will send your Lordship an account in my next.

I have look'd in your Lordship's scrutore and there is no key's there but the key of Priors Haw, the key of the park, the key of Deen gardens, & the key of your Lordships closset in the court, which last I made use of to shut the window shutters which I perceiv'd were open, & then I laid it where I found it. Mr. Hodgkin begs the favour of your Lordship to lend him the centors, for he is going to make a seller in his own house, & they will be of very great service to him, & it will be no damage to your Lordship, and he is willing to make any satisfaction for the use of them. Will Wade presents his duty to your Lordship & desires me to let you know that all things under his care are well. Mr. Ly[n]wood was satisfied with your Lordships [receipt & has deliverd your Lordships*] bond into my custody. They have not yet begun to plant the quick upon the Common, for it is not yet got.

All the rest of your Lordships commands shall be carefully obey'd by

> Your Lordships
>   most humble and
>   most faithful s[ervant,]

Deen, January 27th, 1724.   D: EATON

[*Direction endorsed:*—]
        To the Right Honble. the Earl of Cardigan, these present.

[*Seal*]

[**4**]   [*Monday, 1 February,* 1724/5.]

My Lord,

I have receiv'd the honour of your Lordships letter. On Wednesday last I examined into the affairs of Deenthorpe, & I find that there is only one man there who has no legal settlement there except James Townsend, who your Lordship knows built the house he lives in; & if we should remove Joseph Starsmore, the person aforementioned, then old Widow Cornil would immediately fall upon the parish, for he maintains her, being her son-in-law. There is indeed some others, but they have certificates from Deen.

As to the plowing, old Will Wade plows about twenty acres, John Braughton about four acres, and Jenkin Harrisson about twelve acres, & the tenants of Weldon about five acres. John Braughtons land is very cold land, & ought to be plow'd and laid high this year & sown with ray grass. Jenkin Harrissons land will all of it bear good trey foil, & may be made fit for it this spring. The land that old Wade plows may some of it be sown with trey foil & some with ray grass, & the land that Weldon tenants plow seems to me to be harsh enough for cinq foil. But I think it is no great matter whether this last is laid down or plow'd, for the land is naturally very bad, & there is only six acres of Wades land that can be laid down this spring.

On Friday last Edward Worth came & brought me the remaining part of Leicestershire timber mony, & I believe has clear'd the account; but I cannot certainly tell whither he has or not, for he left all his vouchers & papers behind him; so I only gave him a receipt for what mony he paid. Thomas Bell has clear'd his account, and Lummis & Spencer promise to clear theirs on Friday next.

I have agreed with Will Rowlat for his land for 26 shillings. And Thomas Rowlat of Brigstock was with me, & tells me that the Duke of Montagu has enclosd more of his land than of Will Rowlats, which I will enquire into, & I believe I can agree with him for it at a very low rate. I was at Boughton on Saturday last, but neither Mr. Booth nor Mr. Walter are in the country.

To day wee have sold all the coppice wood in the park, both of this new sale & of the other old sale that remain'd unsold, & have receivd most of the mony for it. To morrow I must go to Weldon Sale to pitch upon some more wood for your Lordships use, where I expect to see Mr. Langtro & shall talk with him about Priors Haw Park. I have been twice round the park since your Lordship left Deen & I cannot see any disorders.

I have serch'd in your Lordships scrutore & have found the right key, I believe, but I could not find Wilcocks's bond. I cannot prevale with John Parsons to fix a time for the payment of 50£. Mr. Lynwood promises to clear his [Leicestershire*] arrear before I leave this country.

Mr. John Lynwood intends to go to morrow to Benefield & to make a sure bargain for the land. I intend to go on Wednesday to Wardly, & there I will observe all your Lordship's commands very strictly. The inclosed is a letter which Mrs. Bradshaw receiv'd from her son's master that he was apprentice withall. 'Tis true he has always been a very great friend to her son, but since he is a Quaker and a creditor, he may perhaps, if he could get mony into his hands, pay himself in full, tho' he pays the others but in part. He is a man of very good substance & promises very fair, but she begs your Lordship's advice in it. The Common goes on very well now, both for plowing & fencing, & the ground turns up very rich. The man that casts the ant-hills works very hard & has done a great part of Sheep Close.

When Ward of Stoke[1] came on Thursday last, he declar'd his resolution that he would not buy the barn floor nor anything else that is at Winsals. But he insists on Mr. Lynwood's leaving the great hovell, which is worth 10£. at least to remove, but a great deal more to stand, & he will not buy the floor at any price, and he insists upon penns to be made for his conveniency. I think it is as unreasonable for him to refuse the barn floor at a moderate price,—for it is an extream good one and certainly very necessary,—as to desire the great hovill to stand, a third part of which I am sure would be sufficient for him. In short I don't like the man,—I think he is unreasonable in everything he requires.

Your Lordship knows best what bargain you made with him, but I am a stranger to it; but I know a man who is very substantial (& I

---

[1] Probably Stoke Doyle.

believe would be a better & more peaceable tenant and afford your
Lordship more satisfaction than can be expected from Ward), who would
buy all the things & wheatcase & every thing else that is any ways
necessary, of Mr. Lynwood, & give the same rent for the farm that Ward
is to do. The reason why I write this is by cause Ward seems to think
that he has an hard bargain of it.

I hope I shall clear the last years wood account this week.
I am,

> my Lord, Your Lordships most humble
> and most faithful servant,

February the first, 1724.   D: EATON

[5]   [*Saturday*, 6 *February*, 1724/5.]

My Lord,
I receiv'd yours of the second. I have deliver'd your Lordships
orders to the tenants of Deenthorpe. I have sent your Lordships letter
to Ward & have ordered him to be with me on Munday. I have sent
Mr. Whitwells mony today by Walt: Harrisson. I have finished Mr. John
Billinge's account. I cannot find Wilcocks bond & Mr. Lynwood is
very possitive he never had [it]. Mr. Langtro was not at Weldon Sale.
I intend to go to Kirby this afternoon.

I was at Wardly on Thursday and have examined into what your
Lordship orderd as followeth: I find your Lordship was misinform'd as
to the plowing the land, for I am sure it could not have been done better.
And for the cutting of the hedges, those that Mr. Roberts has cut this
year he promises both to cock-hedge & ditch; those that have been cut
formerly in all the lordship have suffered very much, partly by the un-
skilfulness of labourers & then by the neglect of tenants after they have
been cut, that a great many fine hedges are quite ruin'd. I think there
ought to be a clause in every lease to oblige all tenants to cock-hedge &
scoure the ditches of all the hedges they plash.

John Manton will give fifty pounds a year for his farm, & bear a
third part of the tax, and be oblig'd to maintain his wife's mother, who
has lived upon the farm this forty years, as long as she lives. I think
that what he proposes is very reasonable, for I have look'd upon all his
land, & I find that the close that is valued at 25s. per annum is worth
more, but the rest is dear enough of 18s. per acre, take it alltogether;
for some of it (that has not been lately plowd) I think is but indifferent
land, and I do realy think that it would not be let for 55£. per annum
together, for whosoever takes it will examine it thro'ly first. John Mantons wife dyed about a week since, and if he quits the town his wifes
mother must of necessity fall upon the parish.   I have got Harriss's
lease.

I beg leave to advise your Lordship to one thing, which I am sure
will be of great advantage to Mr. Brudenell, viz: that whereas the land
that Mr. Roberts is now a plowing, which I look upon to be about 50
acres, cannot recover it self under three years at least, and in the mean
time cannot be worth above a mark an acre, now if his Honour would be
at the charge of sowing trey foil, which must be sown & rol'd in immediately after Mr. Roberts has sown his barly & oats, it will make the land

worth 20s. an acre the first year, & the trey foil will continue till the natural grass kills it, which will be four years at least. This, my Lord, I will be bound to make good, for I think I never saw better land for trey foil than this is; but the soil is not so rich as the other side of the lordship is. The charge will not be very great, for Mr. Dawson of Weldon has a large quantity of seed by him, which I believe for ready mony I could buy for 2s. a strike at the most.

The park sale came to 57£. Mr. John Lynwood has contracted with Mr. Worley for about 400 acres of land and another house in Benefield which was not proposd before, but it will be made a good house for him.   Mr. Worly will not let Jonas be his shepherd, but insists upon his imploying John Harrisson, which I think is an hardship. Mr. John Lynwood begs your Lordship would assist him in this & write to Mr. Joy about it; but I have not agreed with Richard Harrisson, for fear that Jonas must stay at Deenthorp (from whence he cannot remove without a certificate). If so, I think he will be a better servant than the other.

J. Lummis & J. Hinks will be at Hamby tomorrow, when I will send Christopher Dexter's valuation of the alterations of Mr. Lynwoods house, & on Munday I will take a particular of the moveable goods. The ant hills are laying on heapes.   I have sent the hound whelpes & spanniels to quarters & have put the hounds into the little kenell.   I intend to draw a plan of Mr. Lynwood's house, &c., & bring it with me, which I hope will be on Thursday next.

I am your
      Lordships most humble
        & most faithful servant,

February 6th, 1724.   Dan: Eaton

I beg your Lordships commands about Manton, & likewise about the trey foil for fear it should be sold; I never knew any sold under 2s. 6d. a strike before.

[6]   [Sunday, 7 February, 1724/5.][1]

My Lord,
The inclosed is Christopher Dexters valuation. Mr. Langtro was not at home yesterday, but I will go to him to morrow. Mr. Robinson thinks there can be no trees planted this year, & says it will be better to let them alone for next winter, & in the meantime to prepare the ground for them.

I cannot think of any close so convenient for us (instead of the Green) as that which your Lordship has let to Will Bell. I should be very far from desiring any man's bargain out of his hands, but necessity has no law, for without a piece of grass ground to keep our horses, it is impossible we should hold the rest that I have taken, for we must have 22 acres of fallow this next summer, which [which[d]] cannot be managed with less than seven horses; & we are oblig'd to lay what grass ground we now have for hay, bycause before I knew that Mr. Lynwood was to have the Green, I had got all the anthills cast in all the closes. And this can be no great inconveniency to Will Bell, by cause I heard him say that he did not

---

[1] Date reconstructed from internal evidence. See 5 and 7.

greatly want it. I beg your Lordships answer to this, that I may prevent his plowing, for which I think he has liberty by his bargain. I think to draw an exact plan of Mr. Lynwoods house & places adjacent, for there will not be a great deal more trouble in drawing it exactly than in drawing it indifferently.

To morrow I will collect mony to pay Mr. Goode. I fear I shall hard[ly[^i]] clear John Spencers account of last years timber before I leave this country, but there will not be much behind.

I am your Lordships
    most humble & most
      faithfull servant,

Deen, Sunday morn.   DAN: EATON

[7]   [*Saturday*, 13 *February*, 1724/5.][1]

My Lord,

On Saturday last I drew a letter of licence & composition for Mrs. Bradshaw, & she sent it to her friend Mr. Thruckston, & has desir'd him so soon as he has got it sign'd to send it down that your Lordship may see it. On Munday Mr. John Lynwood with me met Ward at Winsals farm, & he has agreed to buy the barn floor at a price that shall be fix'd upon it by two men chose by Mr. Lynwood & him. He likewise has agreed to pay for the trey foil seed that was sown by Mr. Lynwood last year, & has agreed that he may remove every thing from the farm except a little hovell of three bays & the barn & stable.

I likewise on Munday collected mony of Deenthorpe tenants, & on Tuesday I paid Mr. Goode a quarters tyth due at St. Thomas. He refus'd to allow a quarters tax, for he says that the tax by Act of Parliament is due but every half year, & his tyth is due quarterly, so that if he should dy before Lady Day, his successor must pay the half years tax, tho' he receives but a quarters tyth.

Likewise on Tuesday I deliverd your Lordships commands to Mr. Langtro after as good a manner as I could. He says that the substance of what he said to Lummis was this, that he believ'd him to be the person that advis'd your Lordship to cut down the hedge row, by which my Lord Hattons hedge had receiv'd a great deal of damage, or otherwise that he caus'd it to be cut down without your knowledge. He owns that he did not treat Lummis with so much good manners as he would have done any other of your Lordships servants, for some private reasons which he did not discover to me, but he says that he shall make it his study to continue good neighbourhood between your Lordship's and my Lord Hatton's family. I told him, amongst other things, that I was very well assur'd that had your Lordship known beforehand what damage Lord Hattons hedge would have suffer'd by it (which indeed is very great), you would not have sufferd the backing to have been cut down. He treated me very civily, but I hear by those that were by that he was very rough with Lummis.

On Wednesday & Thursday last I survey'd Ashleys field & the little meadow & that close of Will Wade's which John Peak is to have, & have

---

[1] Date conjectured from internal evidence. See **4, 5,** and **6**.

sent the contents inclosed. Your Lordship was pleas'd to say in your last that you would have John Parsons have one of our closes that lye on the other side of the lane, but I always thought that he was to have two of them, and I have bought trey foil of Mr. Dawson to sow upon the other, in order to make it fit for a cottage pasture; and John Parsons's farm will not be very convenient without them two closes.

I deliver'd your Lordships commands to Mr. John Lynwood concerning his quitting the house at Lady Day; but he beggs that he may stay in it 'till his house at Benefield is ready for him, for if he goes to Mr. Jones's he does not know what to do with his goods, for to lay them on heaps would do them a great deal of damage. Mr. Worly will get the house ready for him as spedily as possible, and in the mean time, if your Lordship has no private reasons to the contrary, I think he might stay in one part of the house while the workmen are altering the other, without any damage to them or your Lordship; for he may fasten those two doors which come out of the new building and out of the kitchin into the old building, & live in those two parts. I beg your Lordship would consider of & consent to this, for I think indeed that he cannot remove so soon as Lady Day without suffering great damage in his goods, & I would have him have no reason to exclaim against your Lordship. He says he will willingly quit it so soon as the old building is made fit for your Lordship to live in.

Christopher Dexter & John Winsall say that Stanion stone will be the most proper & that about 14 loads will be sufficient, which Will Wade tells me your Lordships team can fetch, for every body here is busy in seeding. The reason why the slaters could not go on was by-cause they could not run their slate out of the log for want of frost, but this last frost will help them.

The quick will be all planted upon the Common on Munday next, & I think it is as well done as ever I saw any. John Peak desires me to let your Lordship know that they now lose some deer, not many, & that they have no fodder at Presto Foddering & not a great deal any where else, & the park indeed is extreamly bare of grass. I deliver'd your Lordships letter & proposals to my Lord Hatton yesterday & his Lordship promised to write an answer & send it to me to day.

Mr. John Lynwood begs very hard for the Green, as well as Deenthorpe Meadow, & while he stays at Deen I think he cannot do without it conveniently. I had come to Hamby to day had not John Lummis told me that your Lordship expected that I would draw a plan of Mr. Lynwoods house before I came; for since Mr. Robinson told me that there could be no trees planted this year, I thought that might have been done soon enough when I come back; but I am going about it to day. John Lummis tells me likewise that your Lordship would have me measure the close that Thomas Meadows & John Winsal have taken, which I will do. I have sent the papers which your Lordship orderd me to look in your scrutore for.

I am your Lordships most humble & most faithfull servant,

DAN: EATON

I have indeavour'd to perswade John Lynwood to take Richard Harrisson for his shepherd, but he says he likes John as well.

[Direction endorsed:—] To The Right Honble. the Earl of Cardigan,

[Seal] these present.

On 13th February Lord Cardigan was fox-hunting at Hanby (see 7), the "hunting house" in Lincolnshire which he shared with his friend Lord Gower. On the 24th February, 1725, Cardigan House was burnt down (B.D.p.210), so it may be assumed that he then went to London. The winding up of accounts and tenancy affairs referred to in 1 to 7 were in preparation for the New Year on 25th March when tenants moved and new leases came into force.

[8]   [*Saturday,* 27 *March,* 1725.]

My Lord,
    On Thursday last all the new tenants took possession of their farmes & Walt Harrisson is remov'd to Mrs. Walkers house. I could not perswade Jonas & his wife to go to John Spencers house, by cause they say that as Will Barnes's wife was a thief once, she may perhaps be so still, therefore they durst not go to live with her. They lye in the chamber of that little place your Lordship intended for Mrs. Wilkins, & get their victuals in the kitchin of Walt Harrissons house, where they us'd to live. This they intend to do till your Lordship shall order them another place.
    I have been to day at Stanion, and all the farmers & most of the rest have paid their rent.   John Peak desires me to ask your Lordship whither you would have any part of the park laid for hay this year or not.   I told Elisha Harrisson what your Lordship orderd me concerning Richard Harrissons close, but he insists upon it, that your Lordship let it to him your self, at 9s. per acre.
    All things here are well, & Mr. Lynwood['s] house goes on very well.
                    I am your Lordships
                        most humble and
                            most obedient servant,
                            D: EATON

Deen, March 27th, 1725.

P.S.   Christopher Dexter & the glassier beg that [your Lord]ship [*MS torn*] would be pleasd to order them [? their mon]y.

From 28th March to 9th April the absence of letters indicates that Lord Cardigan was at Deene, but between 10th April and 15th August he was away for most of the time, as Dan wrote forty letters to him during this period. In April and May Cardigan was certainly in London for he made twenty-three attendances at the House of Lords in those months (Journals of the House of Lords, XXII). By 3rd June he was at Bath and stayed there until at least 17th June (24, 29). About 1st July he was back in London until after the middle of August, as the following group of letters ends with 48, dated 15th August.

[9]   [*Saturday,* 10 *April,* 1725.]

My Lord,
    I receiv'd the honour of your Lordships letter by Thomas Hutchinson. What your Lordship was pleasd to write concerning Leicester-

shire I had perfected before I receiv'd it. For the week [that^d] [after^i] your Lordship left Deen I went into Leicestershire, for I knew there was several affairs to settle. The first thing I did, I made matters easy between John Spencer & Brightman concerning the repairs of Stonton Hall, & windows & fences, &c., & they are both satisfied. George Woodcock has paid his Lady Days rent to Dunmore, & he promises to return it to your Lordship as soon as possible. Beau Woodcock promises to pay all his rent at the first of May next. Mr. John Lynwood intends that your Lordship shall receive the mony of Spencer & Freeman for his penns, &c.

Mr. Iliffe's rent is secur'd & to be paid at the second day of May, but he beg'd of me to continue the seizure of the goods that are in his house at Cranoe, for he says that it will be of service to him, which I have done. He desired likewise that his son might be tenant to that house he lives in, and not himself, which I told him I would acquaint your Lordship withall. Your Lordship may easily know the cause of this request. I cannot see that it will be any disadvantage to you, but it will certainly be of service to him.

Bates's rent is secur'd, but I had the greatest difficulty to secure Thomas Johnson's, for he, poor man, when wee came to seiz for six pounds due to your Lordship at Lady Day, had but one poor cow of his own, which I could not bear to take a way. So I have contriv'd the following method to make matters easy & your Lordship safe, viz: that whereas we seiz'd [a gread^d] a great many cattell of Will Bryon's that were joisted with Johnson, I have made him promise the payment of forty shillings at May Day, tho' he did not owe so much to Johnson, & Johnson himself is to pay 20s. then. Then I told Will Bates that if his son would pay the rest & become surety for the rent, I would let him have the Warren & a little close that Rebecca Briggs had (for she had nothing but joisters upon it), & that little close would find him with hay in winter. So I orderd him to bring his son to Stonton, which he did on Wednesday last, & I met him there & he gave his note for 2£. 5s. 5d., which with the tax paid is in full of Johnsons 6£., & he became joint tenant with his father. By this means, my Lord, poor Johnson keeps his homestead, which your Lordship intended for Bates, & it will keep Johnsons cow, & he is very thankfull. He is to pay 30s. a year & Bates 5£. 10s.

Freeman of Cranoe has by his ignorance given the parishoners a great deal of trouble concerning a man and his family that he brought into the town, who came from an extra-parochial place; & it would have been a great deal worse had not his Honour Brudenell fortunately been at Oakham when it came before the Bench of Justices, and knowing them to be your Lordships tenants, he tells me that he thinks they will have but little further trouble, bycause there was an order granted to remove them. I was with his Honour to day & he desir'd [me^i] to let your Lordship know that he will write to you next post. He is very sorry to hear that your Lordship is not well. I have been about his affairs three days this week, but the particulars are too tedious to mention.

I went to deliver your Lordship's commands to Elisha Harrisson, but he was not at home. Richard Harrisson will be here to morrow, when we shall bargain with him. I went with J. Peak & Will Wade, & have pitch'd upon that part of the park for hay that is next to Fallow Close & Cooks field; the wood that lies in Priors Hall ridings will go a great way towards fencing of it, and as soon as it is done I will measure it & then it may be mown by the great. Godfrey has not yet bargained for Parsons's hay & there is none of it remov'd. I shall receive Corby rent on Tuesday; they tell me they are all ready. I have receiv'd some of Deenthorpe rents, & I hope I shall receive the rest upon the 20th of this month.

There is no mony uncollected of last years wood account but what is in Thomas Bailys hands of Stanion & Clem Barret of Bulwik: 2£. 7s. 6d

I was yesterday morning in the gardens & there is a very good quantity of fruit of all sorts.   Christopher Dexter will give me the plan of Mr. Lynwoods house & I will send it to your Lordship on Munday. The house goes on very well; there is as many masons as can conveniently stand to work.

Mr. John Lynwood has brought three or four loads of his goods to the Hall & they are put into the steward['s] parlour. He begs that he may put the rest of them in to the long grainary over his stable, which I think, if your Lordship approves of it, will be more convenient than bringing them down to the Hall. There is two other grainary's there, wherein he proposes to lay his beans & malt your Lordship has bought of him, which Will Wade is to keep the keys of, so soon as it is measured.

I sent three horses & a cart to Mr. Brudenells use, before I receiv'd your Lordships letter. I hope I shall finish Mr. Brudenells affair on Wednesday, & then I will send your Lordship a particular account of it. I have nothing else to inform your Lordship at present.

I am your Lordships most humble
        and most faithful servant,

Deen, April 10th, 1725.   DAN: EATON

I beg the favour of your Lordship to frank the inclosed: it is to my poor sister that marryed the trooper.

[**10**]   [*Tuesday*, 20 *April*, 1725.]

My Lord,

I have bargained with Richard Harrisson for 8£. a year wages and the keeping of one cow constantly, for which he is to shepherd all your land in Deenthorpe & to be constantly in your business; & he is to have the keeping of two sheep in lieu of his killing all the moles.

Your Lordship did not fix who should have a cottage pasture in Deen before you went; I have therefore inclosed the names of those people who I think stand the most in need of the pasture. There is six of them, but since the pasture will keep but 5 cows, your Lordship must determine who are to have it. Widow Sutton I think deserves one more than Richard Wilkins, for tho' he has three children he is better able to work for them than this woman, who besides her own two small children maintains her husbands mother, who otherwise must be an immediate charge to the parish.   Mr. Jones desires to know what sea-coal your Lordship intends to have.   Those people that your Lordship shall be pleasd to fix for the pasture promise to stock it with their own cows, & never to let it any more.   Last [*sic*] I was yesterday with the rest of us at Glapthorne viewing the oaks.

Last night I receiv'd the honour of your Lordships letter. We are going to day to view at Corby, & to morrow I will execute your Lordships commands at Stamford, &c. There is in this country extraordinary promising crops of all sorts of grain, & more grass than ever I knew so soon in the year. The park looks extreamly well, & the deer begin to mend.

I do assure your Lordship I am never idle. I will take care for wagons, and of every thing else according to your Lordships command.

I could neither prevale with John Reddyhoofe to bring the doors of the rooms in the house that John Winsal is to live in again, nor to mend the windows, notwithstanding I threatned him very severely; so that John Winsall & his old parents live very uncomfortably, for there is no doors to any of the rooms, nor windows to the house.

I am your Lordships most humble
    & most faithful servant,

Deen, April 20th, 1725.   DAN: EATON

[*Endorsed in another hand*:—] Daniel Eaton's Letters, 1725.

[**11**]   [*Sunday, 25 April, 1725.*]

My Lor[d],

I have procur'd two wagons which will be in Town on Fryday, the seventh [the^d] day of May. I desire your Lordship would send me word where they are to take up the goods, that I may let them know. I have bargained with them for three shillings and four pence per hundred. If your Lordship wants another wagon, I can get one at a weeks warning.

I have inclosed a plan of the inside of Deen Church. The arches are 20 foot high from the crown to the floor. I have likewise inclosed a plan of the alcove room floor & north side, & the south side is the same except the chimny. They have raisd the timber of the first floor at Mr. Lynwood's house, and proceed very well. The little houses in the back yard are finishd,—I mean the slating.

John Kingston excercises the young hounds at the ram, & they are all well, and every thing else here. I am,

    Your Lordships most humble & most faithfull servant,

Deen, April 25th, 1725.   D: EATON

[**12**]   [*Sunday, 2 May, 1725.*]

My Lord,

I receiv'd the honour of both your Lordships letters. Will Wade has bottled one hogshead of small beer, but I cannot tell whither I can send it by one of the jocky wagons or not. The owners of them are both to be with me to day, but I doubt the post will be gone first. I belive one of the wagons will be in Town on Wednesday night next, but however they will both be there on Fryday night at the farthest. Your Lordship shall have an exact account by the next post.

The chestnut mare has not foled but we expect her every day. The horses according to your Lordships order are gone into Lincolnshire. The padocks cannot both be laid for hay till your Lordship has given orders where to dispose of your colt & Mr. Billinge's & the dog-rams. One of them has been laid a great while. I have orderd all the coppice keepers to be ready to view those trees to morrow that Mr. Peircy & Mr. Tryon shall think proper to come down; I am glad your Lordship took this method, for now there is no danger of our displeasing you. Mr. John Lynwood says that Simson went forward for London on Thursday last, & will pay the bills.

As soon as the roads are better I shall order the seacole to be brought in by the boon teams, and I desire to know where your Lordship would have it laid. Mr. Roberts does not know the exact survey of Tookys grounds, so I must measure them. I am sorry the draught of the alcove room did not please your Lordship; I am sure I laid down the length, bredth & heigth, and scituation and size of the windows & chimny very exactly, and likewise the partition. Mrs. Markland had a years wages due to her yesterday. Mary Ellis was paid to January 9th, 1722 [*i.e.* 1722/3].

There is six cupples of hounds come from Lord Gowers. John Kingston goes out with the young hounds tomorrow morning to see whether they will hunt or not, for as yet he has only walk'd them in couples & aw'd them at sheep. He says they are very tractable. Tom Hutchinson goes with him on the bald horse that Mr. Billinge used to ride, who is now very sound and Tom hopes he will continue so. John Hinks cut the willows on the backside of the Parsonage orchyard a great while agone, and he says that nobody has sayd anything to him about them either at the time of cutting them or since.

I cannot hear that Mr. Goode said any thing of your Lordship when he came out of the church, or of any body else, but told the churchwardens, in a great heat, that if they did not get the rubbish out of the church yard before the Visitation, he would present them. But he is now very well satisfied at its being levelled & sown with hay seed as it is.—If I can hear anything further, I will let your Lordship know.— That part of the park that is to be for hay is finished, and the[r^d] hedge is very well made. There was more wood in Priors Haw ridings than did it; the rest I have orderd to be fagotted & brought to the Hall. I hope this week I shall finish the wood account, & then I will send your Lordship an abstract of it. The building goes on very well.

Will Wade has sent a trunk of butter, & all things under his care are well.

I am your Lordships
Most humble and most faithful servant,

D: Eaton

P.S. Your Lordship did not say any thing about the cottage pasture, & the poor people can not tell what to do with their cows.

Deen, May 2d, 1725.

[**13**]   [*Tuesday, 4 May, 1725.*]

My Lord,

The wagons will certainly be in Town on Fryday night,—both of them. I have sent the small beer by one of them at 3*s.* 6*d.* per hundred, which is the price they have for carrying their wood.

I receiv'd the honour of your Lordships letter. The chestnut mare has not yet foled; Tom will obey your Lordships commands both as to her & the other so soon as they will take horse. I have appointed Munday next for collecting Leicestershire rents, & when I am there I will take a very particular account of all things concerning Hurst's Meadow, &c.

Mr. John Lynwood has a greater stock of cows and heffers in the Green & Deenthorpe Meadow than they will well bear, but I will give your Lordship a more particular account next post. Mr. Brudenell, Mr. Tryon, & Mr. Peircy were here yesterday, & they mark'd 27 trees to come down, which we afterwards view'd; & tho 7 of them are small ones, the[y] come to 85£. 17*s.* 6*d.* at our view & I hope they will be sold so on Fryday next.

All things at Deen are well. I am,
        Your Lordships most humble & most faithfull servant,

Deen, May the fourth, 1725.   D Eaton

[**14**]   [*Thursday, 6 May, 1725.*]

My Lord,

The chestnut mare has fold a very fine colt fole of her own colour. Tom Hutchinson goes to day with your Lordship's pad mare to my Lord Gowers, for she now goes to horse very keen. Mr. John Lynwood has 9 very good cows & heffers in the Green and 12 more in Deenthorpe Meadow, and he has a very good stock upon his land in Benefield. The pheasant in the garden has laid thirteen eggs. Dan Whitworths letter came too late for me to send an horse by the jocky wagons, so I intend to send one by the carryer on Sunday.

I have just now receiv'd the honour of your Lordships letter. I have collected Stanion & Corby rents & as much as I could get of Deenthorpe. There is due to Mr. Lynwood from Will Wade 11£. 0. 0.; from Ward about 10£. for the barn floor & trey foil; from Freeman, &c., I think 13£., and from me 6£. 10*s.* 0*d.*; & I believe there will be 5£. more due from me to him when I have had all his dung, for I believe he has near 200 load. I don't hear any complaint from the new tenants. Will Dunmore has returnd 50£. to Mr. Keck.

The little bay mare that John Goodwin used to ride has had the strangles very violently, but wee think she is something better.

I am your Lordships
        Most humble and most faithful servant,

Deen, May 6th, 1725.   D Eaton

I beg your Lordship would let old Guelder keep his cow, for he is very old and infirm and past his work, & I think cannot live a great while. Then his pasture will fall to somebody else.

[**15**]   [*Sunday, 9 May, 1725.*]

My Lord,
We have sold all the trees in the park that were view'd at our view, except one which is not sold.   There is 145 yards of unbleech'd flaxen cloth bought at Brigstock Fare; it cost 7£. 8s. 10d., which is but about 1s. per yard. The maids are whitening it.   There was no good, finer cloth there, but if your Lordship would have any finer, there is a man lives at Stockerson can furnish you with any sort and any quantity. I bought some of him yesterday for shirts at 2s. 6d. per yard, which my mother tells me is very good & very cheap.   I think it will be more for your Lordships advantage to mow the grass in the plantation than in the south padock, for that will cut as much grass, very near, as this, and ought to be mown to kill the weeds.
The front wall of Mr. Lynwood's house is got up something higher than the wall of the old house was.   The young hounds behave themselves extreamly well. Tom   & John Kingston go out with them each other day. I shall go into Leicestershire to morrow, where I shall execute your Lordships commands. The bay mare is almost well. I shall send an horse for Dan Whitworth today by the carrier.   John Peak is very thankfull that your Lordship will let him come to Bath. I shall take what care I can in his absence.
I have nothing else to inform your Lordship of at present.
         I am your Lordships
            Most humble and most faithful servant,

Deen, May 9th, 1725.   DAN: EATON

There is a trunk of butter sent by the carrier with the horse.

[*Seal*]

[**16**]   [*Thursday, 13 May, 1725.*]

My Lord,
On Munday last I went to Stonton and met your Lordship's letter as I went. The tenants have paid their rent very well; what remains in arrear I have appointed the 11th day of June next to receive it. Beau Woodcock has paid all his Lady Days rent except 10£., which he begs your Lordship would stay for 'till you receive Lady Days rent of the rest of the tenants, but he promises to pay it before if you require it.
On Tuesday morning I sent for Langton men to [meet*(ms. worn)*] Mr. Elliot, J. Lummis, Will Dunmore, & my self at Hurst's Meadow, &c., which they did. And we find that nine tenths [at least[i]] of that brook which parts Hurst's Meadow from Church Langton Field is intirely upon ground that belongs to Church Langton, as it does most plainly appear by a numerous quanti[ty] of old meers which are in the said meadow; and there is apparently a large quiantity[*sic*] of grou[n]d in the said meadow which belongs to this town. And it does likewise appear that so often as your Lo[rdship's] tenants have scowred the brook, they have been trespassers upon Church Langton people, their land lyinge [o]n both sides, almost all the way.

When your Lordship has read this account, which we all of us ag[ree to] be right, your Lordship cannot blame the people for insisting upon their priviledges. They talk'd very [smo]othly &, we think, offer very fairly, viz: that they will resign all their land to your Lordship a[s] it now lyes with the brook, if you will be pleasd to set them out a piece [to them^d] of your land in any place of the said meadow which may be [an^i] equivalent, allowing a sufficient quantity for your Lordship's right of common upon theirs.

As for Thorpe Langton people who lye against Widow Wades ground, they are more troublesom people, and your Lordships advantage by agreeing with them will be so small that we hardly think it worth the while to take any notice of them.   Stonton pays no town duties to any of the Langtons.

Thomas Hutchinson is gone to Hamby with directions what to do.   Yesterday I went the preambulation of Glapthorne, which had not been done of eight years before.   The hounds continue to behave themselves very well.   I have got all the last years wood mony except what was in Mr. John Lynwoods hands and in Clem Barrets of Bulwick.

There is a very great quantity of both fruit of all sorts & kitching stuff in the gardens; the gardener is doing nothing particularly now but keeping the garden clean.   Christopher Dexter says he can make the staircase as your Lordship would have it without altering anything that is done.   Will Dunmore has order'd [25£. more to Mr. Neil], which with 50£. paid to him before is 75£. in all. We have [⅓ *line missing*] for [. . .£. . . .s. . . .d.] by the scoe for [½ *inch missing*] dy to buy it by the [1⅓ *line missing or undecipherable*].

All things are well at Deen. There is abundance of grass in this country, and no [bad?] grain [ex]cept my own, which is upon land that was Mr. Lynwoods.

I am your Lordships

Most humble and most faithfull servant,

May 13th, 1725.   Dan: Eaton

[**17**]   [*Saturday*, 15 *May*, 1725.]

My Lord,

The house goes on very well; the front wall is finished.   The chestnut mare is hors'd; I sent Ned Vines to Burleigh with her yesterday, and he returnd to day.   The hounds are all well.   I intend to measure Mr. Brudenells farm on Munday & Tuesday next.   I have nothing particular to inform your Lordship of.   All things are well at Deen, and the deer mend very fast.   I am,

Your Lordships most humble and most faithful servant,

Dan: Eaton

Ned tells me that my Lord Notinghams groom would have the mare cover'd three times, & she had three fine leaps.

[**18**]   [*Tuesday*, 18 *May*, 1725.]

My Lord,
I receiv'd the honour of yours. I have inclosed an abstract of our account of wood. The reason why your Lordship had it not sooner was bycause there was some in Corby Sale that was not sold, and still there is about five pounds worth there to sell which we had view'd too dear. Your Lordship will find some difference between this abstract and the account I sent you of Leicestershire timber, which arises from some old trees that we took in the closes since our first view.

Since your Lordship was resolved that there should be no allowance for dodderells, we thought it the most certain way to do your Lordship justice about the bark, to view all the old great trees in Corby Sale by them selves; & wee sold the bark at 2*s*. p. Li.[1] which is more than three shillings p. Li. was there to be an allowance for dodderell, for they generally lye amongst these old sticks; and we have sold all the bark of Corby saplins and Stanion timber and saplins at 6*s*. 6[*d*.] p. Li.

I was at Corby yesterday, and have set things strait about John Lummis's rent and arrears to Michaelmas last; and I have allow'd him his wages to that time. He says their [*sic*] is mony due to him for lime, and he will pay your Lordship for Ball when you come into the country.   I have been at John Parsons's, and I find that there is room in his stables for about 26 horses without being crowded: that is, for 13 coach horses or naggs, & for 13 hackneys. What little alterations there is to be made for conveniencies he says he will readily do it at his own charge, if he was sure that your Lordship was resolv'd upon what I told him.   I have ordered the two colts into the park, and likwise the ramms, for there is grass enough.   All the goods got safe to Deen.

I don't rightly understand what your Lordship means by what your Lordship is pleasd to say in yours, viz: that you hope Mr. Brudenell's affairs go on well, for I have not been concern'd in any business for his Honour but in that affair of Joseph Tooky's and the letting of his farm, which I am sure I have perfected to his Honour's advantage. I am going to day to measure the land and I intend to wait upon his Honour tonight.   Mr. John Lynwood has deliverd to Will Wade 25 quarter of oats, 55 quarter of malt, and 18 quarter of beans, which were all the beans he had, his crop yielded so very indifferently. Christopher Dexter was not here yesterday, it being holyday.

I humbly thank your Lordship for what you was pleasd to write about my sister. I am sorry that my Lady thinks her too young for her service; but tho' she is not 2[-] [*the second numeral is obliterated*] years of age, yet I believe that, let the busines my Lady wants her for be what it wil[l] she would be as perfect in it, with two or three month's instructions, as some that have been at it several years, for I think she has a far brighter genius than any of us; and I hope your Lordship would never have cause to repent the charge of her instructing.

The hounds are all well, and John Kingston says they behave themselves extreamly well.   I am,
Your Lordship's most humble and most faithful servant,

Deen, May 18th, 1725.   DAN: EATON

---

[1] i.e. *per libram*, apparently meaning not pound weight but pound sterling, the value of the bark estimated at one-tenth the value of the timber from which it was taken. (*Cf.* **68**.)

[**19**]   [*Thursday, 20 May, 1725.*]

My Lord,
    I have inclosed a draught of the new building in Mr. Lynwood's house, by which your Lordship may see that a convenient little staircase may be [may be^d] made in the place where [the^i] little pent house now is, the foot of the stairs to be at the dining room door; and the coming in to the hall and that room which is now the old kitchin may be by a passage under the stairs. By this method, if your Lordship approves of it, both the hall and dining room will be very much enlarged, and there may be three very good chambers in the new building, whereas otherwise there can be but two. There may be a door broke out of the old kitchin for a passage into the celler, which will be much better than where it is. The workmen can not proceed much further without your Lordships resolutions about the staircase. Now the front wall is done, the house looks extreamly beautifull upon the park, and when it is finish'd I think it will in reality excell romances.
    I have measured Mr. Brudenells farm, but when I went to Loughfenham, his Honour was gone to Stamford Race. We want Richard Hill to make ironwork for the house and for shoeing the cart horses. The roads here are so very bad that I fear we shall not get pit coal at any rate. It was thirteen pence per hundred (when I was at Stonton), and there is none brought into this country yet. Therefore I think it would be the best way to lay in a larger stock of seacoal than ordinary. Here is 21 chaldron come which is very good, and there is boon teams which have not been, enough to fetch the rest of the 30 chaldron your Lordship orderd me to speak for.
    Thomas Hutchinson is return'd from Chatsworth and has brought the colt safe to Hamby. He was forced to leave the grey mare there bycause she did not go to horse. The groom promis'd to take great care of her and send her to Hamby as soon as she is hors'd.
    All things at Deen are well.
    I am your Lordships
        Most humble and most faithful servant,

Deen, May 20th, 1725.   DAN: EATON

[**20**]   [*Monday, 24 May, 1725.*]¹

My Lord,   Rothwell, Munday, one o'clock.
    I receiv'd the honour of your Lordships letter of the 20th instant. I have, according to your command, inclos'd a short abstract of my several accounts. I have paid Mr. Blyth in full for oats & beans he bought. I am very glad to hear that your Lordship has got Hougham and Marston living again, and have obey'd your commands as to the bells, &c. I have already examined all Will Wades bills. John Lummis has deliver'd 45 quarters of lime, and there is about 20 quarters more ready burnt which we shall want for slateing & ceiling the house.
    The sale hedges in Corby Woods are kept up very well. I have not

¹ Dated from internal evidence. See **16**, **19**, and **21**. Rothwell Fair of 24 May is the only one late in the month in the years under consideration and Dan had just received a letter of 20 May.

been in Stanion Woods about this three weeks. As for the horses in Corby Woods, I have been there to day, and there are three of John Lummis's, two of Will Meadows's, one of Thomas Meadows's, one of John Peaks, one of Sam Jones's the keepers, and a little two year old filly of my own, besides your Lordships. I have a mare in Stanion Woods which I sent on Fryday last, for I was told there was abundance of grass, more than there was when I was there. I intend to go round those woods to morrow, and by Thursdays post will inform your Lordship particularly about things there.   I intend to go to Stamford and take a cart with me on Wednessday & execute your Lordships commands there.   There is not one stick cut in Bangroves to continue Priors Haw Riding.

I am extreamly sorry John Parsons's bill upon his son should deceive my Lady, but I am resolvd I will be servd so no more.   Mr. Lynwood tells me that he has sent his accounts according to your Lordships desire.   I am forced to be at Rothwell Fare to day about some business of my own.   I shall most carefully observe all your Lordships commands.   I am,

Your Lordship's most humble and most faithfull servant,

DAN: EATON

P.S. I expect your Lordships letter to day about the staircase. The masons have but this days work without it, but I left Deen before the post came in. I shall be at home early to night.

[21]   [*Thursday, 27 May, 1725.*]

My Lord,

I have been in all those woods that Thomas Bell looks after, and there is a great number of deer in all of them, but especially in Oakly Purlues. They have done a great deal of damage to the last years sale there by croping the ash, for I think there can not be a streight ash pole in all that quarter when it goes sale again, for there has none escap'd. I saw a great many fine deer in most of the woods as I rode through them; they have made pads in Oakly Woods like sheep tracks in a fallow field.   There is no horses in any of the woods but in Sow Wood, and there is one of John Peak's, one of Thomas Bells, & one of my own. The horse that Thomas Bell rides, he tells me he puts him into Corby Haw.

The weather is very wet so I did not go to Stamford yesterday, and shall not till I see a prospect of fair weather to bring the goods home in.   We are going on with the stair case.[1]   The hounds are very well and perfectly aw'd from sheep.   Will Wade has sold all the heffers but two that are kept for your Lordships use.   Thomas Hutchinson tells me that the colt he brought to Hamby is a very strong one—four years old, but not fourteen hands high.

The roads are so very bad that the wood goes out of the sales very slowly. I have nothing more to say at present.

I am your Lordships

Most humble and most faithful servant,

Deen, May 27th, 1725.   DAN: EATON

[1] This refers to Little Deene.

[**22**]   [*Sunday*, 30 *May*, 1725.]

My Lord,

John Parsons tells me that he has all his last years wool by him and he promises to pay the 50£. upon bond as soon as he sels it.   Mr. Brudenell, Mr. John and Mr. Charles Tryon din'd at the Lodge on Fryday last with their Ladys.

By making the stair case, as in my last, we shall preserve that seller which Christopher Dexter told me your Lordship ordered should be fill'd up, but I have order'd them to dig a passage to it under these stairs, which will be very convenient and a little charge; it will make a small beer celler for 14 hogsheads, or otherwise what your Lordship pleases.[1] John Lummis is gone to London; he promises to return next week. In the mean I intend to be frequently at the sale to look after things.

All things are well in and about Deen.   I am,

Your Lordships most humble and most faithful servant,

Deen, May 30th, 1725.   DAN: EATON

[**23**]   [*Tuesday*, 1 *June*, 1725.]

My Lord,

Mr. Goode sent his son yesterday for his quarters tyth due at Lady Day last and I paid him, deducting the half years tax, for I thought that your Lordship would have order'd me to have paid him sooner if you had not forgot.   The hounds are all very well, and John Kingston tells me they found a fox yesterday and pursu'd him three quarters of an hour, and behav'd themselves very well.—The weather here continues extraordinary cold and wet, & the grass has grown very little this fortnight. Will Wade says that all things under his care are well; he bought six cows at Rothwell Fare for feeding.   I receiv'd the inclosed yesterday from Mrs. Lynwood.   I am going to day into the woods to look after things.   I am,

Your Lordships most humble and most faithful servant,

Deen, June the first, 1725.   DAN: EATON

[**24**]   [*Thursday*, 3 *June*, 1725.]

My Lord,

I should have put the inclosed from Mrs. Lynwood in my last; the other I receiv'd to day, as I have likewise the honour of your Lordships from Bath. The mony I was to pay at Stamford was not included in the account. I have inclosd a scrap of the largest payments in my account, the shortness of which I hope your Lordship will excuse till next post.

I am going with the wagon to Stamford today, and I will go to

---

[1] This refers to Little Deene.

Mr. Langtro, and to Norgrave again to morrow. I was there once and
he was not at home. I left word at his house that if he did not bring
the mony to Deen in three days, he would certainly be serv'd; but it is
six days since, and I have heard nothing. His name is Charles.

Mr. Billinges's ball is sound and fat. I don't know that any body
rides him now since Jack Kirkham is come to the kenell.   The colt I
have bought is of the coach breed, 5 years old, 15 hands and an inch
high; has a star in his forehead and one white foot; he is a very
nimble, handsome and sound horse. I bought him of young Burdit of
Cotterstock as much for the sake of hooking in my Lady's rent as for
the covering my own mares, which now I hope will cost me nothing.
He is coal black and very gentle.

I do assure your Lordship that I never lay any of your letters out
of my hands till I have obey'd your commands exactly, and if I have
not answerd every thing in writing, you may be assurd that it is done;
but next post I will be very particular.   Mr. Tryon of Bulwick is not
in the country.   I doubt Mr. Lynwoods house at Benefield goes on
but slowly since Mr. Worleys confinement.   Wheat bears a pritty good
price still; I have sold mine for 30s. per quarter to deliver it at
Peterborough.   I shall have as strict an eye as possible over thing[s]
both at the dogkenell and else where.

I am your Lordships
Most humble and most faithfull servant,

Deen, June 3rd, 1725.   DAN: EATON

[Seal]

[25]   [Friday and Sunday, 4 and 6 June, 1725.]

My Lord,   Deen, June 4th, 1725.

I receiv'd the honour of your Lordships letter with the draughts of
Little Deen this morning. In the first place I think the sash window
which your Lordship would have made in the place where the sundial
should be, will be very convenient and uniform, and it is impossible
that the chambers can be made according to this design without it. And
there must be either a window or a large sundial or some such
thing in that place, but I think the former will look the best. And the
door stands in the middle of the building within two inches, which
cannot be discern'd. Tho' the front wall is finish'd, that part of it may
be safely taken down, since it is not roof'd.

They are now going on with the stair case according to this
draught, and it makes no alteration as to the celler. Wee desire to know
whither your Lordship would have a door out of the staircase upon the
columnade. Everything else in the draught we understand rightly. We
shall make no use of the form of the door [case^i] your Lordship was
pleasd to send 'till you come; there is an handsome plain one already
fix'd upon the south side of the house, & we had put the old door trees
into the staircase, which will do very well. There can be no objection
to the window but the little charge of plucking down that part of the
wall.

Immediately after I had finish'd my letter on Thursday it began to rain, which continued almost all the day & continues still, very wet weather, so that I cannot tell when I shall fetch home the goods for fear of wet, & I would have one journey serve for all. I went to Mr. Langtro yesterday, & he has receiv'd no orders yet concerning the riding; he told me he would write to my Lord Hatton about it, this post.

I went likewise in to Corby & Stanion Woods; the roads in them & to them are so bad that the bark can hardly be carryed out, & it is a sad wet time for the tanners. I went likewise to Mr. Norgrave, but he was not at home. But for fear he should not be at home, I took Thomas Bell with me, & I gave him orders to be with him by four of the clock this morning for fear he should be gone out early this morning. & I orderd Thomas Bell to bring me the mony, or otherwise to bring Mr. Norgrave to me this morning to show a reason why he would not pay it; which Thomas Bell did likewise this morning, & brought me the inclosed letter, for [he^d] [Mr. Norgrave^i] said he could not possibly come himself. We have take[n] care for wood for lath. I have paid James Ashly 20£.

June 6th, 1725. Mr. Brudenell sent for me to Luffenham yesterday; his Honour and the family are very well. The chiefest things that Mr. Lynwood is to leave behind him are the two coppers & cistiron, which wee cannot value; there is some coal, about 200 load of dung at Winsalls, three hovills at home and one in Newland, a role in the garden, & some other things. I think the hovills at home can be of no great use to your Lordship, but we shall value them to morrow. There is about 170 quarter of oats and 10 quarter of beans at the Hall, and 5 quarter of malt; and there is at Mr. Lynwood's oats 25 quarter, beans 18 quarter, malt 55 quarter.

The surveyor of the roads could not come in a wors time, for they are very bad; but I shall take care to attend him according to your Lordships command. My accounts are very regular; I am sure there is not one article in them that your Lordship can dislike when you come, but I should have been more particular if I had not gone yesterday to Luffenham. To morrow we will value the things at Mr. Lynwoods as near as we can. I have sent the horses into the woods. And I think Thomas Bell, Thomas Meadows, & Thomas Hutchinson & every body here do their duty.

I am your Lordship's
Most humble and most faithfull servant,

DAN: EATON

[In another (contemporary) hand:—] Lady C. word how much due to Jo.

[26]   [Tuesday, 8 June, 1725.]

My Lord,

Yesterday & Sunday we have had such a vast quantity of rain that all our meadows are very much flooded. Tho' the flood was very great in the park, yet the cascade being taken a way, the pond head was not over flown. I went to meet John Lummis & his father, who came to Corby last night. I have some reason to think that, considering his former circumstances, J. Lummis's fortune with this wife will be very prodigious. Mr. Fell embrac'd all J. Lummis's children with as much eagerness & tenderness as if they had been his own grandchildren, and told his daughter that the more carefull she was of them, the more she would oblige him. He promises to settle something upon every one of them before he leaves the country. He is a very infirm man, having the dead palsy on one side of him.

I am going to day to make a valuation of Mr. Lynwoods things.

All things in and about Deen are well. The 20£. that Mr. Elliot should have paid my Lady I sent by John Lummis.

I am your Lordships

Most humble and most faithfull servant,

Deen, June 8th, 1725.   DAN: EATON.

[27]   [*Thursday*, 10 *June*, 1725.]

My Lord,

The inclosed is a valuation of things Mr. John Lynwood intends to leave behind him; whither your Lordship intends to have them all or not I cannot tell. Wee were not able to value the coppers & cistern.

I went yesterday to Boughton to have paid Mr. Walter a years chief rent due to the Duke of Montagu at Michaelmas last, and likewise to have setled the affair about your Lordships chief rent for Stanion and for Corby Hundred rents due upon Boughton, which I gave him as good an account of as I could; & he promised to write to the Duke by the next post.   He told me that he could not deduct the tax of the chief rent, so I would not pay him. I told him that it always us'd to be deducted, which we could prove by our acquittances, but he says Mrs. Hunt sold it to the Duke as a rent-charge, therefore he must acquaint the Duke with it.

The house has gone on very slowly, for this fortnight the weather has been so wet. Nothing can be remov'd out of the sales, and one half of the bark is spoild. I go into Leicestershire to morrow, being the day appointed for receiving the rest of the rent. The hounds and all things else at Deen are well.

I have just now receiv'd the honour of your Lordships letter of the 5th instant. No wood neither out of the park nor in it 'till the roads are better. The bark in the park is all well pill'd, and must be carry'd out as soon as it is dry, but nothing else shall be remov'd till the ground is hard. All the rest of your commands shall be carefully obey'd by

Your Lordship's most humble and most faithful servant,

Deen, June 10th, 1725.   DAN: EATON

[28]   [*Saturday*, 12 *June*, 1725.]

My Lord,   Deen, June 12th, 1725.

Soon after the post went out on Thursday I went to Stamford, for it look'd like a fine day. But as soon as I got thither it rain'd very hard

& continu'd till night, so I could only bring the china, which I pack'd up with my own hand, and it is come very safe. Mrs. Denshire will bring the courtains, &c., when she comes to Deen, but the four large glass sconces, I think it will be the safest way to send two footmen for them. Mr. Brudenell advis'd me not to pay for the goods till his was remov'd.[1]

I went into Leicestershire yesterday. I have inclosd the arrear for Michaelmas rent. The meadows are all under water and the weather continues very wet still.

I am inform'd that Mr. Tryon of Bulwick has given orders for all his fawns both male & female to be kill'd, & that he intends to leave this country. Mr. Worley is come home, but I think Mr. John Lynwoods house goes on very slowly. I don't think it will be finishd by Michaelmas. The quick and the oats upon the Common grow very well. All things in and about Deen are well.

I am your Lordship's
> Most humble and most faithful servant,

> > DAN: EATON

[29]   [*Thursday,* 17 *June,* 1725.]

My Lord,
John Kingstons two horses that he used to ride are come out of the marshes, & we have turnd them into the park. The gray mare that he rides is so founderd that I think it would be the best way to have her hors'd, for she may bring a very good fole tho' it is late in the year. The hounds continue to behave themselves very well; they kill'd a wild catt and two couple of rabots on Munday last. Will Wade says that all things under his care are well. The weather continues so wet that things go on very slowly & nothing can be got out of any of the sales.

Mrs. Chambers was with me yesterday to desire me [to[i]] beg the favour of your Lordship to let her sell ale. I told her I had some reason to think it would not be granted, but she says that she hopes your Lordship will not deny it, by cause her husband is not able to work to maintain his family.

I have just now receiv'd the honour of your Lordships letter. John Hinks has the best crop of melons in this country & a great deal of other fruit. My Lord Exeter's gardener has lost almost all his melons & other fruit by the severeness of the season. John Kingston told me this morning that the hounds are perfectly aw'd from sheep, and do everything as well as can be expected. There are no horses here fit to come to Bath but the grey mare, Lord Langdale's ball, Lummis's bay horse, & your Lordships pacing mare. Perhaps old Ball would come, but the little bay mare is not perfectly well yet. I will be with Nalgrave to morrow morning early.

I understand the meaning of the door under the columnade very well & always did, but by the draught it look'd as if there was to

---

[1] This refers to a sale at Wothorpe. See p. 33, note 2.

have been an other door to have opened upon the columnade, which I see by your Lordships letter you did not intend.

I have nothing else worth letting your Lordship know, at present.
I am your Lordship's
Most humble and most faithful servant,

Deen, June 17th, 1725.   DAN: EATON

[**30**]   [*Sunday*, 20 *June*, 1725.][1]

My Lord,
I went on Fryday to Brigstock, but Nalgrave was not at home; his wife told me that I might certainly meet him at Oundle market. I therefore went to Oundle yesterday & saw him, & as soon as I told him your Lordships resolution, he paid me the mony without any more words to the contrary. Wheat was sold there yesterday at 1£. 17s. 0d. per quarter, and all other grain bore a proportional rate. The meaning of this rise of grain I think must be from the late great transportation, which has so exhausted the old stock that it will hardly last while new comes; butt here is very great crops both of wheat & beans every where in this country, but I think the barly is not altogether so good.

Mr. Lynwoods house goes on very well now they have 8 hands at work, but it was at a stand during Mr. Worleys confinement. The walls are but so high as the chamber floor.   The weather continues very bad; we had a fine day on Fryday, but it rain'd much yesterday & rains now.   I hasten the workmen at Little Deen as much as possible.
All things are well in and about Deen.   I am,
Your Lordships most humble and most faithfull servant,

DAN: EATON

I told Mr. Fell, Lummis's father in law, what your Lordship order'd me, & he desir'd me to present his duty to your Lordship & return you many thanks.

[**31**]   [*Tuesday*, 22 *June*, 1725.]

My Lord,
I have got all Deenthorpe rent and arrears due at Michaelmas last except Mr. John Lynwoods, Nicholas Harrisons, & two of the cottagers. I have gott all Bulwick but Johnson's & Dalby's. And for Deen I have receiv'd Edmun [*sic*] Starsmore's, John Parsons's, John Peak's, John Hodgkin's, & Will Guelder's, and nothing of any body else.

Mr. Pywell has lately marryed a woman whose father I know can give [all(?)[d]] her 600£. if he pleases. Pywell promised me his Michaelmas rent upon the 20th instant, but has not brought it. He has a better stock upon his land than I ever knew him have.   Robert Wade, Junior, of

[1] Dated from internal evidence. See **24**, **25**, and **29**.

Weldon has very plainly been guilty of forgery in altering the receipt that Mr. Lynwood gave him last for his Michaelmas rent 1723, which your Lordship will be a judge of when you come to see it.

John Kingston tells me that the hounds guide a scent very well & are at good command. He knows all their names but some of those six couple that came last from Lord Gowers.

Mr. Jones's merchant that he buys his cole of sent to him yesterday for mony for the coal he bought of him about a month since; therefore he came to me and beg'd of me to pay him the remainder of your Lordships last years bill for coal. I ventur'd to let him have 15£. in further part of it. So there is about 3£. behind. If I have done wrong in this, I beg your Lordships pardon; he told me that his credit would be destroy'd without it.

We have nothing but rain yet. I intend this week to state the accounts with every body in Deen that have bills upon your Lordship.

I am your Lordships
Most humble and most faithful servant,

Deen, June 22d, 1725.   DAN: EATON

[32]   [*Thursday, 24 June, 1725.*][1]

My Lord,

I was on Tuesday at Shortwood[2] to look after things there. I could not find any irregularitys, but the weather is so extreamly wet that nothing can be got out of the sale. We have no sign of summer here but long days & green leaves, for the weather is as cold & the roads are much worse than ever they were in winter.

I was at Cotterstock to have got Mrs. Stewards arrear of chief rent, but Mr. Guilliam was not at home. In examining into Mrs. Stewards particuler of her estate, I find that one of your Lordships cottages of 0£. 6s. 8d. per annum is included, which I [i]ntend to let Mr. Guilliam know, for it signifies nothing talking to her.   Yesterday wheat was sold in Upingham market at 2£. 2s. 6d. per quarter, barly at 1£. 12s. 6d. per quarter.   Everything continues here as in my last.

My Lady sent orders to have a buck kill'd for Lady Strafford, & we killd one which prov'd the very best that has been in the park this seven years, which makes me hope that the rest are good; for this had not a very fine skin, which I impute to the coldness of the season, but he was extreamly fat.

I am your Lordships
Most humble & most faithfull servant,

DAN: EATON

P.S. I have receiv'd a letter from Mr. Webber about going with young Mr. Denshire to Mr. Goode & I shall be ready according to order.

---

[1] Dated from internal evidence. See **27, 28, 30, 31, 33-35**.
[2] N.W. of Glapthorne village.

[**33**]   [*Sunday, 27 June, 1725.*][1]

My Lord,
   I went yesterday to Weldon with young Mr. Denshire & took
Mr. Goodes answer. Today it is to be sent to the Clark of the Peace
& to morrow he carrys it to London. I am very glad this troublesome
business is over. Things continue here as in my last, the weather
very wet & cold. We sent a very good buck to Luffenham yesterday.
Grain bore the same price at Oundle yesterday as it did on Saturday
last, but it advanc'd at Stamford & Kettering. I have nothing material
to inform your Lordship of.
   I am your Lordship's
      Most humble and most faithful servant,

Deen, June 26th [*sic*], 1725.   DAN: EATON

[**34**]   [*Thursday, 1 July, 1725.*]

My Lord,
   I went on Tuesday last to Cotterstock, & I saw Mr. Guiliam &
told him of the mistake that was in his particular. I desir'd him to look
in the old lease that Lord Brudenell[2] granted to Mr. Steward, which
he did, & we found the cottage and an old barn which is now standing
in Mrs. Steward's yard very particularly describ'd; & he is very well
satisfied that these are your Lordship's undoubted right, & says that he
had not perus'd this lease when he drew that particular, & that he will
exclude these things in all the particulars he makes for the future.
They treated me very handsomly, & paid me the arrear of chief rent.
   Yesterday morning I receiv'd the honour of your Lordship's by
John Peak. I will send a particular of Leicestershire arrear to Will
Dunmore with orders for him to receive it as soon as possible.
   My Lord, I remember very well that your Lordship sent me
orders concerning wheat, but they were conditional and not possitive;
& I remember that by the next post after I receiv'd the honour of
yours, I let your Lordship know how I had sold mine, which I had
told your Lordship before was as good as any in this country; & I
expected positive orders in answer [to that[d]], which if I had had, your
Lordship might have been furnishd with wheat before it began to rise.
But it was as much impossible either for Will Wade or my self to
foresee the rise of wheat as it has done, as it was to foretell the weather;
therefore I can't help thinking that we are both blameless. I have all the
letters by me that I have had the honour to receive from your Lordship
in my life.
   I dont doubt but I can furnish your Lordship with one wagon or
two at an hours warning, but if your Lordship could fix any day for
their being in Town about 10 days hence, you may depend upon as
many as you want. Mr. Goodes [*sic*] said very little at passing the
answer. The old man desir'd young Mr. Denshire to take notice that

---

[1] This letter seems to have been written on Sunday 27th rather than on Saturday
26th. Oundle market was on Saturday.
[2] Francis, Lord Brudenell, the 3rd Earl of Cardigan's father.

the words which he made a squabble about before were intirely left out. They would have had us din'd with them, but we refus'd.   I heard that there is deer in Shortwood, so I went yesterday to let his Honour know, & he intends to hunt there on Saturday next.

We have had three fine days here & have a good prospect of a fourth. Your Lordships hay & treyfoil in Halbanks is in very good order & they are carrying it today. I have sent John Goodwins bay mare to Oxford; there was none more proper.

I am your Lordship's
Most humble & most faithful servant,

Deen, June [*changed to*] July the fir[s]t, 1725.   DAN: EATON

[**35**]   [*Sunday*, 11 *July*, 1725.]

My Lord,

I receiv'd the honour of both your Lordships letters by the cook and the post, with the rule, for which I return your Lordship many thanks. What lead me into an error concerning the deer was that when Mr. Peircy was at Deen Park, he said that your Lordship had given leave to Mr. Brudenell to hunt in Shortwood. Therefore I, thinking to oblige both your Lordship & his Honour, was so hasty in letting his Honour know, for fear the deer should be gone, it being but a very small wood that is now standing. But since this cannot be help'd now, I can only crave your Lordships pardon & promise to take no notice of such things for the future.

Thomas Watson's grey mare is come from Chatsworth.   She was cover'd five times, the last time upon the 23th of June. We have put her into the park till your Lordship is pleasd to give further orders about her.

The carpenters [had*d*] [would have*i*] began to raise the roof of the house to morrow if the masons could have work'd yesterday, but it rain'd all day; but I hope the roof will be intirely finish'd this week for the slaters to begin to work to morrow sevenight. The window in the front looks very well.

As to Thomas Hutchinson, it is [*about 2 letters deleted*] very natural for people to lay blame upon any body rather than themselves; therefore to avoid this as much as may be, I can only say that if my own mare had been taken so good care of when I rid her, as she ought to have been, I should not have sold her. And I declare that I have been always as careful [of*d*] of your Lordships horses as I have been of your business. I always ride them gently & feed them well while they are with me; but when they come home, whither they are taken care of or not, is not in my power to say.

As to the bay mare, I have not been upon her back this ten weeks, & but seldom before. Her ilness was the strangles, which she had in such a violent manner that I thought she would have dy'd; but she was very well recover'd when she left Deen. They would not let Thomas Hutchinson bring her from Oxford again. I never saw Thomas drunk twice in my life, and I believe he was careful in the park in John Peak's absence, but as to the stable affair, I cannot say whither he was [*deletion*] or was not. He says that he knows nothing of the horse's being bowel-gall'd. I sent him yesterday to [Hamby[d]] Stroxton with orders to bring the nutmeg-grey mare & the cropt guelding to Deen today, & I sent mony according to your Lordships order.

To morrow we shall do what your Lordship has orderd us about the dogs. I have look'd upon Mr. Brudenell's stable; the charge of repairing it will not be very great. Will Hawksby was not at home yesterday, but he is with me now, & I shall bargain with him to morrow.

All things in and about Deen are well.

I am your Lordship's
Most humble and most faithful servant,

Deen, July 11th, 1725.   DAN: EATON.

[36]   [*Tuesday*, 13 *July*, 1725.]

My Lord,

I have receiv'd the honour of your Lordship's letter of the 10th inst. We have yesterday executed your Lordship's commands concerning the currs in Deen & Deen Thorpe. I do assure your Lordship that you have been misinformed concerning Mr. John Lynwood's dogs, for he has but one bitch, & I know her to be very harmless. Mr. Joseph Lynwood had four about two months since; but he, considering in the first place that they might displease your Lordship, and in the next place, that he had better mind other business than shooting (for they were all springing spanniels), hang'd three of them of his own accord, and he promises to dispose of the other in a few days.

I have bargained with Will Hawksby to repair the stable at the dogkenell & to make it compleatly strong & neat for 30s., your Lordship finding wood, &c. Mr. Leaver was here yesterday, & he tells me that he believes your Lordship would have orderd me to have paid Mr. Goode his quarters tyth due at Midsummer last, immediately after it became due, and likewise to have paid the tenant at Deen Parsonage for damages in the church yard,[1] if you had not forgot. Before Mrs. Chambers desir'd me to write to your Lordship, she had brew'd against Deen Feast, which she sold; but I told her your Lordships resolution that she should not proceed.

It will neither be safe to send the bucks to London by the jocky wagon, by cause of their being so long upon the road, nor advantagious to the carrier [I mean the wagoner[i]] to be in Town on Saturday, bycause the lying in Town on Sunday with his team will be far more expensive then on the road; therefore I will order the bucks to be in Town on Saturday night by the carrier, and the wagon to be in Town on Munday.

I cannot find in my accounts that I have paid Sinnot any mony, & what your Lordship has paid him, or whither you ever paid him any, I have intirly forgo[t]. I have told John Peak of a buck for Lord Brudenell, but I will remind him again before the day.

I have been with Will Pywell again about his rent. And he surpris'd me very much, for he told me that to be very plain with me, the reason

[1] See **32-34, 38**.

why he had not paid it before was bycause he thought I had no authority from your Lordship to receive it; & therefore he will pay none till your Lordship comes to receive it your self at Deen. I gave him the most perswasive words I could invent, untill I found him inflexible; & then I told him I wonder'd what reason he had to think himself endow'd with a better understanding than all the rest of your Lordships tenants. Your Lordship knows that I have never deserv'd this usage at his hands.

Thomas Hutchinson has brought the nutmeg grey mare & the crop guelding. They are in good order & are in the park. There is only those two horses your Lordship bought at Bath & Lummis's bay horse fit to come to London when your Lordship sends. I have nothing else to say at present.   I am,
Your Lordships most humble & most faithful servant,

Deen, July 13th, 1725.   DAN: EATON

[**37**]   [*Thursday, 15 July, 1725.*]

My Lord,   Kettering, July 15th, 1725.
By Mr. Fell's desire I am come [with him[i]] to Kettering; he was taken very ill yesterday & sent for me, & is gone forward for London.[1] The reason why he has left the country so soon is bycause he is af[f(?)ᵈ]raid he shall not live to alter his will. He was very much out of order when he went from hence & I think he can not live long. He is very delirious, but in one of his intervals yesterday he desir'd me to assure your Lordship that he is extreamly well satisfied in his daughter's marryage, & he desir'd me to let your Lordship know it.   John Lummis & his wife are gone with him to Northampton & intend to go with him to London; & John Lummis intends to wait upon your Lordship on Saturday night next, & I don't doubt but he will shew your Lordship a very good reason for his leaving the country with his father Fell.

They are raising the timber of the roof of Little Deen, & I hope the slaters will begin on Munday or Tuesday next.   I orderd the post, by a messenger, to bring my letters to Corby this morning, & the post came to let me know that I had no letter, for I left Deen this morning before the post could come in.   I have seen Haimes the carrier since I came hither, & he tells me that he cannot possibly bring the bucks to London, for he has not one horse at home; therefore I must contrive to get them to London by Saturday night (if possible) some other way.
I am your Lordship's
Most humble & most faithfull servant,

Thursday, 11 o'clock.   DAN: EATON

[**38**]   [*Sunday, 18 July, 1725.*]

My Lord,
I receiv'd the honour of your Lordship's letter; I have been with Pywell, & find what your Lordship suspected to be true, for he has no

---

[1] See **26**.

mony. I think it was a strange sort of excuse, but now he promises to bring me the mony at the latter end of this week.

I was forc'd to send one of the jocky waggoners horses to London with the venison, for I could get no body else to bring it, which hinderd the wagon one day, & it can't be in town before Tuesday night.

The twelve chairs for Lord Gower are not remov'd from Woothorpe, they are to be carryed with Mr. Brudenell's goods when he removes them, which will save a great deal of trouble; & it was Mrs. Denshires advice & Mr. Brudenell's desire that nothing should be paid for till all were remov'd. I intend to wait upon his Honour to day to know when he intends to fetch his goods, that I may safely pay the mony.

The three squares that are broke upon the staircase are 19 inches long & 15¾ inches broad. Mrs. Bradshaw did not tell me or I should have let your Lordship know before. I have paid old Goode & his tenant.

What Mr. Leaver and I were talking of concerning the house was that a flat roof would look much more noble than what was intended, & yesterday Christopher Dexter & I computed the utmost charge of this alteration, which will be 80£. extraordinary. The same timber will serve again, & the slate, for we propose a double slated roof instead of lead, but the present garret windows will become useless, for we propose them to be sash'd. This alteration will not only make the front beautiful & noble, but will be attended with [two^d] a very great conveniency, for the garrets will hereby become very handsome bedchambers. The timber of the roof is rais'd according to the first design, but if your Lordship approves of what we propose, it may be taken down without damage or much trouble. I hope to receive your Lordships answer to this on Thursday next.

In the mean, the masons must take down that chimny that is at the east end of the old building in order to raise it answerable to the other chimnys, & the carpenters may fix the ceiling joice,[1] &c., in the lower rooms. The seven garret sashes, both glass & wood, are included in this computation, & likewise the lead for the gutters.

John Peak tells me that he has carryed half a buck to Mr. Robinson, & as he is to carry half buck [sic] to Mr. Allicock by your Lordship's former orders, therefore he will at the same time carry half a buck to Mr. Stratford at the same time, & he will carry half a buck to Mr. Kirkham & half a buck to Major Creed as soon as he can.

Mrs. Bradshaw can give no account of what soap she receiv'd last year, but only that she receiv'd eight barrells in October last which she expected were all soap, but two of them prov'd to be gunpowder, which she did not discover till about a fortnight since;[2] & the jocky wagons never have a particular of what goods they bring, but only of the number of the parcels; & as they are always paid as soon as the goods are weigh'd, they never make any bill.

Will Wade has bought some very good wheat & it is brought in at 1£. 14s. 0d. per quarter; he has bough[t] but 5 quarter, but he intends to buy 5 quarter more. The grain in this country is very backward & harvest will be very late, but here is vast crops of wheat & beans. All things are well in and about Deen. I am,

Your Lordship's most humble & most faithful servant,

Deen, July 18th, 1725.   DAN: EATON

[1] joists.   [2] See **40**.

[39]   [*Tuesday, 20 July, 1725.*][1]

My Lord,
I went on Sunday last to Luffenham, & his Honour tells me that he cannot fetch his goods yet this half year, but he tells me that my Lord Exeter has given Mr. Richards a very particular charge concerning them;[2] therefore he thinks I may very safely pay for them, which I intend to do on Fryday next, & I will take care to send my Lord Gowers chairs.
Mr. Tryon has procur'd two hogsheads of [French*d*] wine for your Lordship which we sent for from Peterborough yesterday, & they are come safe to Deen.   The hounds, &c., are all well at Deen.
I am your Lordships
Most humble and most faithful servant,

[*Seal. Date of postmark* 21 [*July*]. *The rest of the page is torn off and signature missing.*]

[40]   [*Thursday, 22 July, 1725.*][3]

My Lord,   Deen, Thirsday morning, 7 o'clock.
I have this moment receiv'd the honour of your Lordships letter. I will to day take a par[t]icular account of every thing your Lordship desires, & if I find that the utmost expences of Little Deen don't exceed your Lordships expectation, I will then order the workmen to proceed according to my proposall, which I have a great deal of reason to think your Lordship will not repent.   I don't think there has been any wast of lime,—the new staircase has taken up more than was expected,—but by the next post your Lordship shall have a very particular account of everything.
I am very sorry for your Lordships loss in Alder's affair. I knew him very well when I was in London. It is a great pitty that honesty & ingenuity are not always companions. I shall as much as in me lies use my best endeavours by carefulness to repair your Lordships losses, & the vast trust your Lordship reposes in me I hope I shall never abuse.
Mrs. Bradshaw says that she thinks there was but six barrells of sope come to Deen in October last, & there was one barrel of gunpowder in the house before, & Mr. Bradshaw has put the three barrells in an out house for fear of damage.[4] She has been distilling a great while.
The antelope is well in the park & I don't doubt but may be catch'd when you[r] Lordship desires it.   One of the footmens saddles is at Hamby, but here is one that I used to ride upon will do very well. Thomas Hutchinson rid the horse your Lordship bought at Bath to help John Peak kill a buck in the park, [he*d*] and he fell with him & has bruis'd him very much, so that he can hardly do his business.   I am,
Your Lordship's most humble & most faithfull servant,

DAN: EATON

---

[1] Dated from internal evidence. See **38, 41** and remnant of postmark.
[2] The goods mentioned here were evidently those bought at a sale at Wothorpe. See **38, 41**, and **118**.
[3] Dated from internal evidence. See **35, 37, 38, 41, 42**, also ASR 106b.
[4] See **38**.

[**41**]   [*Saturday*, 24 *July*, 1725.]

My Lord,

I was yesterday at Stamford with Mr. Richards to have paid for the goods at Woothorpe, but finding his account to differ from that your Lordship sent me, I therefore brought the mony back again. He says he will readyly wait upon your Lordship when you come to Deen, & will bring the account that is sign'd by the appraisers to shew you, for he says that he is chargeable not only with the inclosed additional summs, but likewise with the poundage, which is not one farthing advantage to him.

I have inclosed as perfect an estimate of the charge of finishing Little Deen according to the former design as is in my power to make. I can't conceive how any body could think as this could be done for 60 or 70£. It is true the new staircase & that other sash make a very considerable addition to the charge. But I believe your Lordship will find that in this estimate I have come very near the mark, and by such time as the hall is pav'd and wainscoated, the dyning room floord & wanscoated, [&*i*] the chambers & garretts floord [&c.*i*], I am very much mistaken if this 170£. does not amount to 300£. I think that this is the charge that this house must of necessity cost your Lordship tho' you only follow the former design.

Therefore if I might advise your Lordship, I would have it made one of the prittiest little houses in England by following my last proposalls, & I find that it will be compleated under 80£. extraordinary, as I have told your Lordship before. But perhaps your Lordship may suspect that I speak without thinking, as some have done before, but if I can't prevail with Christopher Dexter & John Winsal to undertake it, I shall never consent to have it done. They told me this morning that they would undertake it & find all materials at that price & compleat it. If your Lordship will be pleas'd to send me orders to make a bargain with them, by the next post, then if I don't make such an agreement with them as will be both for [L*d*] your Lordship's advantage and satisfaction, I will patiently bare the blame. I remember that if your Lordship had not proceeded after this manner about 9 years agone, the beautiful canell in the gardens had not been made at so cheap a rate.[1]

The three long gutters on the roof will take 25 hundred weight of new lead; they will want 30 tun of freestone, all which, as likewise everything else, they shall furnish if I bargain with them. The seven sashes will be worth 17£.; the stone cornice to adorn the battlements will be worth 2s. 6d. per foot; with severall other things two [*sic*] tedious to mention here; but I shall take care to draw the articles very copiously, if your Lordship will give me leave.

The goods came all very safe & right except the box of wax-candles, which I find, by a particular that Lummis sent me, were not sent.

Thomas Hutchinson had one of his ribs out; he went on Thursday to the bone setter, and is now much better.

If I make a bargain with Winsall & Dexter,[2] I will oblige them to

---

[1] Dexter had been previously employed at making the canal at Deene, and Winsal in mason's work about the pond head (ASR 118).

[2] For this agreement, which was found by Miss Deborah Webster at Delapré Abbey in 1961 (ASR 106b), see Appendix 1.

finish the whole by a certain day, and then your Lordship can have no further uneasiness.

All things in and about Deen are well.

I am your Lordships
Most humble & most faithful servant,

Deen, July 24th, 1725.   DAN: EATON

[**42**]   [*Tuesday, 27 July, 1725.*]

My Lord,

I receiv'd the honour of your Lordship's letter.   The strength of the walls of Little Deen was the first thing I consider'd before I proposd an alteration. Christopher Dexter was not here yesterday nor to day, it being Gretton Feast; but if I find those four sashes will do for the garrets, I will oblige Christopher Dexter to allow the same price for them that they cost.   The buckets for the carabines are at London, but the pistols, &c., are here and that other saddle is come from Hamby.   Dan Whitworth went out with his brother Francis on Sunday last & is not yet return'd, & I know nothing of the wine.

Pywell has not pay'd anything. I sent very particular orders to Will Dunmore about collecting & returning the arrears to Mr. Keck, but have not receiv'd an answer.   I shall give orders to Dan about black cherry brandy as soon as he comes home.   I shall obey your Lordships commands concerning Thomas Watson as soon as he comes to Deen. I have spoke to Will Wade about the hides, &c., & he says that he always charges him self with all hides, tallow, &c., in his bills, & I remember that Jeremiah Richardson always used to charge himself with them in his bills at Hamby, so that I cannot tell how this mistake can be.   John Peak will take care to have the brace of bucks in Town on Fryday by a messenger, which I think, since it is as cheap, is a much better way of sending them than by the coach.   Will Wade tells me that all things under his care are well.

I am your Lordship's
Most humble and most faithful servant,

Deen, July 27th, 1725.   DAN: EATON

Mr. Janvers's letter was charg'd 0£. 1s. 9d.

[**43**]   [*Wednesday, Thursday, 28, 29 July, 1725.*]

My Lord,   Deen, July 28th.
The wine was all sent in by Mr. Tryons order. The first hogshead was fetch'd from Colliweston, the other two from Peterborough. The venison we have sent by a messenger who is to be in Tow[n] on Fryday. Haimes refusd to carry it, but here is at Weldon a very carefull & responsible young man who, if he might be constantly employ'd, would at any time go up with one brace, two brace, or three at a minute's warning, which I think would be a very great conveniency.

July 29th, 1725.   I have receiv'd the hounour [*sic*] of your Lordship's letter. The four sashes that were taken from your Lordships bedchamber, &c., are too narrow by half a foot, but when Mr. Tryon comes
I will consult with him whither we can by any means make them serve.
I don't doubt but by the next post I shall send you a copy of such a contract[1] as will be of satisfaction to your Lordship, and likewise a particular
of the linnen, &c., as your Lordship desires.   I don't doubt but in a
short time I can hear of such a servant as will suit the dairy, &c.

All things at Deen are well, & the hay in Newlands is in a fair way
of being well got.   I am your Lordships
            Most humble and most faithfull servant,

                                                    DAN: EATON

I am extreamly glad to hear that your Lordship has quitted Hamby,
that unhealthy expensive place. Hicks of Tansworths lease is not yet
expired; I think there is two years in it.

[44]   [*Thursday, 5 August, 1725.*][2]

My Lord,
        Master Brudenell[3] is safely arriv'd at Deen and is extreamly well, and
without flattery I think he is the finest boy that ever I saw of his age.

When I was last at Luffenham, Mr. Brudenell desir'd that I would
not let Hawksby do any thing at his stable at the dogkenell till he had
seen your Lordship, for he intends to have it rail'd for coach horses, for
his Honour intends to set his horses there when he comes at any time to
Deen; otherwise Hawksby had begun to work to day. We had no timber
fit for him to work up before. His Honour spoke to me about getting the
stable altered according to his mind, before I told him that I had bargained with Hawksby pursuant to your Lordship's command.

The person that is to come to London with a wagon on Fryday
se'night is the same that brought the last load of goods down; he goes into
Essex with a load of wooll & from thence to London.   All things in
and about Deen are well.

I was at Tansworth to day & I find that Mr. Hicks never had a lease
of your Lordship's land. He had a lease of the land he held of my Lord
Westmoreland wherein there is two years unexpired. I remember that in
talking with him about Mr. Inot's tyth, he told me that he was in the
same case with land he held of my Lord Westmoreland as with your
Lordships land, & then said that he would not put himself to charge of
suit, bycause it would not be above two years before my Lords lease
expir'd, without making any distinction, which caus'd me to make this
mistake & to inform your Lordship wrong. I have not yet enquird into
the value of the farm but I will do it as soon as possible.
        I am your Lordships
            Most humble and most faithful servant,

Thursday evening, eight o'clock.   DAN: EATON

¹ See **41** and Appendix 1.
² Dated from internal evidence. See **35-38, 42, 43, 45, 47, 48.**
³ This is James, Cardigan's second son, born on April 20th, 1725 (B.D. 224).
Dan reports on him as "Master Brudenell" in many subsequent letters.

[**45**]   [*Saturday, 7 August, Sunday, 8 August, 1725.*]

My Lord,   Deen, August 7th, 1725.

Mr. Faulkner was here to day & has measured the chimny's of the dining-room, the chamber over it & the chamber over the hall at Little Deen; but I think a good Weldon-rag chimny piece for this latter will do very well, since it is not a very large room.—He is gone to Luffenham.

I have receiv'd the honour of your Lordship's of the 5th inst. I sold my horse to Mr. Leaver for ten guineas & his mare, which I valued at six guineas, & I sold her immediately to Mr. Brudenell at that price. If Mr. Leaver does not cut the horse, another guinea is due to me now; if he does cut him, I am to trust for this guinea 'till he is well again.

Mr. Brudnell intended to have had him, but his Honour was inform'd that he was too little for the rest of his set. He has been at Luffenham 5 weeks, & since his Honour dislik'd him I was forc'd to sell him at an under rate, bycause I had not a standing of my own to keep him in, & I durst not make bold with your Lordship's any longer, tho' I bought meat for him all the time he was here. He cost me 18£. 10s. 6d., therefore considering the advantage of covering mares, I cannot say that I lose by him; but I am sure I have sold him above five guineas under his value, for he is fifteen hands and & inch & a quarter high, & the most beautiful and gentle creature that I ever saw, & he runs in the chair like a lap dog.

I have deliver'd your Lordships commands to Mr. John Lynwood & Thomas Parsons.[1] The latter says that he will submit to your Lordships pleasure. I have seen the wagoner to day & he desires that the goods may be ready by 12 o'clock on Fryday next, for if he can possibly, he will leave London that night. The person that brought the venison last is him that will bring it always; the other could not undertake two brace, he having but one horse. Master Brudenell continues extreamly well. There has been a great deal of your Lordships hay got very well in Newlands these three last days, & there is a good crop of it. Lummis's bay horse has been so lame lately that he was forced to have his sole drawn, so that here is no hacks but those two that were bought at Bath. Walter Harrisson has a mare that I believe he would lend if your Lordship desires it.

Sunday morning. It has been a very wet night & rains now very fast.

I am your Lordship's
Most humble & most faithfull servant,

DANIEL EATON

[**46**]   [*Tuesday, 10 August, 1725.*]

My Lord,

I receiv'd the honour of your Lordship's of the seventh inst. I have nothing material, but that Master Brudenell continues extreamly [well[i]]. I have provided horses to be in town on Saturday night. The weather here continues very wett, & here is not an ounce of ripe grain in this

---

[1] The saddler of Deene.

lordship.   John Colton assures me that he never saw young hounds perform their business so well in every respect as these do.
I am your Lordships
Most humble & most faithfull servant,

Deen, August 10th, 1725.   DAN: EATON

[**47**]   [*Thursday*, 12 *August*, 1725.]

My Lord,
Master Brudenell continues extreamly well.   I have receiv'd the honour of your Lordship's letter of the tenth instant. Lummis is with me, and we are going to Tansworth to enquire into Hicks's farm.
Mr. Tryon has sent to me to go to Colliweston tomorrow, & I will likewise then wait upon his Honour & let him know what your Lordship desires about the stable. I have sent to Corby for one of Lummis's horses; I had provided another, but he is very glad your Lordship has order'd his horse, & he has writ to his wife to send the best he has. I shall carry the 14£. with me to Colliweston for Mr. Jacksons malt. I have deliver'd your Lordships commands to John Peak.

Jack tells me that when they hunted last in Laxton Wood, Mr. Kirkham shot a fox before the hounds after they had run him sharply some time, which they tore to pieces, & it has given them very good blood.
The inclosed came from the keeper of Badminton Park[1] to John Peak.
I am your Lordships
Most humble & most faithful servant,

DAN: EATON

P.S.   J. Lummis has this day receiv'd a very kind letter from his father.[2] He desires me to present his humble duty to your Lordship, & returns your Lordship many thanks for your trouble in going to him, since he left London. He is overjoy'd at it.
Deen, August 12th, 1725.

[**48**]   [*Sunday*, 15 *August*, 1725.]

My Lord,
Master Brudenell continues extreamly well.   I have been at Tansworth with Lummis & wee think that the best land in Hicks's farm is worth about 9s. per acre. In another field the land is worth about 7s. per acre. The other field is not so good as either of these, but we think what plow'd land there is in it does not come far short of the latter, & it is worth about 6s. per acre.

---

[1] The seat at that time of Henry Somerset, 3rd Duke of Beaufort (1707-1743) (C.P.).
[2] i.e. father-in-law.

What land your Lordship has upon the place call'd Tansworth-Old[1] (we are infor[med] that you have some there, but we cannot learn how much), it is no[t] worth above 3s. per acre. We think both the meadow & lay-grownd are but very indifferent. We could not be inform'd of the quality of ground your Lordship has in Tansworth Lordship.

I have been with Mr. Tryon & have paid him the 14£. for Mr. Christopher Jacksons malt, & have stated an account with Mr. Rowly concerning Bristol water, & have receiv'd £1., 15s., 11d., the ballance, for your Lordship had formerly paid him two guineas, which I suppose by your letter to him you had forgot. I saw Mr. Brudenell & I told his Honour what your Lordship orderd me, & he says he does not heed what is done at the stable, so Hawksby shall begin to morrow. Mr. Janvers is going to Luffenham to day & he will do what your Lordship orderd me there, & save me the journey. I am oblig'd to go to Stocking on Tuesday, & I shall [call at^d] wait upon his Honour as I come back.

These last ten days of wet weather have almost broke me, for I had a most fine crop of tray foil cut down about a fortnight agone, and it is all spoil'd, & the seed most of it shell'd. It rains now; I hope God will send us better weather or we shall be all ruin'd.

The undertakers at Little Deen proceed as well as possible, but the weather has been a great hinderance to them.

I am your Lordships
Most humble and most faithfull servant,

Deen, August 15th, 1725.   DAN: EATON

Lord Cardigan was probably at Deene for most of the time between 16th August and the end of October, 1725. The indication from 49 is that he was at Cottesmore on 11th November, probably for the start of the hunting season. Early in November his eldest son, Lord Brudenell, then at Queen's College, Oxford, contracted a serious illness from hunting on a wet day (B.D.,p.247). By 6th December he was "mending as fast as can be expected" (Lord Cardigan to Lord Hatton, B.M.Add.MSS.29,569). Lord Cardigan's visit to Luffenham on 20th November was undoubtedly to see his brother James Brudenell.

11 November, 1725 — 21 December, 1725

[49]   [*Thursday, 11 November, 1725.*]

My Lord,

We have been with Lord Hatton & he says he will find out an equal number of men to view the woods with those your Lordship has pitch'd upon; and after we had told him your Lordships reasons for having the wood view'd out of hand, he desir'd us to present his humble service to your Lordship & to assure you that his men should be ready to view with us to morrow if possible. His Lordship desir'd us to leave the list of

---

[1] Old has the same meaning as "wold", a tract of open country.

our names with him, which we did, and he told us that he intended Mr. Bradshaw of Rockingham should be [of^d] one of his men. Both in the viewing and signing the books, &c., we shall carefully observe all your Lordship's directions.

Mr. Billinge is in a sweat in bed and cannot answer your Lordships letter. He has a feavor upon him, but is something better since he has been blooded. He could not go with us to Kirby, so only Lummis & I was there.   I have asked Thomas Hutchinson his reason for his so flatly refusing to come to Cotchmore, and he says he had told John Peak he would help him kill a doe.   I shall observe all the directions your Lordship has order'd Mr. Billinge.

Master Brudenell is extreamly well.   All the trees are come from Oakly.   On Munday next Little Deen will be finished if the weather is good.

I am your Lordship's
Most humble and most faithfull servant,

Deen, November 11th, 1725.   DAN: EATON

[50]   [*Saturday*, 13 *November*, 1725.]

My Lord,
Master Brudenell is very well, and Mr. Billinge is better than he has been. We was viewing in Bangroves yesterday with Lord Hattons servants & wee agreed very well in our opinions, which we think was chiefly owing to the judgement and good nature of Mr. Bradshaw and Mr. Peak of Cottingham. We cannot view today bycause two of my Lord Hattons keepers, who are persons imploy'd, and Mr. Bradshaw must kill does to day, but on Munday we have appointed to meet at Deen Wood, for we all think that it will be better to view a day in one wood and then a day in the other rather than to finish one wood intirely before we begin the other.

I am going to Tansworth to day to inquire about the affair between Hicks and Simson, & I intend to enquire of the miller of Southwick about the holding up of the water in Cotterstock Meadow.   Last Munday being so very wet a day, we could do nothing in Glapthorn Field, &c., and I don't know when to appoint an other day.

I am your Lordship's
Most humble and most faithful servant,

Deen, November 13th, 1725.   DAN: EATON

[51]   [*Tuesday*, 16 *November*, 1725.]

My Lord,
Master Brudenell is very well & Mr. Billing is very well recovered.

We were viewing in Deen-wood yesterday, & tho' we had several disputes, yet I believe we finished our days work to your Lordship's advantage. The saplins are more numerous & better than I expected to have found them, for I never was in that wood before. We shall view in

Bangroves to day if it is fair, but it raines now very fast. John Spratt could not get an horse sooner than today. Pywell has paid his rent according to promise.

I am your Lordship's
Most humble and most faithful servant,

Deen, Tuesday morning, November 16th, 1725.   Dan: Eaton

[*Direction endorsed:—*]
To the Right Honble. the Earl of Cardigan.
These present.
[*Seal*]

[52]   [? *Saturday*, 20 *November*, 1725.][1]

My Lord,

I should have gone to Stonton to day & from thence have waited upon your Lordship at Luffenham to night, but yesterday I lam'd my horse in going to Southwick to enquire of Laurence Barnes about the water at Perio Mills. I went from thence to Cotterstock in order to have gone to Tansworth to make inquiry about the affair between Hicks & Simson, but was stop'd by the waters (for when I should have gone before I was stop'd by excessive rain). I have seen young Hicks & the affair as he relates it seems to me to be intirely against Simson, but my further enquiry will be more satisfactory.   From Cotterstock I came to Glapthorne, where I receivd almost all that was due to my Lady of Lady Day's rent. And I have made some discovery's there which will be of great advantage to your Lordship, and at a proper time I will make your Lordship acquainted with them.

John Lummis, Thomas Bell, Joseph Meadows, young Will Meadows, & Sidney went yesterday into Leicestershire to set out the underwood ready for us to view it & sell it to day, but neither I nor Mr. Billing had an horse to ride upon. So I sent to Corby last night to order old Meadows to go to Stonton very early this morning & to [order them to view and[i]] sell the wood as if I had been there; for there will not be four acres of underwood in the whole, & I believe they can and will sell it as well without me as with me.

I am forc'd to send the twenty pounds by John Hinks, bycause I cannot get to Luffenham.

I am your Lordships
Mos[t] humble and most faithful servant,

Deen, Saturday, three o'clock p. noon.   Dan: Eaton

Letters **54** *and* **55** *in the following group deal with the alteration of the post route between Uppingham and Kettering (See Appendix 7 below). In these letters also come the first references to the long series of negotiations for an exchange of woods between Cardigan and Hatton, his nearest neighbour.*

[1] Date conjectured from internal evidence. See **48, 50, 51, 54, 57, 60, 63**.

[53]   *[Monday, 6 December (or possibly 29 November), 1725]*[1]

My Lord,

The inclosed came to me on Saturday and I forgot to shew it to your Lordship. We are in great wants of the iron, for Richard has none to work upon. Mr. Jones begs that your Lordship would order him some mony for this years coal; what he has already deliver'd comes to just 36£., and if your Lordship would be pleasd to order him a part of it, he says it would be of very great service to him.

    I am your Lordships

      Most humble and most faithful servant,

Deen, Munday morning.   Dan: Eaton

[54]   *[Thursday and Saturday, 9 and 11 December, 1725.]*

My Lord,

On Munday last it rain'd all the morn till ten of the clock, at which time we were ready to have attended my Lord Hattons servants in Bangroves, but none of them came. On Tuesday it rain'd incessantly, and in the evening of that day I receiv'd the honour of your Lordships letter, and carryed the inclosed to my Lord Hatton immediately; and according to your command went to Upingham yesterday to meet the surveyor of the roads. Lummis was with me, but we could not perswade the gentleman to leave Uppingham last night, so we came from thence to Corby, and made an appointment to meet him this morning at Liddington.[2]

My business at Corby was to meet the copy holders to talk with them about their right of common in the three purlue woods, and I see most plainly that it will be no difficult matter to accomplish your Lordships desires herein. And we have thought of an other affair which, if it is possible to bring it about, will be of vast service both to your Lordship & the town of Corby, but since I have so much other business to write to night, & it is so late, I cannot now let your Lordship know the particulers.

This morning we went to Liddington & there met the surveyor. My Lord Hattons keeper was with us, who shew'd us the best road cross the meadows; but the waters being out, the gentleman saw the worst of every thing. And I must own I think that water, in a dark night, very dangerous, and I think that there is no way of altering it but by making a courseway cross the meadows, which will be a great charge. From thence we came to Gretton, and from Gretton we came thro' the woods that the post is to come till we came to Kirby Grounds; then we turn'd down to Kirby and stay'd there about an hour. Then we came again into Weldon road and continued it to Weldon. I could not perswade the gentleman to come to Deen, so I left him there about eight of the clock to night, & have promised to be with him before nine to morrow morning.

I wrote the former part of this letter on Thursday evening, expecting that Mr. Billinge would have met your Lordship a hunting yesterday.

---

[1] Date conjectural. See **54, 55.**

[2] The Surveyor was an official of the Post Office who had come down to survey the proposed alteration in the post route between Uppingham and Kettering.

Yesterday morn we went with the surveyor from Weldon to Kettering, where we stay'd with him till evening.

Amongst other discourse I cited several clauses in the petition that was deliver'd by Bunning & some others to the Bord, and he acknowledg'd them to be most [. . . . . . ly^d] detestably false & groundless, which were as followeth. First that the road by Weldon was so very bad in winter that it was not passable. Secondly that the road thro' the Forrest[1] that way was so very intricate that [it would that^d] a boy could not find the way in a dark night. And thirdly that this way the mails would be in continual danger of being rob'd.

To the first of which the surveyor agreed that he never desir'd a better post road, & that tho' it was a mile or two about, he believ'd it would be sooner gone in winter than Rockingham road (which is now hardly passable). To the second he agreed that by Weldon it was almost impossible for a boy to loose his way, whereas by Rockingham there might be a great deal of danger of this, by the boy's being forc'd to go over those two black lonesome plains, the Lawn, and the Shire. To the last he allow'd that it was certainly more safe for the post to go by [three^d] six towns in the same distance than three. Besides, he agreed that the posts, coming by these six towns, would certainly advance the revenue.

Bunning, who was with us all this time, had nothing to say in his own defence for signing that petition, but that he had never been this road before, but believ'd what the gentlemen told him. The only objection that the surveyor made to this road was the dangerousness of the water, which we could not plead against, but promised that your Lordship & my Lord Hatton would get it mended; and he promised us that he would represent the whole affair in a favourable manner to the Commissioners.

When I go to Stamford for the iron, which will be the first day that we cannot view in Bangroves, I think to take Richard wth me, & if he likes it, I think it will be the best to have as much as I bargained for when your Lordship sent me to Stamford, bycause there is the same trouble in bringing home half a tun as a tun; and if it is good, I am sure I have bought it cheap.—I promis'd ready mony.

I do assure your Lordship that I have always forwarded the work in Bangroves and Deen Wood as much as I possibly could; and [2 *letters deleted*] my own thoughts upon this matter I have always conceal'd, and shall allways act in this affair with fervency to procure your Lordships satisfaction.

I am your Lordship's

Most humble and most faithful servant,

Deen, December 11th, 1725.   DAN: EATON

Master Brudenell is very well.

[55]   [*Thursday*, 16 *December*, 1725.][2]

My Lord,

On Tuesday last we valued eight score trees in Deen-wood, but Mr. Bradshaw can come no more this week; therefore yesterday I went

---

[1] Rockingham Forest.
[2] Dated from internal evidence. See **53, 54**.

to Stamford for the iron. There was three or four tun to choose out of, but Richard could pick but half a tun that was right good, so we brought no more. Mr. Taylor was not at home and I could not perswade his wife to take mony for it.

Mr. Bradshaw seem'd to think that this exchange would never be perfected (by what he said on Tuesday morning), for he said we were labouring in vain, he doubted; he was some time with Mr. Lantro on Munday night, but what pass'd between them I can not tell. We have appointed to meet at Bangroves on Munday morning. My Lord Hattons people are so very indifferent about this affair that I fear it will be a long time before it is finished.[1]

When we talk'd with the copy-holders of Corby about their right of common in the two Sow-woods & Bandy Slade, they were very willing to resign it upon reasonable terms. We propos'd the inclosure of Thackly Green to their use, and likewise making the town master of the houses upon your Lordships wast, none of which ever paid any rent; which they like'd very well, but besides this they sayd they expected a sum of mony for a town stock, but did not mention a particular sum. What they proposd further (but I fear it is impracticable) was that they would resign their right of common in Upper Shrub and Neither Shrub without any consideration [? at all[d]] if your Lordship would stub them up to make a cow pasture of them, which they would give as much rent for as if they had never had any right of common thereon. This would more than double the value of the woods, besides the great advantage it would be to the town if it could be done.

I have this minute receiv'd the inclosed from the surveyor of the roads.   Christopher Dexter has been very ill these ten day[s]; he vomits a great deal of blood.

I am your Lordships
Most humble and most faithful servant,

Thursday morning.   DAN: EATON

[56]   [*Tuesday, 21 December, 1725.*][2]

My Lord,
We valued an hundred & fifty trees yesterday in Bangroves, and are going this morning to Deen-wood; but I doubt the wetness of the morning will prevent my Lord Hattons servants meeting us.   Master Brudenell is extreamly well.

I am your Lordships
Most humble and most faithful servant,

Deen, Tuesday morning.   DAN: EATON

Lord Cardigan was obviously at Deene for Christmas and part of January, 1726. He wrote twice from there to Hatton about the exchange of woods (B.M.

---

[1] See Subject Index under Exchanges with Lord Hatton.
[2] Dated from internal evidence. See **54, 55**.

Add. MSS. 29,569, fos. 27 & 29) and letters 57 to 63 were probably all directed to Hanby.

[57][1]   [*Tuesday, 8 February, 1725/6.*]

To Francis Cave, Joseph Starsmore, Thomas Jacklins, Senior, Thomas Barnes, and John Taylor of Deenthorpe.

These are to require you and every one of you to come to Deen to work for my Lord either to day or to morrow at the furthest, which if any of you should refuse or neglect to do, I have his Lordship's possitive commands to raise every one of your rents, for his Lordship will not suffer you to live in his houses for nothing if you disobey his commands.
I am your well-wishing friend,

Deen, February 8th, 1725.   D: Eaton

[58]   [*Friday, 11 February, 1725/6.*]

My Lord,
Master Brudenell continues very well.   I sent your Lordships letter to John Lummis on Tuesday last, and on Wednesday went to Corby, where I sold the rest of Bandy Slade underwood with very little abatement. We likewise sold the hedge pole fagots & some thorne legs in the riding for ready mony, & I receiv'd it.
John Lummis has been in Leicestershire and has partly finish'd that part of his account. He paid me 20£. and 0£. 18s. 3d., which was the difference between his years wages and Sidney's and Corby Court dinner, and a years rent of land in Corby & Stanion due to your Lordship at Michaelmas last, which account I stated with him. There is still unaccounted for upon his wood account 130£., whereof his lime bill and some few expences, &c., come to 30£. The rest he is in hopes of paying into my hands on Thursday or Fryday next, or greatest part of it, and to return[2] that in arrear that is not paid to him. He is very much disturb'd at your Lordships letter, but did not seem to think that it sprung from my informations. He paid me the mony he receiv'd at Glapthorne.
I orderd Thomas Bell to be as expeditious as possible in collecting the wood mony under his care, and to pay it to me.   I was at Glapthorn to day, where I receiv'd as much of my Lady's mony within 4£. as I was to pay at London; the sum to be paid is 139£. 1s. 6½d. I beg your Lordship would return it to Philip Gaines by some means; I shall send him the receipts by Sundays post with my Lady's directions.
This evening I receiv'd the honour of your Lordships letter of the 7th instant. I have given orders to Thomas Batt to begone early in the morning, with written directions what he is to do. I wonder that the letter should be 4 days coming hither.

[1] This is evidently the "inclosed order" mentioned in **63**.
[2] i.e. to report.

I believe the cellar at Little Deen will be intirely finish'd before Saturday se'night. Christopher Dexter has put up the partitions of four of the garrets, which are now ready for the plaisterers.

John Chambers says that your Lordship promis'd him a close to keep him an horse.   Mr. Jones begs that your Lordship would order him some more mony for last years coal, and likewise that he may become tenant to Tomsons close at Lady Day next.   Old Guelder begs that he may have Spratts close when he is remov'd.

The suddain advancement in the price of wheat in this country is very surpriseing, for in one month it is risen from 32s. to 50s. per quarter; but my brother had fortunately pursu'd the directions I left with him when I came to Hamby, and we have secur'd for your Lordship 56 quarters of good wheat, which according to our markets is already worth more by 25£. than we are to give for it. When I was at Stamford I bought an hundred weight of clover seed, which I beg your Lordship would permit the cart to call for as it comes from Hamby, & then it may bring the glassiers glass, &c.; for I have spoke to him to come on Tuesday next to alter the blew room windows & to do several other things that are to be done.

The deer in the park are now extreamly poor and dye very fast, insomuch that John Peak is afraid that notwithstanding all our care, more than thirty brace of the old deer either are dead or will dye, & all the fauns.

I intend to go to Kirby to morrow to know when we may go on with viewing.   I have nothing further to inform your Lordship [of^d].   I am, Your Lordship's most humble and most faithful servant,

Deen, February 11th, 1725.   D: EATON

[59]   [*Wednesday*, 16 *February*, 1725/6.]

My Lord,
    Master Brudenell continues very well.   I went on Saturday to Kirby, but did not meet with Mr. Hawkins, so I went again on Munday, and we have appointed Munday next for viewing Bangroves, so I hope we shall finish that work next week.   I am sorry there should be a mistake about the plates. I remember the cook told me to send the pewter plates, but I went to Glapthorne on Fryday, & left directions in writing with the gardener & Mrs. Bradshaw what to pack up. I wrote down all manner of herbes, and the soop plates, &c.; I knew the silver ones could not be got to, & I did not suspect their sending china. The gardener says he has no spinnage worth sending, and that sorrell would be spoil'd in one day.

I go to morrow morning into Leicestershire, and I hope I shall clear that account.   I have paid Mr. Joseph Lynwood.   I hope your Lordship will like the mending of the lace.   The prices of the wheat we have bought are very different: we bought some at 4s. 4½d. per strike, some at 4s. 6d. per strike, some at 5s. per strike, and the last, which is to be deliverd the latter end of April, at 5s. 3d. per strike; it is all very good.

Richard will tell your Lordship why he stay'd so long.

I have reduc'd John Radoff's arrear to 26£. at Lady Day last, & discharg'd his bill.   Your Lordship did not say whether Mr. Jones is to have Tomsons close, or Guelder Spratt's, or not.   There is two teames plowing every day upon the Common, so I hope it will be done in due time. I have not heard anything yet of oats from Mr. Plythe [*i.e.* Blyth].

The glassier is here and I am giving him directions what to do. I desire to know if your Lordship would have the window in the passage room to the blew room alter'd.   I have nothing else to let your Lordship know at present.

I am your Lordship's
Most humble and most faithful servant,

Deen, February 16th, 1725.   DAN: EATON

[**60**]   [*Tuesday,* 22 *February,* 1725/6.]

My Lord,
Master Brudenell continues extreamly well.

On Thursday last I went into Leicestershire and have receiv'd all the arrears except Thomas Watts's of Glooston. I told Will Worth what your Lordship desir'd me about his mare, and he is very willing to oblige your Lordship and take her again, but desire[s] that she may first be try'd, for he assures me that she never had any ill qualities, and that if he had thought that she would not carry Lord Brudenell very safely, he would not have sold her to your Lordship at any price. And what makes me the more ready to believe him is that his wife seems very eager to have her again, for shee us'd to carry her single very pleasantly; I think the mare is very well worth the mony.

I spoke to Spencer about the penns, but he desires to be excus'd from paying any thing for them, for he says in the place they now stand they are of no use to him, and he has put up other penns in a more convenient place, which he says will serve his turn very well. I have not seen Freeman, so cannot tell what he will say concerning them.   I receiv'd 20£. of Will Dunmore for Mr. Leaver.   All the underwood is already gone out of the sale.

I was at Slawston, and I find that old John Ward intends to quit that part of his son's farm that he held for the advantage of the widow, he having taken a larger farm at Glooston. Your Lordship may remember that Thomas Bosden and John Bosden, junior, were his partners to the whole farm and paid their rent jointly, but they managed the farm seperately. Now these T. & J. Bosden would very willingly divide this part between them and pay the rent, and continue the same advantages to the widow that she now enjoys; but I find this part is very well worth the mony, and may produce some advantage to your Lordship, and the same to the poor widow as before.

Brightman desires that he may have Hurst's Meadow one year longer.   Thomas Hutchinson went with me, but came back again; I find he would gladly stay at Deen while grass comes, that he may keep his horse without charge.   On Fryday I went to Gretton and paid Mr. Horton the remainder of his tyth of Bandy Slade; he treated me very handsomely, and gave me a guinea to buy me a pair of gloves.   On Saturday I went to Corby and receiv'd forty pounds more of John Lummis, and eight guineas of Thomas Bell.   Those people that have hounds in Leicestershire beg your Lordship would let them be brought home: they

are two years old, but very troublesome.   Yesterday we valued 250 trees
in Bangroves, and to day we valued 300 trees in Deen Wood, and we think
we have about three days work in Bangroves and two in Deen Wood.
My Lord Hatton's servants cannot attend till Fryday next; then they
promise to go on without intermission 'till we have finished.

I have paid Mr. Jones the remainder of his bill for last years cole,
I having paid him 20£. in part before. Four of Stanion teams brought
four chalders to day, and there has not been an ounce of cole of any sort
burnt in the house since your Lordship left Deen, before to night. I told
John Winsal of the Lodge what your Lordship orderd me concerning
Strarsmores part of the house, but he says he will not have it at that
rent, & he says likewise that he thinks your Lordship is very hard upon
him [to make him^i] pay so much rent for the other.

I have receiv'd the honour of your Lordships letter. The glazier has
finish'd the window in the blew room according to your Lordships desire.

I durst not carry above six score guineas to my Lord Gower on
Fryday for fear I should not be able to answer my Lady's return, since
I have told your Lordship how we are all of us to be five days engaged.

Will Wade has bought five hogs & kill'd them, and there is nine
little ones of your own that are feeding.

I have no good news to tell your Lordship about the park; we have
taken several old deer into house, but they have all dyed. But there is
about 15 brace of old deer that we thought in the most danger of any,
that have always haunted the old park and would never go to the foddering, which I believe we shall preserve by some good hay which I have
caus'd to be carryed into the dogkenell barn to fodder them night and
morning, with all that will come to eat with them.   When I was at
Glapthorne, Hicks of Tansworth did not meet me; and since I did not
see him, to tell your Lordship the truth I forgot both his hound and the
other, but I will write to John Meadows about them by the first oppertunity.

The coach horse that was mine, his eyes are very well again, but the
little London horse's eyes are very bad. The two horses that came from
Hartford shire are very well, but I think they are very plain horses; one
of them comes four years old, the other comes five.   I have nothing
further to acquaint your Lordship with.

> I am your Lordships
>> Most humble and most faithful servant,

Deen, February 22th, 1725.   DAN: EATON

[**61**]   *[Tuesday, Wednesday, 1, 2 March, 1725/6.]*

My Lord,   Tuesday Evening.
Master Brudenell continues very well.   We have finished valuing
the timber in Deen-wood this evening, and shall finish in Bangroves to
morrow; and on Saturday morning your Lordship will receive by the
post an abstract of the books.

I have receiv'd the honour of your Lordship's letter by Will Barnes.
I shall take care of everything your Lordship desires therein.   The
coach horses are all well except the little London horse, whose eyes are
no better yet.   I hope those deer that are now alive will continue so,

for they seem to mend since we have given them a little good hay; for I believe it was the badness of the hay that destroy'd them more than the badness of the weather. But I find that our deer have escap'd as well as any of our neighbours, for there is a great many dye every where. Mr. Bradshaw says he shall lose more than half his deer of all sorts. The hound that Hicks of Tansworth kept dy'd mad some time since, and the other hound that was at Glapthorn Mr. Gach kept, and he is dead; they thought him poison'd. There are no other hounds there.

The partitions in the garrets of Little Deen are all done, but the cellar is not yet quite finished, for contrary to their expectation they met with a surly solid dry rock which they had very great labour to get thro'; but now I think nothing can hinder the celler from being finish'd on Munday or Tuesday next. But the workmen will have [h^d] as hard a bargain in proportion as that about the finishing the house.   I am,
    Your Lordship's most humble and most faithful servant,

Deen, March 2d, 1725.   DAN: EATON

[62]   [*Friday, 4 March*, 1725/6.]
My Lord,
    Master Brudenell is very well.   I have cast up the wood books, and Bangroves amounts to 865£. 0s. 0d. and Deen Wood to 730£. 0s. 0d., which is a difference I did not expect before the two last days of viewing; and I believe Bangroves contains more ground by 70 acres than Deen-wood. We have not valued the timber upon your Lordship's wast by Deen-wood side.   The teams are gone to Stamford to day for two lasts of oats, and they will be at Hamby on Munday. I shall send to Stanion for three horses to assist them.   I have nothing else to inform your Lordship of.
    I am your Lordship's
        Most humble and most faithful servant,

Deen, March 4th, 1725.   D[AN:] EA[TON][1]

[*Direction endorsed:—*]
        To the Right Honble. the Earl of Cardigan
        at Hamby Grange near Grantham in Lincolnshire.

[*Trace of Seal*]

[63]   [*Monday, 7 March*, 1725/6.]
My Lord,
    Master Brudenell is very well.   We shall finish Little Deen cellar to day, but the paving we shall let alone till your Lordship comes to Deen. One half of it is so good a rock that I think no pavement can be better, so I shall set the masons to secure the common stable wall, and after that I think the next thing that ought to be done is to build the lime kiln.

---

[1] Corner of MS. is torn off.

Your Lordship's hedges are not yet finished, but will be in proper time. As soon as I came from Hamby I sent the inclosed order to Deenthorpe labourers,[1] and two of them possitively refus'd to obey it; one of the other three I must own made a reasonable excuse, so that we have had but two of them, and they have been great part of the time employ'd in the park.   I have inclos'd an abstract of the whole arrear as I have brought it into my Lady Day's account.

The bearer hereof, Sam Lee, begs that your Lordship would accept of him for an helper in the stables or a postillian. As to his capacity for the latter I can say nothing, but I believe he would do very well for an helper. Your Lordship may have a satisfactory caracter of him from Mr. Bryon Hull, whom he serv'd last; I believe he is very sober and honest.

Wee are going to sell the poles in Sheepclose Spinny to day, for now the ground is a little hard, they may be got off without much damage.   I am,

Your Lordship's most humble and most faithful servant,

Deen, March 7th, 1725.   DAN: EATON

Lord Cardigan was in London during April and early May, 1726. Nine attendances at the House of Lords are recorded in the Journal of the House of Lords.

19 APRIL, 1726 — 1 MAY, 1726

[64]   [Tuesday, 19 April, 1726.]

My Lord,
I was at Uppingham on Wednesday last to wait upon his Honour, where was Mr. Roberts, who has prevail'd upon his Honour to wave the repairs of Wardly Church 'till your Lordship comes into the country, and then to leave out the battlements and partition, &c., and make all the old timber serve again (if possible).   Whither these things are for his Honour's interest or not your Lordship will discover when you come to see the church again; but I can't help reciting the motive by which he induc'd his Honour to adhere to his proposals, which I think a very extraordinary one, viz: that if the church was to be repaird after this manner, it would exhaust so much mony from the tenants, who he said were all very poor, that his Honour would be in danger of losing his rent hereafter, or of getting it with much difficulty.[2]

I take it, my Lord, that he had a double end in this: in the first place to save his own immediate expence, and in the next place to keep his Honour still in the dark as to the value of his land. I don't doubt that if all the leases were expir'd, but Wardly estate would bear as much yearly advancement as the repairs of the church will this year come to; by which

---

[1] See 57.
[2] From time immemorial there was a common law obligation on parishioners to contribute to the repair of the parish church. This was done at this time by raising a rate on occupiers of land: W. Tate, The Parish Chest, 92-94.

it is plainly evident that Mr. Roberts continues still to impose upon his Honours goodness. There is no difficulty atall from the articles of agreement being sign'd and seald, for Christopher Dexter will most willingly relinquish the bargain if they allow him a trifle for the trouble he has had in this affair.

Will Wades family are all perfectly recover'd, and no body else fallen. We have lay'd Presto for hay. Will Wade intends to go to Grantham on Saturday next to buy sheep. James Ashley was here on Sunday, but has not made up the account. I paid him 26£. and he says he must have 50£. more to clear the account, which I have promised him on Fryday next. All things here go on very well. The plaisterers are not yet come.

I am your Lordship's
Most humble and most faithfull servant,

Deen, April 19th, 1726.   DAN: EATON

[65]   [*Thursday, 21 April, 1726.*]

My Lord,
The plaisterer is not yet come; we have everything ready for him.
I am sub-poena'd by Mr. Bellamy to be at Grantham to morrow at 10 o'clock in the 'fore noon; so I intend to go by Cotchmore and let James Ashly have mony to clear the account. He told me that my Lord Gower told him that your Lordship had orderd me to let him have what mony he had occasion for, and that my Lord Gower had already paid more than his share of the years expence came to. I think to lye there to night, and if possible I will state and clear the account. I intend to come home by Stamford, where I shall appoint Christopher Dexter to meet me to look upon some dales for chamber floors at Little Deen, but I shall not bargain for any 'till I let your Lordship know the price and what sort of dales they are.

I am going to Glapthorn this morning and I hope I shall clear my Lady's account. We should have view'd the oaks in [B]andy Slade to morrow and on Saturday had it not been for the sub-poena, but on Munday we begin without fail. My mother is remov'd to Chambers's, and Guelder to Spratt's. I beg of your Lordship to let me know whither Mr. Lynwood ought to pay the window tax for Little Deen for the last year or not, for he refus'd to pay it, and I did not think it right to pay it without your Lordship's order. I am,
Your Lordship's most humble and most faithful servant,

Deen, April 21th [*sic*], 1726.   DAN: EATON

[66]   [*Sunday, 24 April, 1726.*]

My Lord,
I was at Cotchmore on Thursday last and pay'd James Ashley 60£. to cleare the dogkenell account to Ladyday. He told me that he could not possibly make up the account that night, so I went forward for Stroxton and lay there that night. He promises me to pay every body

before Thursday next, and come hither that day to state the account. If your Lordship intends to build a dogkenell at Stroxton this year, this is the only cheapest time to build in, for in about 7 weeks time labourers will not work under 14*d.* per day.

John Black should have orders now to lay in coles, for people begin to go to the pitts; he says he wants mony very much. I could not get from Grantham on Fryday, but yesterday I came by Stamford, where Christopher Dexter met me. We could not find any right clear dales in the town. Mr. Collington has a large quantity that are right good wood and very well season'd, out of which there might be pick'd an hundred clean dales, I believe; they are twelve foot long, and the price is eleven pounds an hundred when they are pick'd.

I receiv'd the honour of your Lordships letter and deliverd the inclosed according to your command. Needham the plaisterer came on Fryday; he has set his men to work, but goes away himself to day and comes again ten days hence. He drew the inclosed yesterday. The masons shall begin upon the kill to morrow. Will Wade has bought 60 sheep for the Common; he thinks they are not very dear, but I have not seen them. We shall buy no more till Holy-Thursday-Fair.[1]

I am your Lordship's
Mos [*sic*] humble and most faithful servant,

Deen, April 24th, 1726.   DAN: EATON

[**67**]   [*Tuesday, 26 April,* 1726.][2]

My Lord,
We were viewing timber in Bandy Slade yesterday. The leaf is very forward, therefore we intend to day to fix one day this week for the sale, for the sooner they are down, the better for the bark. Since your Lordship comes to Deen so soon, we shall not make any possitive bargain for the bark till you come. His Honour has sent last night to speak with me at Luffenham this morning. It is very early and I hope to be back at Corby by ten of the clock to continue the view, where I have order [*sic*] the wood-men to meet me. I am,
Your Lordship's most humble and most faithful servant,

Tuesday morning, 5 o'clock.   DAN: EATON

If your Lordship has any thing to be brought from London, here is a jocky wagon which will bring it down either next week or the week following, which your Lordship thinks proper; he is the same that brought the goods last year. He will call at Mr. Webbers on Munday next.

[**68**]   [*Sunday, 1 May,* 1726.]

My Lord,
James Ashly was here on Thursday and brought his accounts, which are very clear, but not perfect, by cause the earth stoppers and keepers

[1] This was at Grantham. See **137**.
[2] Dated from internal evidence. See **65, 68**.

& apothecary's of Oakham, Grantham, and Stamford are not paid; and your Lordship has not declar'd what boardwages James and the rest are to have at Woethorpe. They expect more than they us'd to have at Cotchmore, &c.

Yesterday we sold the timber in Bandy-Slade, which comes to 206£. And since your Lordship's coming to Deen is uncertain, we have agreed with Mr. Peach for the bark at 6s. 6d. in the pound for the saplins, without any allowance to be made for doderells, which we think is as good as eight shillings if the doderells were to be allow'd, for we are assur'd that a great number of them will not peel. The bark of the large trees we have sold for 3s. per Li[1] without any deductions, as the saplins; this we look upon to be the utmost value of the bark, tho' Mr. Peach pleaded very hard that we would consider him something in this years bark for the vast loss he had last year. But I told him we could not do any such thing, but must leave that intirely in your Lordship's breast.

We go into Leicestershire to morrow to sell those few oak trees there; and on Tuesday is the rent day. I intend to set out one or two of those very old trees in that wood above the bowling-green in Deen Park, and have them cut down for your Lordship's use: there is a great many there that are very much decay'd, and nothing growes under them. All things here are very regular.   I am,

Your Lordships most humble and most faithful servant,

Deen, May the first, 1726.   DAN: EATON

On 23rd May Cardigan wrote to the Duke of Montagu, from Deene (Mont. Corr. I. 106), where it is likely that the Earl spent much of this summer, keenly interested in the building work in progress at Little Deene. Towards the end of July he left for Yorkshire, and the next two letters found him at York and Grantham respectively.

7 AUGUST, 1726 — 17 AUGUST, 1726

[69]   [*Sunday, 7 August, 1726.*]

My Lord,
I have been at Brampton and Dingly to enquire about the Hundred rent and to demand it. I cannot learn from the oldest men in both towns that ever it was demanded before, so that I doubt it will be a difficult matter to redeem it. My Lord Griffin said that he knew nothing of it, and bad me enquire of his agent, Mr. Peach of Harborough, which I did; and he told me that he never heard of it before, but he would enquire into the affair. I did not deman'd it of Sir Geoffrey Palmer bycause I had a message to deliver, but I left a particular of it with his steward, who promised me to make Sir Geoffrey acquainted with it.

[1] i.e. 3s. per pound sterling as indicated by "in the pound" just above, meaning that the bark of a tree is to be estimated at 3s. for every £1 of the price of the tree. See 18.

I have been in Leicestershire, where I have clear'd the arrear to a farthing; but Thomas Watts has not yet paid what Will Dunmore laid down for him. There is some wood remaining in both the woods, which I repremanded Will Worth for, and he promises me to cause it to be remov'd in a fortnights time. I find John French still inflexible; his brother cannot prevail upon him to be reasonable. In all this circuit that I have been, the crops of all sorts of grain are very indifferent. New wheat at Harborough was worth 4s. 10d. per strike.

I have stated Lummis's old account of wood, and there is due to your Lordship upon the ballance 58£. 3s. 6d., which he promises to pay to Mr. Gibson on Thursday next. I told him I believ'd it would be acceptable to your Lordship any where, and I gave him directions where Mr. Gibson lives. He with his wife set out for London on Tuesday next.

The hounds are all well; none of them have fallen since your Lordship left Deen. John Kingston tells me they behave themselves very gallantly. They killd a young fox the other day in one of Laxton woods.

There is about 20 loads of your Lordship's oats extreamly well laid together and thatch'd, and by Wednesday next all those in the Great Close will be secur'd if the weather continues fine.

I am your Lordship's
        Most humble and most faithful servant,

Deen, August 7th, 1726.   DAN: EATON

[*Direction endorsed:*—]
        To the Right Honble. the Earl of Cardigan at York.

[*Further contemporary endorsements:*—]
                17 - 17
                 6 - 18   2 - 1
                _____

                24 - 15

[*Seal*]

[**70**]   [*Wednesday*, 17 *August*, 1726.]

My Lord,
        I have receiv'd a letter from Lummis wherein he says that he has paid to Mr. Gibson 48£. 3s. 3d., and to Philip Gaines upon my Lady's account 10£., which clears the ballance of his account, and my Lady has paid me the 10£.

We have got all the hay together to the old park corner that was in the plantation and in New Wood and round the grain in Lammas Close; there was sixteen load of it, and it is extreamly good. All the oats in the farthest part of the Common are laid together and well thatch'd, and I never saw grain better got. They are going today to carry the hay in Langly; I believe there will be about 24 loads of it and it is likewise extreamly good. The labourers began to mow in Newlands yesterday, which falls a pritty good crop. The rest of the oats will not be ripe till Saturday. They are likewise mowing in Presto, but to morrow they must begin to mow the barly in Lammas Close.

One of the chamber ceilings at Little Deen is intirely finish'd and the other is almost done; they are very handsome.   John Kingston tells me that Lady is dead; she was chap-fallen. The rest of the hounds and the horses are very well.   I have nothing else material to inform your Lordship of at present.
I am your Lordship's
Most humble and most faithful servant,

Deen, August 17th, 1726.   DAN: EATON

[*Direction endorsed:—*]
        To the Right Honble. the Earl of Cardigan at Grantham.
[*Seal*]

The letters from **71** *to* **147** *are quite the largest consecutive group in this correspondence, and imply long absences from Deene by Lord Cardigan. During September, October and part of November he was at Bath. The evidence from Dan's letters is supplemented by some from William Elmsall, his Yorkshire steward, and other writers (Bru. MSS. F.iii. 170, 171, 268, 273). In early December letter* **99** *is directed to the Earl at Ditchley in Oxfordshire, but just before Christmas (* **102**, *18th December) Dan wrote that he was not sure whether his master were still at Bath. There is a very short gap in the letters over Christmas, when Cardigan and his family were almost certainly at Deene.*
Several subjects run through this long series of letters during the autumn and winter of 1726-1727: the management of the woods took up a great deal of Dan's time and he had trouble with the labourers over their "bottles" (the faggots of wood traditionally allowed to them). It is not surprising that he felt overburdened with work and had to engage someone to help him to write up his accounts (**81**). *Then there was much sickness and also madness among the hounds, which Dan reported in detail. In letter* **92** *is the first mention of brickmaking and brickmakers, a recurrent theme during 1727. Lord Cardigan was in London directly after Christmas and his presence in the House of Lords is recorded in each month from January to the beginning of July, 1727. On 27th June he took his oath of allegiance to the new King, George II, and was put on the Committee for Privileges (Journals of the House of Lords, Vol. XXIII). During April and May Lord Brudenell and his two sisters were ill with smallpox, and the new baby, Robert, was sent down to Deene to join his brother James ("Master Brudenell"), now aged two.*

11 SEPTEMBER, 1726 — 1 JUNE, 1727

[**71**]   [*Sunday, 11 September, 1726.*]

My Lord,
        Mr. Elliot was here on Thursday morning last, and he tells me that George Taleby of Glooston assur'd him that Edward Spence of Slawston intends to quit his farm very shortly. Whither this is his real intention or not I cannot say, but it is very plain that if he intends to

hold it, he will impoverish it, for he lays all the mannor[1] it produces upon his own farm, and declares he will not lay an ounce upon your Lordships land. He likewise tells Mr. Edwards that whereas he is under no obligations to enclose, he shall expect some considerable advantages. I am very much mistaken if he did not in my sight sign an agreement to your Lordship wherein he has bound himself to enclose at your Lordship's pleasure. This declaration of Spence's has made Mr. Edwards think the difficulties of compleating the enclosure will be very great; but what I have told Mr. Elliot concerning Spence's agreement he says he does not doubt but will make him easy.[2]

Needham has been here, and I have measur'd all his work that is finish'd, and have enclosed a particular. His prices are all under even the red column in the particular your Lordship gave me (except the stucco bead work, which is not there mentioned). They cannot proceed in their work till the architraves of the doors and the window jaums are finish'd in the hall and dining room. So they are all gone, but Needham promises to come again upon the first notice. In the mean, Thomas Nickols the joiner will go on with those things as fast as he can. If your Lordship intends to have a wainscot door for the front of Little Deen (which I think will be better than a sash), here is season'd English oak planks that will make a [g^d] very good one.

The hounds and horses are very well; they kill'd a bag'd fox and an hare on Fryday. I did not shew Needham the prises in the particular your Lordship gave me, since I found his prices under the mark; but your Lordship may enquire the price of stuco bead-work. You may be satisfy'd that all the other work is not over charg'd.

My Lady left Deen on Thursday last. Master Brudenell continues extreamly well. I am,

Your Lordship's most humble and most faithful servant,

Deen, September 11th, 1726.   DAN: EATON

P.S. Needham says the cornices will not seen [sic] too big when the rooms are finish'd.

[72]   [Enclosed in 71.]

[Wednesday, Thursday, 7, 8 September, 1726.]

PLAISTERERS WORK DONE BY JOSHUA NEEDHAM
Measured September the 7th & 8th, 1726

In the garrets at Little Deen:	£	s.	d.
365 yds. of plain-ceiling and partition at 4d. per yd.	6	01	0
158 yds. of rendering at 3d. per yd.	1	19	6
In the chambers at Little Deen:			
107 yards of floated ceiling at 6d. per yd.	2	13	6

[1] So pronounced in Lincolnshire c. 1920; i.e. manure.
[2] See Appendix 3 for the Rev. J. Elliot's letter to Cardigan at Bath, 22 Oct. 1726 (Bru. MSS. F.iii. 268), which throws much light on inclosure difficulties at Slawston.

49 yards of plain ceiling and partition at 4d. per yd.	0	16	4
58 yds. 2 foot & ½ of plain cornice, running measure at 2s. 6d. per yard	7	7	0
51½ yards of cornice in the hall and dining room at Little Deen, enrich'd, at 4s. per yard running measure	10	6	0

In the Bowling-house at Deen:

44 yds. of coves & ceiling, floated, at 6d. per yd. ...	1	2	0
15 yds. 2 foot of plain cornice in the ceiling at 2s. per yd. running measure	1	11	4
24 yds. 1 foot of stuco impost at 2s. 6d. running measure	3	00	10
68 yds. 4 foot of stuco beadwork at 1s. 6d. per yard	05	2	8

In the little room at the Green House:

7 yds. of coves and ceiling, floated, at 6d. per yd. ...	0	3	6
4 yds. 2 foot of cornice in the ceiling at 1s. per yard	0	4	8
10 yds. 6 inches of impost stuco at 1s. 6d. per yd., running	0	15	3
19 yds. 4 foot of stuco bead work at 1.6 per yd. ...	1	9	2

12 yards of plain ceiling in the other little room at 4d. per yd.	0	4	0

Paid at several times in part 33£., 00s. 0d.

[73]   [*Thursday, 15 September,* 1726.]

My Lord,
   Master Brudenell continues very well.   I should have enclosed the list of the board wages in my last, but the post stay'd while I folded my letter, so I forgot it, for which I beg your Lordship's pardon.
   Linthwait has brought the copper bottom and they are putting it in; it weighs 2 cwt., 1 quarter, 24 lbs. Whither the copper is so good as it ought to be or not I cannot tell, but I have sent to Mr. Keep, the brasier of Wellingborough, to come hither before it is us'd, and he shall pass his judgement upon it. Your Lordship knows him to be a man of a very fair caracter. I think this bottom is a great deal thicker than it need to have been, which makes me fear that it is not so good metal as it ought to be, for [by*i*] the contract he was to procure the very best of copper; but I don't doubt but Keep will be just in declaring his opinion.
   I have spoke to Robert Hibbins and he will come in a weeks time to take down the arch of the small beer celler and make a new one.   I am,
   Your Lordship's most humble and most faithful servant,

Deen, September 15th, 1726.   D: EATON

[74]   [*Sunday,* 18 *September,* 1726.]

My Lord,
   Master Brudenell continues very well.   I bargained with the labourers for the trenching that meadow that was John Parsons's that the

Miller has, at 2s. per acre, the ditches to be 3 foot deep and three foot wide. This will improve the ground very much, and I believe it will be finish'd this week.

If your Lordship would have that close that Will Wade has that was Hawksby's done, I believe the labourers will do it cheaper now than at any other time, and whereas the ditches there only want scowering, they will be done a great deal cheaper than where new ones are to be made. And if your Lordship would have a road ditch'd in that close as you formerly propos'd, it will be done cheaper now than at any other time, for the labourers have nothing to do till the sales begin. I have measur'd Philip Days work, and I find it comes to more by the foot than it does by the day. So I shall pay him by the day.[1] He will have finish'd all his work this week.

The hounds and horses are very well.   We have scarce had one fair day since your Lordship left Deen, so that I dare not let teams fetch the gravil bycause the[y] will rut the park very much, nor can we rightly remove the rubbish from Little Deen till the ground is dryer.

I am your Lordship's
Most humble and most faithful servant,

Deen, September 18th, 1726.   DAN: EATON

[75]   [*Tuesday*, 20 *September*, 1726.]

My Lord,
Master Brudenell continues very well.   We have had two very fine days here, in which we have got together all the hay in Newlands. It has receiv'd very little damage, being laid in large cocks before any rain came upon it, and all possible care has been taken of it in every fair blast to stirr it and keep it sweet, so that all the hay there is good; and there is about six score and ten loads of it. I will get it thatched with rushes as soon as possible; we have some cut in the park to do it. If it continues fair to day, we shall get most of the hay in the meadow, which will be very good fodder.

I have nothing else to inform your Lordship of at present.
I am your Lordship's
Most humble and most faithful servant,

Deen, September 20th, 1726.   DAN: EATON

[76]   [*Sunday*, 25 *September*, 1726.]

My Lord,
Master Brudenell continues extreamly well.   I receiv'd the honour of your Lordships letter on Thursday last.   I have appointed the rent day in Leicestershire to be the Munday after Harborough Fair.[2] Your Lordship knows that I receiv'd Corby rents a great while since. I have likewise receiv'd some of Deenthorpe rents, and have given warning to

[1] In August, 1728, however, he was being paid "by the great" (ASR 252).
[2] Market Harborough Fair was on 9 October.

the tenants of Deenthorpe, Stanion, and Deen to clear there [sic] rent by the time your Lordship has appointed.

I have stated the house account for all the time your Lordship was at Deen, and have paid great part of the bills, but I don't intend to pay any of them in full till your Lordship has seen them. I have posted the wood account in your Lordships book, and the Yorkshire rental, and am about the other. Here is continually something or other to take me off of writing. I think my own accounts are very regular, but I fear I cannot trans-scribe them all before your Lordship comes, for from the beginning of them there is above an hundred pages to this day.

We gott the hay, all of it, on Tuesday before the rain came [last^d] in the afternoon, & I think this hay we got last is better than any we got last year. Here has been continual rains since, so that nothing can be done with carts in the park.

On Wednesday and Thursday here was Linthwaits men to fix the copper bottom. I think I never saw a more bungling piece of work in my life than they have made of it. Mr. Keep came hither on Fryday according to my desire. He was unwilling to say anything against another mans performances, but when I told him that if he would not declare his opinion frankly in the case, I was resolv'd to get another workman that would, he then told us possitively that there was more metal by an hundred weight at least than there ought to have been if the metal was good, and that the men that put it on did not understand their business; but as it was vastly thick, it might do good service. The man came on Fryday to hang it, and I sent for Robert Hibbins, and he came yesterday to help him; and Richard is making the iron work as fast as possible. As soon as the copper is finish'd, they shall begin upon the small beer celler.

The male deer begin to look thin with this bad weather; but since there is so much good hay in the park, John Peak says he does not fear losing any. The stakes which confin'd the treys round the plantation were very much decay'd, so we have set the labourers to make new ones of some poles that came from Bandy Slade, which are fit for little else; and these stakes will keep the treys secure.

I went on Fryday a second time to Benefield to speak to Mr. John Lynwood (for the first time he was not at home), and I got a receipt for John Fardell in full, which clears the mony that was due for wood. Mr. Joseph Lynwood has brought in the rest of the oats, so the wood & rent is clear.

What is between Mr. John Lynwood & myself I could not settle, by cause he had mislaid his account and he thought that mine was not right; nor could I prevail upon him to do as your Lordship propos'd concerning the 15£. of John Radoff's. He says he will wait upon your Lordship as soon as you return. He says he should not have thought much to have taken 5£. 10s. 0d. for the barn floor, if he had had the full value for the treyfoil, but he is only allow'd what he paid for the seed, without any consideration for his trouble in sowing it, and it was worth above ten pounds more.

Yesterday Mr. Allen came, and I measured all the stone[1] we have had of him. The floor of the great room and of the little room of the Green House come to 6£. 9s. 4d. The circular steps come to 3£. 6s. 0d., and the steps for the celler at Little Deen come to 1£. 9s. 4d. He told me he wanted mony very much, so I paid him 8£. in part.

[1] Evidently paving stone for the Green House.

His Honour has order'd me to go to Stockin to morrow to measure some work that is finish'd there.   I have receiv'd a letter from Mr. Norgrave, wherein he desires me to order the cony-catchers of Corby and Stanion to meet at some time and place that I shall appoint this week to sign the bonds; which I intend shall be either Wednesday or Fryday next.   I think the sash door at Little Deen ought to be oak, and these planks we have will do very well.

The hounds and horses are all well and J. Colton says that since they have had six couple of old hounds amongst them, they have had very good sport. They found a fox at Jenkinson's Spinny and run him to Collyweston Park and cross the river again, and near Tinwell the young hounds view'd him and kill'd him. And yesterday they found a fox in Laxton Woods and run him very hard for two hours, then earth'd him in a swallow hole.[1] John says he never saw young hounds behave themselves better. He thinks it will be of advantage to them to go to Ashton Old, for as yet they are forc'd to whip off whene'er a fox makes to the forest; but he will not go thither without your Lordships orders. I have nothing else material to inform your Lordship of at present.

I am your Lordship's
Most humble and most faithful servant,

Deen, September 25th, 1726.   DAN: EATON

[77]   [*Thursday, 29 September*, 1726.]

My Lord,
Master Brudenell continues very well.   I was at Stockin on Munday, and was kept there all night by excessive rain; and when I came home on Tuesday I could not pass at Turtle Bridge[2] for the water.

I was forc'd to send a messenger to Stamford yesterday for Linthwait to mend the copper if he can, for it runs in an hundred places at least. He desir'd that we would not put water into it before the stuff he had tear'd it withall was dry, which we observ'd, but it was to no manner of purpose. He promised to send his men to mend it to day, but they are not yet come. If they don't finish it effectually to day (as I don't expect they can), I will discharge the copper hanger to morrow. If we had known as much before, we had no occasion to have sent for him, for the method he takes is exactly the same in every respect with the method Robin Hibbins has continually us'd in hanging several coppers in this country, but particularly Mr. Tryons of Colyweston and Mr. Kirkhams, & I see him take the same method in hanging my mothers, which boils very quick. So that I don't doubt but Robin will finish the hanging of it as well without him as with him.

I have been twice at Bandy Slade since your Lordship left Deen, and there is no coppice wood left in the sale, and not a great deal of timber.   Yesterday I measur'd the thatchers work upon the hovells and penns at Newlands.

I have this minute receiv'd the honour of your Lordships letter. I understand the method your Lordship proposes for the trenching and

---

[1] Alias swallet hole. See Glossary.
[2] Over the Welland at Harringworth. See *P.N.Northants* p. 168.

making a road in the Brick Kiln Close perfectly well. I will take care to excecute all your Lordships commands, and will be very perticular in my next.   My Lord Hatton is in the country; I will enquire when he leaves it.   I have receiv'd a letter from my Lady which orders me to Cliff¹ & Luffenham.   The Scotch cattell are not yet come, which I am sorry for, for our eddishes want them.   The post stays.

I am your Lordship's

Most humble and most faithfull servant,

Deen, September 29th, 1726.   Dan: Eaton

[78]   [*Sunday, 2 October, 1726.*]

My Lord,

Master Brudenell continues extreamly well.   The gardner & I have set out the ground in the Brick Kiln Close in the manner your Lordship has directed, except that the banks between the great ditches and the little ones on each side of the road we have orderd to be 7 foot wide, for 5 foot would be so narrow that no trees could thrive upon it. The gardner intends constantly to attend the workmen, for this work cannot be done by the great. They will go on with those two ditches that are next to the church first, for we think that the great bank had better be 36 or 38 foot wide, if your Lordship thinks proper; for then there may be a row of trees planted upon it [on each side*i*] 3 or 4 foot from the great ditches, which will not only preserve the bank from being trampled into the ditches, but will be very beautiful. This waits your Lordship's answer.

I have been with Thomas Bell to look upon the crabtrees in Bandy Slade. So much of them as are fit for fencing posts we can sell for more, I believe, than oak posts are worth. If not, Thomas Baily will give an equal number of oak posts for crab tree, for this wood they make cogs & rounds of; but we all know that neither crab tree nor apple tree will stand long in the ground for a post. I have given orders to have them cut down; then we can make the best of them.

I was on Fryday at Stanion to see the cony catchers execute the bonds, which they did. Mr. Norgrave and the attorney he employ'd insisted upon 18s. a piece charges, but I told them I had no commission to make any conclusion in this part of the affair, and advis'd them to forbear prosecuting the men for the mony 'till your Lordship's return into the country, which they promised to do. When I was there I collected most of Stanion rents.

I can not hear certainly when Lord Hatton leaves the country, but I hear it will be in a few days.   I have sent home the copperhanger. The copper still runs in three or four places, but now it is come so near the point, I don't fear but it will be stop'd. I think I never was more plagu'd with one affair in my life than I have been with this.

I have some reason to think that Lummis met with a better reception at Hull than I expected he would have done, and I believe his journey answer'd very well. I believe he intends to spend most of his time in London. He has left orders with Sidney to attend the woods constantly,

¹ Kings Cliffe.

and for his reward has promised him all the perquisites which he himself used to have as coppice keeper. He has left his three youngest daughters with one of his sisters at Corby, and allows her something certain for their board. He intends to be in the country the latter end of this month, and intends to stay as long as your Lordship shall require him. He intends for himself only his share of the earnest, so that its very plain he does not intend to get any thing by serving your Lordship, for I am very sure this will not bear his charges riding after it.

Ranter is dead mad, but all the rest of the hounds and horses are well.   The wife of Michael Bywaters is come hither by a Justice's order for an habitation. She is big with child and her husband is run a way from her. I can't tell what to do with her with out your Lordship's orders.   Jack intends to hunt in Weldon Park & Priors Haws, &c., and to shoot foxes if they can to morrow, for they had an hard days work on Thursday last. They are very quiet with the deer in the park.

I have fix'd upon Wednesday next for making the riding strait that is to part the wood that is to go sale this year in Stanion, and as soon as ever the leaf is down the labourers shall begin; but leaves will rot the hedges. They shall likewise begin in Corby Sale as soon as possible.

Philip says that both the bay mare and grey mare are well, and will be fit for hunting whensoever your Lordship pleases.

I am your Lordship's
Most humble and most faithful servant,

Deen, October 2d, 1726.   DAN: EATON

[79]   [*Tuesday, 4 October, 1726.*]

My Lord,
Master Brudenell continues very well.   Yesterday they shot a fox in Weldon Park which run some time afterwards, but the hounds kill'd him. Afterwards they found another and run him very hard a long time, but could not kill him. Either to morrow or on Thursday they go to Oakly Woods.

When Lummis was in the country, he propos'd a method which I think indeed would effectualy prevent Corby people for ever turning any more cattell of any sort into the Southwoods; which was to take each of those woods at twice, and to make no fence between the old spring and the young, and to make no fence between the woods, so that there [m^d] would be always some young spring in one of these woods; which when the cattell were found upon [it^i], your Lordship might recover any damages.[1]

The reason why I did not let your Lordship know this before was bycause I thought the remidy would be worse than the disease, for the young springs lying open, the deer would be harbourd in the old spring, and wou'd entirely destroy all the young ash, as they have done in that part of Oakly Woods which went last sale; for that, by a moderate computation, has receiv'd above 60£. damage by them, and can never hereafter recover it, all the ash being utterly destroy'd.

[1] See **145**.

I am forc'd to send to Stamford again today for the tinkers, for Rowell is come to brew and the copper will not hold.
  I am your Lordship's
    Most humble and most faithful servant,

Deen, October 4th, 1726.   DAN: EATON

[80]   [*Thursday, 6 October, 1726.*]

My Lord,
  Master Brudenell continues very well.   John Winsall was with me on Tuesday, to give timely notice of quitting his close at Lady Day next, for he says he has lost a great deal of mony by it. So that now your Lordship has a fair oppertunity to try the judgement or sincerity of that person who told your Lordship that T. Meadows and J. Winsall had a good bargain of it; for surely he will not refuse this close at the rent, if then he really thought it worth the mony, for Winsal has improv'd it as much as he possibly could in two years.
  I set out the riding yesterday betwixt Burnt Coppice and Harris Wood,[1] and have let it to the labourers to ditch and plash. I am sure your Lordship will like it when it is done. I believe in a weeks time we may begin Corby Sale.
  Lummis sends me word that old Fell has given him a long stable which is worth about 30£. a year, and that he intends to be at Corby before the 24th instant.
  I have taken places in Oundle coach by my Lady's order for the nurse and child, and for the nurses sister to return with the child. They meet the coach at Oundle to morrow, but a nurse's maid my Lady order'd me to hire shall go by the wagon on Sunday.
  I have receiv'd the honour of your Lordship's letter of the first instant. I was yesterday in Bandy Slade, and the greatest part of the wood that remains there is timber trees. There is some few bottle fagots and a few oak tops. I gave strict orders to Thomas Bell and Meadows about them.   The post stays, so I shall be particular in my next.
  I am your Lordship's
    Most humble and most faithfull servant,

Deen, October 6th, 1726.   DAN: EATON

[81]   [*Sunday, 9 October, 1726.*]

My Lord,
  Master Brudenell is very well.   I sent the ball'd gelding to Harborough Fare according to your Lordships command, but he was not sold. Philip tells me that good horses went off very indifferently there.   I have been twice at Benefield, but could not meet with Mr. John Lynwood. I have shewn the contents of your Lordships letter to Mr. Joseph Lynwood, and desir'd him to tell his brother, which he says he will, but he

_____
[1] Both in Stanion. See Index of Places under Wood Names.

says he does realy think his brother has lost both the keys. One of them he says he knows was lost two years agone, and the other he thinks was lost last spring; and this summer he has not come thro' the park, but with a key of the great gate which he did sometimes lend him, and which he has now deliverd to J. Peak.

I do assure your Lordship that I am full as desirous that your Lordship should have a copy of my accounts as your Lordship can be, for it is impossible for me to be easy unless I make your Lordship so. 'Twas this that induc'd me, before I receiv'd the honour of your Lordships last letter, to procure another hand to transcribe my accounts into a book in a regular manner. The person[1] has been at work all this week; he writes full as well and as correct as I can. He writes for Mr. Walter & several others in this country. I don't doubt but your Lordship will like his hand, and I hope you cannot dislike this way of proceeding, for with this multiplicity of business I found I could never transcribe them my self. As to my vouchers, I have not the least objection to your Lordship's taking them into your own custody immediately after your Lordship has allow'd my accounts, for then they are of no service to me, but rather an incumbrance. I wonder'd indeed that your Lordship order'd me to take my vouchers back when your Lordship sign'd my accounts in October last. I believe I shall have done with this man in another week, so that when your Lordship comes to Deen, I hope you will find everything to your satisfaction.

The fagotts from Weldon Sale are all come long since. The weather is now very good and the park dry enough so that I hope we shall get most of the rubbish remov'd from Little Deen this week; then the sashes shall be put up.   The labourers are about the ditches in the Brick Kiln Close. I hope your Lordship will be at Deen before we shall have occasion to begin the sale in the park; if not, I will bargain with the labourers in the manner your Lordship proposes.   I am extreamly glad to hear that the waters have done your Lordship good. I go to Stonton to morrow.

The hounds are all well, and none of them have fallen amiss since Ranter. The horses are all well except that which Mr. Pearcy wrote to your Lordship about. Phillip says that he belives there will be very little difference between keeping the horses here or at Stroxton, either as to cheapness or the benefit of the horses; so that he will not remove without your Lordship's possitive commands, for hay is cheaper, tho' oats are something dearer here than there.   I shall obey all your Lordships commands.

I am your Lordship's
Most humble and most faithful servant,

Deen, October 9th, 1726.   DAN: EATON

[82]   [*Thursday*, 13 *October*, 1726][2]

My Lord,
Master Brudenell is extreamly well.   I receiv'd the honour of your Lordship's and the two inclos'd. I deliverd one to Mr. Hawkins, for my

---

[1] "The person", and "this man" below in this letter refer to John Kirk. See Index of Persons.
[2] Date corrected by internal evidence. See **69-88**, **99** and **101**, which treat of most of the subjects here mentioned.

Lord Hatton has been gone to London above a week, and he promis'd to send it by the next post. The other I deliverd to Mr. Henry Kirkham, who promis'd to give it to his brother[1] that night when he came home; he was gone a shooting.

I likewise told him what your Lordship orderd me concerning the mare, but he says that the knot your Lordship objected against still remains upon her leg. I desir'd him to tell his brother, and if he thought proper, to send her to Deen, but she is not come. I spoke to him about the hops, and he says he could not prevail with his father to let him have any; they sold all theirs from 3£. 15s. 0d. to 4£. per hundredweight. I have got two bags from Mr. Nevile, which were all they could spare, for they had but an indifferent crop this year, and were forc'd to oblige their constant customers, every one a little. They are extreamly good; they weigh very near 4 hundredweight at 3£. 17s. 6d. per hundredweight.

It rain'd here prodigiously all yesterday, but the gravel is all brought to the long walk, and rubbish was carried from Little Deen to mend Bangroves gate-way, Priors Haws gateway, and the miry ditch in Priors Haw Riding while the park was dry, so there is no harm done to it. I had causd the chamber sashes at Little Deen to be put up, or otherwise the wet beating in might have damaged the cornices in the lower rooms.

I was at Stonton on Munday last according to appointment, and collected the rents. The tenants paid very well, and those that are behind promise to clear upon the 14th of next month. John Spencer paid but 20£. Watts of Glooston & John Basset, that usd to be so back'ard, have clear'd. Edward Spence has paid but 16£., and he denies openly and possitively that ever he sign'd any writing concerning Slawston enclosure.[2] If he has forgot, his memory is very trecherous. I think this writing is in Deen liberary, but if there is not two witnesses he will certainly forsware his hand. There were ten people present when he made this denial.   Mr. Edwards is gone into Ireland; he made very little progress in Slawston affair before he went.

Will Worth tels me that the 400£. will be paid at Martinmas certainly, and that your Lordship may depend upon it.   They are brewing as fast as they can, and Rowell says this is very good brewing weather. If to day and to morrow continue fair, they may cart in the park next day, for the distance they are to carry the rubbish is but small, so that if they should rut the park a little, a labourer in a day or two will levell it again.   I am going to Corby to day to set the labourer [sic] about ditching the sale, for this last rain will bring down the leaf so that they may begin to hedge in a weeks time.

I have this moment receiv'd the honour of your Lordship's of the 8th inst.   Ranter did no mischief, for on a suddain [the use of[i]] his limbs were taken a way in the field; they brought him home and he dy'd the next day chap fallen. There is another hound fallen yesterday; he is raving. Jack is gone ahunting, and I have forgot his name. All the rest are well. Jack assur'd [me[i]] that this was secur'd before he did the least damage, and that he has the strictest eye over them immaginable.

Michael Bywaters serv'd your Lordship under Thomas Watson. I am not sure whither he was a servant by the year or not, or whither he serv'd as these little boys now do, viz: for meat & cloths (Mr. Billinge

---

[1] Charles Kirkham of Fineshade, junior.
[2] For references to Slawston inclosure see **71**, Subject Index under Inclosure, and Appendix III.

can tell); which makes me afraid to grant her a certificate (which she is now willing to accept and to go to her father), for this would make her a settlement, tho' her husband had none. But if her husband was servant by the year, we must grant one.   I am,

Your Lordships most humble and most faithfull servant,

Deen, September [*sic*] 13th, 1726.   DAN: EATON

[83]   [*Sunday, 16 October, 1726.*]

My Lord,
    Master Brudenell is very well.   I have been at Corby, but the leaf is not down enough to begin to hedge, and I cannot tell when it will, for it falls very slowly. I found ten men there that wanted employment, so I brought them to Deen to help to ditch the road, which with our own labourers I hope will finish it before the sales are fit to begin. They go on very well; either the gardner or my self are continually with them. The riding in Stanion Sale is ditch'd, but they have not begun to hedge yet.[1]
    They had a most fine chase on Thursday last. They found a fox in Bangroves and run him down the forrest to Apethorpe, then into Cliff Park, then back again thro' the forrest to Winshaw Wood in Stanion, where they chang'd. The young hounds behav'd themselves extreamly well and kept to their business notwithstanding the deer. They are all well.
    I receiv'd the inclosed from Mr. Blyth.   I have nothing material to inform your Lordship of at present.
    I am your Lordship's
        Most humble and most faithful servant,

Deen, October 16th, 1726.   DAN: EATON

[84]   [*Tuesday, 18 October, 1726.*]

My Lord,
    Master Brudenell continues very well.   I have receiv'd the honour of your Lordship's letter of the 12th. The reason why I took no notice of the buck that should have gone to the gentlemen of the Jewell Office was bycause John Peak told me that he had sent a particular account about it both to your Lordship and to Mr. Webber by the very next post after your Lordship let me know of its miscarriage; for he went to Oundle and found it duly enterd in the coach book upon the 16th of September as it was directed, so that if it is lost, the coach man must make it good.
    I will take care to get the nets in order to fish as soon as possible. We are now again removing the rubbish from Little Deen, but wet weather has kept us from it a long time.   Pywell has not paid any of his Lady Days rent, but promises to pay a lar[g]e part of it on Thursday next.   I deliver'd the inclos'd to John Peak as directed.

---

[1] This riding was between Burnt Coppice and Harris Wood. See **80**.

I think what your Lordship proposes about joining those two grounds to Pywells will make it a compleat farm, but I wish Pywell may pay his rent according to promise, that there may be no occasion for this alteration, for I don't think it would bear much advance if it is now at 18s. per acre, as I am inform'd.

As to what your Lordship is pleas'd to mention about John Winsals bearing part of the charge of the fence, I don't think it will bear; for as I take it, he was tenant at will and only by the year. If so, certainly he might quit it without damage to himself if he gave timely notice, as he has done. If he had been tenant for a term of years, the case would then have been alter'd, but I was not present when your Lordship contracted with him. If I was, I have forgot what bargain was made, but I believe he was only tenant at will, by cause your Lordship gave me orders once last year to discharge him; [if so^d] [therefore^i] sure he could not be oblig'd to hold the close while the fence should want repairing. I cannot learn that he intends to take land any where else or to quit his dwelling, but if he should quit his dwelling, I believe his father and mother will not.

I have heard so many different accounts from the Navigation that I think none of them worth relating. In short I find there is no real conclusion made. Your Lordship's presence I think would have been of great service to the country.[1]   I know nothing of any proceedings his Honour has made with Mr. Roberts, but I hear that he keeps his station.[2] Wardly Church is finish'd.

I generally write some part of my letters over night and some part in the morning before the post comes in. I am very sorry that your Lordships collick continues, but I hope your Lordship will return to Deen in perfect health.   I have done nothing at the slates of that place your Lordship mentions at Little Deen, for I always thought your Lordship intended to have the roof intirely alter'd. Your Lordship may wainscot the dining room if you please, for the plaisterers have not proceeded too far.

I suppose Mr. Pearsy has let your Lordship know our misfortune about the hound whelpe that went mad on Thursday last. I was the first that discover'd he was mad, and I took care to kill him as soon as possible, for we could not catch him. I fear he has done some damage among the spanniels, but I sent immediately for the dog doctor, who is come and has drench'd them all. And I order'd Will Wade to buy chaines and we have chain'd them all seperately, and have got a bowl for every one of them, and we shall keep them chain'd till they are out of danger.

Dan Whitworth says that if your Lordship buys two hogsheads of red port & two half hogsheads of white port, he thinks it will be sufficient to serve while the wine of this present years vintage will be fit to drink, which in all probability will be much better than any old wine; but Dan says that he makes this computation upon supposing that the family will not be at Deen before May next.   Our brewing goes on very well and the weather is good for it.

Mr. Kirkham has sent the mare, and I have paid him 12£. for her. Jack Kingston says he thinks she is sound. She came on Sunday & I orderd him to take care of her.   The hounds continue very well since

[1] 'Country' here probably stands for 'county'.
[2] See **64**. In Bru. MSS. (F.iii.273) is a letter from John Tryon to Cardigan (20 Oct. 1726) throwing further light on the dispute between Roberts and James Brudenell senior.

Ruby went mad, and they are all to be drench'd to day. They are most of them chaind seperately, and all possible care is taken of them. They are by Mr. Pearsy's order to rest a fortnight. I have nothing further to inform your Lordship of at present. I am,

Your Lordships most humble and most faithful servant,

Deen, October 18th, 1726.   DAN: EATON

[85]   [*Wednesday, 19 October, 1726.*]

My Lord,
     Master Brudenell is very well. Here is an estray pricket come into the park with a chain about his neck. John Peaks [*sic*] says he believes he belongs to Mr. Jackson of Bulwick, but he will not deliver him out till he receives your Lordship's orders for it.
     We have got ten hogsheads of ale already brew'd, and I think we have malt enought [*sic*] to brew about ten more, therefore I think to send to Stamford on Fryday for a load of Mr. Blyths malt, for here is no good old malt in this country, and I think that 20 hogsheads will be too little for this season of brewing; but one load of malt more will keep the brewer employ'd till I may receive your Lordship's answer either to this, or Mr. Blith's letter, which I enclos'd in mine of Sunday last.
     I believe your Lordship made some agreement with Mr. Blith about malt, but I had no directions about fetching it. The reason why I send without your Lordships orders is by cause we shall want it, and I am sure Mr. Blyth will deliver none that is not good for your Lordships use. This that we are brewing is Mr. Whitwells; it is good malt & I don't doubt but the ale will be very good. The hops are extreamly good, so that we have a sufficient quantity to brew an hundred hogsheads.
     The hounds & spanniels are all duly drench'd, and none of them have been out of order since Ruby dy'd. Mr. Peach has brought the bark mony, it being the usual time of paying for it after Harborough Fare. Wet weather prevents us again for removing the rubbish from Little Dean. I think there is about 60 loads remov'd to the old park and elswhere. One side of the road in the Brick Kiln Close is finishd and part of the other. I'm sure your Lordship will like this piece of work. We cause the earth to be wheeld with wheelbarrows to those places that want to be level'd.
     I am your Lordship's
          Most humble and most faithfull servant,

Deen, October 19th, 1726.   DAN: EATON

[86]   [*Saturday, Sunday, 22, 23 October, 1726.*]

Deen October 22th, 1726.

My Lord,
     Master Brudenell is very well. We have receiv'd the joyful news of my Lady's happy delivery of a son,[1] of which I heartily wish your

---

[1] This was Robert, the Earl's third son (1726-1768).

Lordship joy. Master Brudenell goes alone very strongly; he is not very forward of his tongue, but I think he understands everything that is said to him. I have likewise receiv'd the honour of your Lordship's of the 17th instant. Philip thinks that he cannot give Ball & all the rest of the horses under his care due exercise, therefore he thinks he had better be sent to Stroxton, for John Black has not too many horses under his care for him self & boys to manage; therefore I think to send him either Munday or Tuesday next.[1]

I do assure your Lordship that most of my letters are writ over night, tho' I seldom seal them and conclude 'till the morning the post comes for them. Your Lordship will find by one of my former letters that I did not forget Pywells affair; but I went on Thursday last, and was disappointed; he has only cleard his arrear due at Michaelmas, 1725. I told him what I thought would be the consequence of this slack way of proceeding. I seldom go to Corby or Stanion but I make his house in my way.

I am extreamly glad that your Lordship approves of the method I have taken with my own accounts. The person has transcrib'd all of them to Christmas last, but has not been here this week, being sent for by Mr. Booth; he promis'd me to return on Munday next, which I hope he will do. I stated & transcrib'd Mr. Janvers's account to May last when he was in the country.

The horse that was out of order is the red horse that run at Grantham; he is not right well yet, but I cannot tell what his disease is. J. Colton gives the mare that Mr. Kirkham has sent but an indifferent carracter; tho' she is sound, shee stumbles frequently in her trot & walk.

Mr. Whitwells 40 quarter of malt came in long since, and there has been a great deal of it brew'd for small beer this summer; we have got 8 quarter from Mr. Blyth, which was all he had left. I believe with what we have brew'd, the malt we have will make up about thirty hogsheads for this season of brewing, which Dan says will do very well, for new malt will in all probability be much better than old.

I am sorry I cannot be more expeditious in Slawston affair, for I cannot possibly go thither before Thursday next; for Munday is Glapthorn Court, Tuesday is Corby Court, & Wednesday I had sent Will Wade to Glapthorn to appoint for fishing [before the receipt of your Lordship's[i]]. And I should be there, for I think I can take a new method, which will be less troublesome & I hope more succesful than formerly; for I am acquainted with the millers of Cotterstock & Peri' Mills, & I belive I can at an easy rate hire them to draw down the water as low as I shall think proper.

I have writ to Will Dunmore to meet me at Slawston on Thursday (I have not told him for what), and there I will execute your Lordship's commands rigorously, and if I can bring Spence to any new agreement, I shall take care to make use of such words as shall be particular and comprehensive. Your Lordship I suppose forgot to inclose an order you mention, but your word is a sufficient authority to me for this or the like proceedings, and I am resolved to go on in this affair as the law directs.

Sunday morning.   The rubbish in Little Deen garden is almost all remov'd to the old park, &c. It will be finish'd to morrow and the new road in the Brick Kill Close will be finish'd this week; and we shall do

[1] See **111**.

something this week about levelling the hill before Deen gates, but next week we begin the sales.

I hapned in company with Mr. Legat when I was at Weldon, and he assures me that the Commissioners have possitively concluded with Mr. Wright & Mr. Squires about making the river navigable.[1] They are to have the perpetual profits of the river at eighteen pence per tun to Oundle. They are to make double locks for two boats to go a breast, which are to be drawn up in time of floods; which, being so broad, will be of very great service to the meadows in carrying the water off speedily. They are to compleat it before Michaelmas, 1728, or to forfeit 4,000£. The bargain is sign'd, but the articles are now before Mr. Ward for approbation.

Michael Bywarters' wife is gone to her father's without a certificate, for I would not grant her one. I heard nothing of her husband, and she said she could not tell where he was. We shall not receive her again without another order.[2]

Musick was sent to Cotchmore long since, and Beauty is chain'd at Little Deen, and always has been. Fidler is very bad now, but there is no simpton of madness upon him; he is neither chap-fallen nor raving, but seems to be sick. I fear there is some other distemper among them besides madness. They are all chain'd seperately, and as much care taken of them as possible.

All the sashes are put up and hung at Little Deen.   I can think of nothing else to inform your Lordship of at present.

I am your Lordship's
　　　Most humble and most faithful servant,

DAN: EATON

[*Direction endorsed:*—]
　　　To The Right Honble. the Earl of Cardigan at Bath.

[*Across the endorsement is roughly scribbled what seems to be intended for the monogram* JB, *probably representing the initials of the Honble. James Brudenell, Lord Cardigan's brother. The same symbol appears on* 88, 90, 91, 94, 105, 116, 163.]

[*Seal.   Date of postmark,* 24 October.]

[87]   [*Wednesday, 26 October, 1726.*]

My Lord,
　　　Master Brudenell continues very well.   We had no difficulties at Corby or Glapthorn Court, so I have nothing particular to say upon that score.

We went this morning to fish. We found the water in good order for fishing, for I had agreed with Cotterstock miller at Glapthorne Court to draw it down, which he had done last night. But before we had half finish'd our firs[t] draught, the water was risen two foot perpendicular and the stream become so rapid that it spoild our sport, and we were

---

[1] Referring to the implementing of the Nene Navigation Act. Bru.MSS.F.iii.273. throws further light on this matter.

[2] This refers to a settlement order.

forc'd to leave off; and we had not left the meadows long before they were overflown. We have had very little rain here lately, but I find this flood was caus'd by a great deal that fell between Towcester & Northampton. I have seen the miller of Peri' Mills, and he as well as Cotterstock miller promises to take the water down as low as he can if we let him know the day before we intend to fish.

I shall go to Slawston to morrow, where I will execute your Lordship's commands. I need not mention the hounds or horses, by cause James Ashly tells me that he has let your Lordship know every particular. I am,

Your Lordship's most humble and most faithful servant,

Deen, October 26th, 1726.   DAN: EATON

[88]   [*Sunday, 30 October,* 1726.]

My Lord,

I receiv'd the honour of your Lordship's letter of the 22th instant. Master Brudenell continues very well; we think he has got three or four more teeth than he had when your Lordship was here. He runs about very nimbly and is very merry. I am very sorry that your Lordship's collic is not quite gone. I gave orders to Thomas Bell about the wood mony so soon as I receiv'd your Lordship's first directions.

I do assure your Lordship that I remember that little close of Pywells did formerly belong to that which I rent; this appear'd to me very plain by the old survey; but I pay for no more land than I have, for I measur'd my own close, then charg'd my self with it at 10s. per acre, and deducted the rent of this close from Pywell's, so that consequently he pays 10s. per acre for this little close. He has not paid any more rent yet, since he clear'd his arrear. I measur'd this little close and have the contents by me, and your Lordship has a survey of the rest of his grounds, so I think I need not measure them over again.

We never heard of any mad dog coming this way from any other place. Jewell I believe was not bitt by the whelp that went mad last nor none of the other spaniel bitches, for they were in the little house that morning, unless they were bit the day before; they are all kept chaind a sunder for fear of accidents. Mr. Billing has but one here, and he is chain'd up and likewise mine. Thomas Hutchinson has none that I know of. They have all been drench'd both by the dog doctor and James Ashly. Fidler is well again. I shew'd James Ashly that part of your Lordships letter that concerned the hounds, and he tells me that he has sent your Lordship a very particular account of them.

Lummis is in the country; he has been with Mr. Brooks, who declines making his wood sale this year. He says he is advis'd to the contrary. So we intend to make a good hedge between the woods, but we need not make a ditch, for before our hedge is rotten his wood must be cut.

I think Lummis begins now to manage his own affairs with discretion. He has bought, which I saw confirm'd by a letter from his wife, a leasehold estate of good new houses ensur'd and well tenanted of 160£. per annum for 1,500£., which his wife has given him a commission to receive in order to pay for the purchase. They are most of them chambers for attorneys in Bernards Inn. He intends to quit and let his great house and live in one of these little ones. There is forty five years unexpir'd in the lease. And notwithstanding this advancement of his affairs, to my surprise his way of living seems to be subverted intirely, for I think he now considers the value of a shilling. He is going into Lincolnshire to receive the mony.

The leaf is now down, and Corby and Stanion Sales go on very well; and on Tuesday we shall begin in the park, for the new road will be finish'd on Munday or very near it.

The rubbish is all removed from Little Deen, and I have got all the garrets and rooms in the old appartment cleend and lockd up, and I keep the key. I have likewise set locks upon the other doors & keep them lock'd. There is dales already plain'd for the chamber floors, and the architraves for the new doors are work'd; and wood for the front door, which is to be a sash, is cut out ready to join together when the floor is laid. I fear there is not quite boards enough for the chamber floors, but when the joiner comes again he shall lay them down loose, and then we shall know certainly. He has not been here these ten days, and I think it is no great matter, for the days are now very short and I durst not let him work by candle light, as joiners do at this time of the year. I intend to set the slaters to work about the roof of that little place your Lordship mentions, on Munday.

I went to Slawston on Thursday, where I proceeded after this manner. I went to Edward Spence and demanded the rent due at Michaelmas; and in as severe terms as I could invent, I told him that I had your Lordships commands to seize his stock, which I would do, & sell all after the expiration of five days, if he did not pay the mony before. But I found that if I had seiz'd, it would have been only like kicking against a wall; for he could have paid the mony in one days time, & his cercumstances are so good that this seizure would not have lessen'd his caracter or credit.

I then told him that I had a commission to discharge him from the farm at Lady Day next, unless he would sign an agreement with certain restrictions as to the manureing it, &c., which I particularly mentioned, to which he answer'd, and I think rightly, that it was impossible for him to occupy both his own farm and your Lordship's without your Lordship's being continually jealous of his impoverishing one to enrich the other. Therefore he had some thoughts of turning your Lordship's farm intirely over to his son, if your Lordship would consent; then he should lay all the manure upon it, it produces.

His son was gone to Stamford Fare, and he said he was not fully resolv'd upon this and desir'd some time to consider on it. But I still seemd resolute, and told him that I would not wave the seizure unless he could procure somebody to engage for him that he with his son should come to Deen on Munday next, and bring with them the rent due at Michaelmas; for I would not take his word. And then [he should*] either engage for his son or himself for the payment of [the*] rent under the restrictions I had before told him, or receive a discharge from the farm at Lady Day next, which Will Dunmore promised for him, and to come with them. If I make an agreement with him I will tye him fast to the farm for six years, if your Lordship shall agree to it or think proper; but I will confine your Lordship to him but for one year from Lady Day next; this shall be the substance of the articles if we make any.

I gave the accounts of the Leicester wood to Will Dunmore, and orderd him to collect it as soon as he could. I saw Will Worth and he says the mony will be paid at the time promised.

Here is 23 Scotch cattel come, but one of them stales blood and is like to dye. I have given it a drink which has cur'd several, but I doubt this is too farr gone. The sheep in this country and Leicestershire are rotton again this year. My brother bought 20 which were as rotton as possible. We kill'd one of them that was fat and found it so, so we sold the rest again and lost nothing by them; but people complain very much.
I am your Lordship's
Most humble and most faithfull servant,

Deen, October 30th, 1726.   DAN: EATON

[*Near bottom of sheet, pencilled in another hand:—*] Turnips for the hounds.

[*Direction endorsed:—*]
To the Right Honble. the Earl of Cardigan at Bath.

[*The* JB *monogram across endorsement as* **86** *etc.* Seal. *Date of post-mark,* [. . . .] October.]

[89]   [*Monday, 31 October, 1726.*]

My Lord,
Master Brudenell continues very well. Edward Spence was here to day and has paid the mony, but he would not consent to be tied to his farm any longer than one year. So I have let it to him for one year from Lady Day next, and he is to lay or leave all the manor it produces upon the farm, and is not to mix the crop with that of his own farm, and is to give half a year's notice if he intends to quit it, and then to carry no dung away. He say[s] that if he did sign any paper concerning the enclosure, he has intirely forgot.

I think that a dale floor for the dining room at Little Deen will be the cheapest, but an oak floor will be the most permanent, and I think the best for a ground floor. Your Lordship may cut down a tree next spring that will floor it at one length of boards, and by sawing them out and watering them next summer, they may be fit to lay in the spring come twelvemonth. The hounds continue all very well. The new road is finish'd, and to morrow I shall fix with the labourers about the Park Sale. We have put a stop to the Scotch bullock's staleing blood, & I hope he will recover.   I am your Lordship's
Most humble and most faithful servant,

Deen, October 31th, 1726.   DAN: EATON

[90]   [*Saturday, 5 November, 1726.*]

My Lord,
Master Brudenell continues very well. I receiv'd the honour of your Lordship's of the 31th ult. On Wednesday last I met our

labourers at Dibbins[1] in order to have begun the sale; but they did not care to work without their bottles at any price, it being a custom which they would not willingly brake. So I went to Stanion on Thursday, and their sale is so forward that I think it will be finish'd on Tuesday next, —I mean as to the fencing. So that I have agreed with 20 of them labourers to come to work in the park, and to be paid for their bottles & not to carry them away.

We have concluded, if your Lordship shall think proper, to take all the old wood for sale that made two sales last time, only leaving that part that is next to Dunstanleys gate, which was cut about 13 years since. This will save a great deal of charge in the fence, for if we should take but one part of it this year, we must take the other part next year or the wood would be all destroy'd, for it has stood too long already by seven years.

Now as this sale will afford abundantly more wood than your Lordship can want for your use (for I heard your Lordship say once that you would have the whole sale for yourself), I think I have contriv'd a method to make your Lordship easy, as to the carting that part a way that we shall sell, which is to break a sheet of the pale & place a good gate in one of Jenkin Harrisson's closses (only allowing him a trifle for damage that it will do him), and then no team but your own need ever come in to the park.

My Lord Hatton's servants kil'd nine deer in Cowthick on Wednesday, & they hunted it again yesterday, but I can't tell what they did.

I went to Mr. Kirkhams today, but he was not at home.   I went likewise to Mrs. O:Bryon, but I could not be honour'd with an audience. So I told my business as well as I could to one of her Irish servants, who brought me her answer, that she could not see how Blatherwick could owe anything to Corby manor, but she would enquire into the matter, and if she could find that it was due, she would pay it. I intend to go to Mr. Jackson[2] and get him to write to her by me to explain the case.   I am orderd to go to Stockin on Munday to measure some more work there.

Munday se'night is the day appointed for receiving Leicestershire rents that are behind, when I don't fear but all or within a trifle will be cleard; and I don't fear but Northamptonshire rents will be cleard without any severe methods.   I have receiv'd very little more wood mony that I had when your Lordship was here; but due warning is given to every body to have it ready by the last of this month, and I hope by Christmas the whole will be cleard.

My accounts are all transcrib'd very correctly to Michaelmas last. The person[3] is going a way to day, but promise[s] to come on Tuesday & finish them to this day. I have 650£. by me, but I will send your Lordship an abstract of my accounts by Thursdays post, when they will be all examind and transcrib'd.

I paid Mr. Blith 30£., but have not paid James Ashly for he said nothing to me about mony. But he is to be here again in a day or two; then I will pay him what he desires. My disbursments are very numerous. I have 22 pages of disbursments since Midsummer last, & I am sure your Lordship cannot dislike one article in them. I shall have a great deal more mony than Leicestershire rents come to, but then it is impossible

---

[1] i.e. Deepings.
[2] Mr. Jackson, squire of Duddington. See **92**.
[3] i.e. John Kirk.

that the wood account should be clear; for Northamptonshire estate will not supply my current account.

I cannot send your Lordship all the particulars,—but I have paid nothing that I thought ought to be let alone. I serve your Lordship in every thing to the best of my capacity, and I wish that your Lordship was continual here, that you might take all the mony into your own hands, and make what payments you thought proper. I am so far from getting anything by the payment of mony that, as poor as I am, I would most willingly remit a part of my small sallary to be freed from this plague. Nights are so dark that it will be impossible for me to return from Stockin on Munday, so I can't write by the next post.

There has no hound gone mad from Little Deen since your Lordship left Deen. They are all well, & the horses, except the red horse is as he was. They kill'd a fox to day after a good chase, very farely. When they come home they are all put to their respective places.

I am your Lordship's
Most humble and most faithfull servant,

Deen, November 5th, 1726.   DAN: EATON

When your Lordship order'd me to pay 25£. to J. Ashly, it was if he desir'd it, and not that I should send him the mony. I should when he was here have spoke to him about it, but he went away before I was aware.

[*Direction endorsed:*—]
To the Right Honble. the Earl of Cardigan at Bath.

[*The* JB *monogram across endorsement as* **86**, *etc.* *Seal.* *Date of postmark,* 7 November.]

[**91**]   [*Tuesday, 8 November, 1726.*]

My Lord,
Mr. Brudenell tells me that he believes your Lordship will come to London before you come into the country, but he is sure he shall be able to satisfie me of this on Thursday next. If so, as your Lordship's coming to Deen will be uncertain, I will send on Sunday next to London the book wherein I have caus'd my accounts to be transcrib'd. Your Lordship may perhaps find more time to look them over in London than in the country.

His Honour intends to dine at Deen to day to see Master Brudenell, and certainly sets forward for London on Sunday next. All the family here and little Master Brudenell are extreamly well.

I am your Lordship's
Most humble and most faithfull servant,

Luffenham, November 8th, 1726.   DAN: EATON

[*Direction endorsed:*—]
To the Right Honble. the Earl of Cardigan at Bath.

[*The* JB *monogram across endorsement as* **86**, *etc.* *Seal.* *Date of postmark,* 9 November.]

[*Saturday*, 12 *November*, 1726.]

My Lord,
    Master Brudenell continues very well.   I went on Thursday last to Duddington and Fineshade to have spoke with Mr. Jackson and Mr. Charles Kirkham, but I found neither of them at home. Yesterday I was at Brigstock Fair. Mr. Walter sent me word that he should be there & would state the account about the chief rent, but I could not see him, for he was gone home before I got thither. Lean cattle and fatt hogs sold very well. The price of wooll here is from 14*s*. to 16*s*. per tod.
    The cattel are all well upon the Common, and that which stale'd blood is recover'd.   The hounds and horses are all well, and the red horse is much better than he was. Philip tells me those under his care are in very good order.   John Peak says there is some very good does in the park, and he thinks they will be no better this year, so that if your Lordship intends to have any kill'd, now is the time. His Honour has sent for and had a brace to Luffenham. The rutting heat is over, and John Peak says they have not lost one male deer, which he scarce ever knew the like before.
    This week has been so wett that there has been nothing done in the woods. This morning Stanion labourers came in order to have begun the sale in the park; but, contrary to what they had propos'd before, they insisted upon the very same terms which Deen and Deenthorpe labourers had done, viz: to have their bottles, or otherwise they would not work. So I could do nothing with them, but call'd them fools for coming, and sent them back again. So that now we can't tell what to do. There has been some snake in the grass amongst Stanion men, for they seem'd rejoic'd when I first propos'd it to them. Both this and Deen-thorpe Sale shall not be begun 'till I have your Lordship's directions.
    I have found out a brick-maker whose name is Thomas Newson. He lives at Toucester; he did formerly work with Horn for your Lordship. He says he will make brick for your Lordship upon the same terms as Horn used to do if your Lordship pleases to employ him, and he says that now is the time for diging the earth that he is to work up next summer. He will come in a day or two after he shall receive a letter from your Lordship or me.
    I have been at Luffenham to day to pay into his Honour's hands all the remaining part of Lady Cardigan's Lady Day's rents, that his Honour may pay her Ladyship in town. His Honour assures me that your Lordship intends to come by Deen, so I need not send my accounts to London without orders. They are all transcrib[d] from the beginning of them to this day. I have continually ballanc'd them at Christmas and Midsummer and the ballances are regularly transferr'd. The inclosed is the same hand they are transcrib'd in, and is an abstract of Ladyday's rent with my disbursements since Midsummer.[1]
    Munday next is the day appointed for receiving Leicestershire arrears, & I hope they will be all paid. If there should be any behin'd, I will let your Lordship know the particulars. I will likewise send your Lordship a bill of Northamptonshire arrears as soon as I come from Leicestershire, and have reduc'd them as low as I can.   I am,
        Your Lordship's most humble and most faithful servant,

Deen, November 12th, 1726.   DAN: EATON

    [1] See **93**.

[**93**]   [*Enclosed in No. 92*][1]

[*Saturday*, 12 *November*, 1726.]

DANIEL EATON'S ACCOUNT   November the 12th, 1726.

	£	s.	d.
Disburs'd as appears by the first column . .	122	15	6¾
by the second	71	12	6
by the third	49	19	8
by the fourth	21	16	10
by the fifth	62	14	1½
by the sixth	46	10	4½
by the seventh	38	18	3
by the eighth	35	1	10
by the ninth	17	5	8
by the tenth	69	9	0
by the eleventh . . .	59	12	6
by the twelveth	33	7	11
by the thirteenth	34	6	5½
by the fourteenth . . .	90	3	0
by the fifteenth	33	12	9
by the sixteenth	36	5	10
by the seventeenth . . .	76	1	10
by the eighteenth . . .	36	18	4
by the nineteenth . . .	45	13	3
by the twentieth	09	7	8
by the one and twentieth .	74	6	6½
by the two & twentieth .	159	12	7
Total	1225	12	5¼
Charge . . .	1959	6	9½
Discharge . . .	1225	12	5¼
Due by Cash and Arrears	733	14	4¼

[**94**]   [*Wednesday*, 16 *November*, 1726.]

My Lord,
    Master Brudenell continues very well.   I was at Stonton on Mun-
day, where I receiv'd all the arrears except those upon the inclosed
paper.   Mr. Elliot presents his duty to your Lordship. Mr. Edwards
is not yet return'd. Will Worth's mony is ready for your Lordship. Will
Dunmore has collected part of the wood mony, & I have orderd him to
be as expeditious as possible in collecting the rest. I have receiv'd the
honour of your Lordship's letter (which, I suppose by the contents of
it, was wrote upon the tenth inst., but it was not dated). I am extreamly
sorry that your Lordship is not perfectly well yet. I hope you are much
better than you was when at Deen. I hope the air at Little Deen will
agree with your Lordship better than any other place.

[1] This is the account of Dan's disbursements referred to in **92**. It was written by
John Kirk.

I have been at Weldon to Pywell, but he was not at home. I have orderd him to be with me to morrow morning. I believe he will pay his rent better hereafter than he used to do, for he ow'd 30£. to the tanner Peach which he has paid off this summer, and several other debts he has paid within these two years, & he has a pritty good stock upon the farm.

I will send your Lordship a bill of Northamptonshire arrears as soon as I can reduce them into a narrow compass. I think Leicestershire tenants pay their rent very well; I believe there will not be a shilling behind in three weeks time. I believe I shall send Northamptonshire bill of arrears about Sunday or Tuesday next at the farthest.

Lummis is now gone to London again. I believe he intends to take the house[1] off of your Lordship's hands, but I fear he cannot manage this affair in a short time, for as yet his wife thinks it is his own.

I have been to day and measur'd the board that is plain'd for flooring the rooms at Little Deen, and I find there is of pure clean [new*] dales enough to floor the dining room and the chamber above it, within about six dales, which I think there will want; but there is not old boards enough to floor one half of the other chamber. All these boards will be dry enough to fix in the spring. They are now laid with their faces downwards upon the bridgings in the chambers.

For wainscotting the two chambers and dining room and making the stairs there will want near 400 dales, and wainscotting the hall surbase high; and I think the sooner these are provided the better, for if we had them now, they would not be dry enought [sic] to fix before the middle of next summer, but they might be work'd up and made ready now. I shall take care to have timber cut out for sleepers for the dining room floor.   I think the cellar must of necessity be pav'd, for tho' the bottom of it is hard, yet without a pavement it can never be wash'd and kept clean as cellars ought to be to prevent their smelling. But as the hall is the last room to be finish'd, we have time enough to consider of this hereafter.

I don't fear but the causeway will answer the end when the bridge is made.[2] I think it ought to be sown with oats and ray-grass in the spring.   We have done breewing [sic]: there is thirty hogsheads of new ale and thirty six of old ale in the cellar; and there is only six pipes empty, and we are thrashing out the barly in order to make malt to fill them. The barly is very good. I suppose your Lordship would have it made at Mr. Plyth's [i.e. Blyth's] malting, so we shall send it when it is ready.

We have got a most fine brawn which has been up in the tray a long time, and is fit to kill when your Lordship pleases.   I have sent Philip with the two mares to Cotchmore with directions.   I have deliver'd your Lordship's commands to the gard'ner, who will take care to execute them; but there was but very few haws this year, and those are all gone.

Dan Whitworth is gone to Cotchmore to day to bottle off and pack up the wine and put it in a readyness, and then wee shall send a cart for it, which may return the same day when it has nothing to stay it there. I could not rightly understand this part of your Lordship's letter, for you did not say whither the wine was already in bottles or whither Dan should bottle it when he came thither; which made me send him

---

[1] In Corby. See **121**.
[2] The causeway was probably in Brick Kiln Close.

before the cart, by cause when we know certainly how many bottles are fill'd, we can then send so many empty ones by the cart in their stead.

I saw Mr. Hawkins since I gave him the letter & he assur'd me that he sent it to Lord Hatton by the post. I have appointed a day for receiving Corby rents.

The oats cannot be thrash'd before the barn is made. I have bargain'd with Christopher Dexter to make it 19 yards long, 17 foot wide, and nine foot high from the bottom of the groundsill to the top of the wallplate. He is to have 16£. I cast up the quantity of work there would be in it before I bargain'd, and it came to more by the square. Your Lordship is only to find materials. I likewise bargained with the masons to make a stable there at 1£. 3s. 0d. per rood, and they have work'd up all the stone that was brought. And I have caus'd the walls to be thatch'd, that the winter can't hurt them, for there is no such thing as getting any more stone there this winter.

Christopher Dexter has had two sawyers at work about cutting out timber for the barn a great while, and intends to get it fitted for setting up as fast as he can; but I doubt we can't get materials to make the walls (which are to be three foot high) which the fram'd barn is to stand upon, till towards the spring. If it should come an hard frost, we may bring some of the [m^d] [oats^i] in to this barn to thrash them.

I am now throughly convinc'd that there is some anonimous distemper among the hounds, for yesterday morning Lemon, who' always was in the four stall stable at Little Deen, after eating her meat in the morning very well, was taken in the same manner to all appearance as Fidler had been some time ago; but she dy'd at night, without any symptoms of madness upon her, no more than Fidler had, who after three or four days recover'd and is now very well, but has an eye struck out with a thorn. I have inclos'd a particular where every hound is plac'd.[1] There is one of them lame in the shoulders, but I have forgot its name.

I can think of nothing else at present. I hope your Lordship's directions concerning Deen and Deenthorpe Sales will be particular. I don't think they can be done this year without allowing the labourers their bottles.

I am your Lordships
    Most humble and most faithfull servant,

Deen, November 16th, 1726.   DAN: EATON

The spaniells are all well.

[*Direction endorsed:*—]
    To the Right Honble. the Earl of Cardigan at Bath.

[*The* JB *monogram across endorsement as* **86** *etc.*   Seal.   Date *of post-mark,* 18 November.]

---

[1] See **96**.

[**95**] [*Enclosed in No.* 94.]

[*Monday,* 14 *November,* 1726.]

ARREARS OF RENT due to the Right Honble. the Earl of Cardigan at Lady Day, 1726, for land in Leicestershire, November 14th, 1726.

		£	s.	d.
STONTON				
	John Berry	3	00	0
CRANOE				
	Thomas Woodcock	3	00	6
SLAWSTON				
	John Bosden	3	00	9
	Christopher Basset	6	08	2
	Total . .	15	09	5

[**96**] [*Enclosed in* **94**]   [*Wednesday,* 16 *November,* 1726.][1]

A PARTICULAR OF THE PLACES WHERE THE HOUNDS AT
DEEN ARE CHAIN'D.

At Little Deen:
    In the four stall stable, Dutchess, Beauty, Daphne; & Lemon was there but is dead.
    In the cart horse stable, Bluecap and Abigale, who is stifled.
    In the hay barn, Fidler, who has lost an eye.

Old hounds in the dogkenell court where the wallnut tree stands:
    Betty, Jugler, Di'mond, Lady, Rockwood, Lovely and Ringwood.

In one of the little houses there is an hound whelp that was bit by a mad dog at Glapthorne; it has been drench'd several times.

In the coach-horse stable:
    Fairmaid, Countess, Lilly, Roman, Rival, Madcap and Trouncer.

In the hunter's stable opposite to the coach horse stable:
    Young hounds: Mistris, Pealer, Maukin, Junier and Lively.
    Old hounds there: Singwell, Lilly & Curious.

[**97**]   [*Saturday,* 19 *November,* 1726.]

My Lord,
    Master Brudenell continues very well.   Here is a brick maker sent hither by my Lord Gower from Staffordshire; he came on Thursday last.[2]

---

[1] Dated from internal evidence. See **94**.
[2] This is Jonathan Lewtener.

I have shewn him the clay that is to be made use of, and he likes it very well, but he says he allways had 7s. 6d. per thousand for making brick, and he will not bate one farthing of that price. I have told him that I believe your Lordship will not give that price, bycause you may have them made cheaper, viz: at 6s. 6d. per thousand, by Thomas Newson of Toucester, who I mentioned in my former letter. If we don't employ this man, I find my Lord Gower has promised him to be satisfied for his journey. He stays at Deen to wait your Lordship's answer.

I have receiv'd a letter from Mr. Blyth wherein he desires me to present his duty to your Lordship, and let you know that he is very sorry that his maltsman should part with all his old malt when he had sold your Lordship 40 quarter. But he says that he has now some new malt which is right good; and he will, if your Lordship pleases, let you have 32 quarter (to make the 8 quarter we have had, 40 quarter) at 1£. 12s. 0d. per quarter, tho' he now sells at a greater price.—Barly in our markets is from 22s. to 25s. per quarter; wheat 2£. per quarter; old beans 24s. per quarter; old oats 13s. per quarter.

I have been round to those tenants in arrear, but have done little. I have threatned them very possitively unless they have their mony ready by Thursday next. I have paid John Hinks several payment[s] upon account which discharge his bills within one month of this time. His year ends at Christmas; then I shall state his account in the book, and Will Wades the same; but I think for the future to state their accounts evevery [sic] half year as I do my own.

The hounds and horses and cattle upon the Common are all well. I am your Lordship's

Most humble and most faithful servant,

Deen, November 19th, 1726.   DAN: EATON

[98]   [*Monday, 21 November, 1726.*]

My Lord,
Master Brudenell is very well. The hounds and spaniels are very well, and the horses, except that the grey horse has the grease fallen again into one of his heels; it began to run on Saturday night last.

I have receiv'd the honour of your Lordship's of the thirteenth instant. I shall most thankfully comply with any method your Lordship shall be pleas'd to take for reducing my accounts into a narrower compass. I have not receiv'd any mony of Pywell. I saw him today, and he says that Mr. Goode owes him 27£. 10s., which he promises to pay him at his return from Hougham, which will be in a day or two; so that on Sunday next at the farthest he will bring 30£. at least. I have receiv'd but 10£. of John Parsons; he says he has 15£. more at London. There is very few of the small rents behind. We have begun to plow upon the Common in order to kill the grubbs if possible.

I expected to day an answer to mine of the 12th instant. There can be nothing done at the sale in the park or Deenthorpe Sale unless your Lordship allows the labourers their bottells according to the old custom. They all of them say that your Lordship promis'd them possitively, when they agreed to work without wood in the Park Sale last year, that you would never hinder them of their wood for the future. I don't remember that I was present when any such promise was made; your Lordship only knows whither you made them such a promise or not.

As to the sales being hinderd or put off by this delay, there is no great matter in it, for both Stanion and Corby labourers will work at these sales without wood, provided that Deen and Deenthorpe labourers may work with them and have their wood; for they fear if they should break this custom here, it will not be long before some other labourers serve them in the same manner. I have taken a great deal of pains in this affair, and I find it will be almost impossible to subvert this their resolution; and since the advantage to your Lordship (I think) is but a trifle, sure it cannot be worth while to perplex ones self about it.

I have nothing else material to inform your Lordship of.   I am,
        Your Lordship's most humble and most faithful servant,

Deen, November 21th, 1726.   DAN: EATON

[99]   [*Saturday, 3 December,* 1726.]

My Lord,
    Master Brudenell is very well. His Honour has now got sixteen teeth.   I have receiv'd the honour of your Lordship's of the 28th ult. I have spoke for two pieces of shaloom [*sic*] which is now at the fulling mills, but there is not a piece in the house, for I bought but two pieces last year; it was the year before that there was a piece to spare.

Will Pywell has paid 18£., and could pay no more bycause he could not get his mony out of young Mr. Goode's hands, for the old man would not let him pay him till St. Thomas; there is 15£. 7s. 4d. behind. I do assure your Lordship that I have no partiality for him, but I would not tear any man into pieces for a debt that may certainly be got by fair means.

John Parsons has 15£. 15s. 0d. in his son's hands, which he will order to be paid to Mr. Webber if it is not now upon the road towards Deen.   I will speak for another piece of shaloom for I believe two pieces will not be sufficient.   As I have Will Worth's mony in my hands, Mrs. Denshire will certainly not be disappointed.   I have bought old oats as the hunters have wanted them; some at 13s., some at 13s. 6d. per quarter, and old beans, right good, at 1£. 1s. 4d. per quarter; but I have bought but 8 quarters of these. I wish I had bought more, for they are now worth more mony.

I have receiv'd a letter from Mr. Blyth wherein he says that he never did make malt for any body, but he cannot help serving your Lordship upon every occasion. He likewise says that he will have good malt ready for our team to bring back, and if the frost prevents our fishing, as I fear it will, on Munday they shall carry a load of barly and bring a load of malt home.

I wrote to Mr. Charles Kirkham [about the mare[i]] in the most perswasive terms I could, and repeated the message I deliver'd so particularly to his brother about her, but he told Jack Satchell that he had nothing to say to the affair. The mare is not worth a shilling, for she is glanderd as well as broken winded. We have kept her by herself at grass and have fed her with corn & hay, but I fear the dogs must have her in a short time.

Mr. Blith will take care about oats as soon as he conveniently can.
If the frost continues, I go to Corby on Munday, and will speake
to those laboures [*sic*] to come to help forward Deen Park Sale, and will
let them part of the fence. Deen labourers finish'd the lopping of the
hedgerows on Thursday, but we set them to lop all the pollards in the
sale, which will I believe furnish stakes enough for the whole fence
without mangling the parcells of underwood.   After a long debate the
brickmaker[1] complies with your Lordships terms. He shall lie at Little
Deen this winter. I believe he is honest; he has thrash'd very hard in
the barn ever since he has been here.[1]

I have got that little place your Lordship formerly gave me directions about at Little Deen very well slated without lime, so it may be
pointed at spring. I have likewise causd the great gates and the little gate
into the back yard to be well repair'd, and I keep them always lock'd. I
have tax'd Deen labourers with the contents of the letter I receiv'd from
your Lordship on Thursday last, and they can't denie but that your
Lordship's promise was after that manner, tho' they had before told me
to the contrary; they are not able to make any defence to this. I told
Deen labourers at the time of their submission that I very well knew the
reason why they did so; & that they might think themselves very happy
that they were not the first persons call'd, for I knew ful well that some
of them would have prov'd as obstinate as any of Deenthorpe, and that
by their submission (after so much obstinacy) they could not claim any
title to your Lordship's future favours.   I have no more to say at
present.   I am,
Your Lordship's most humble and most faithful servant,

Deen, December 4th, 1726.[2]   DAN: EATON

[*Direction endorsed:—*]
To the Right Honble. the Earl of Cardigan.
[*In another hand:—*] at the Earl of Litchfields at Ditchly, near Enstone,
Oxfordshire.

[*Endorsement crossed by a hook-shaped mark, conceivably a "J".   Seal.
Date of postmark, 6th December.*]

[**100**]   [*Tuesday, 6 December, 1726.*]

My Lord,
Master Brudenell continues very well. For want of consulting the
almanack I committed a blunder in the date of my last letter, for I wrote
it on Saturday tho' it is dated the 4th.
I could not send the team to Stamford yesterday as I propos'd, the
weather was so extreamly bad, and it continues so to day. But I went
yesterday to Corby, to have talk'd with the labourers about working in
Deen Park, but was disappointed, for three parts in four of them were
gone to Great Easton Feast, it being such weather that they could not
work in the wood. There is but one days work to do in Corby Sale or

---

[1] Jonathan Lewtener.
[2] Dan should have written December 3rd. See **100**.

thereabouts before it is fit to view, and there is about three or four days work to finish Stanion Sale.

If the weather should alter (for now it snows & rains very fast), I will go to day to pay Mr. Whitwell, but if not I will certainly pay him to morrow. I have receiv'd a letter from Lummis: he says he shall be at Corby on Fryday next. Jack Kingston has been at Cotchmore and hunted there one day, and they kill'd a fox. The hounds, spanniells, horses and cattel are all well. We send 30 sheep to London to day, if the drover comes, which are fat upon the Common, and I have writ to Simpson to pay the mony to Mr. Webber. I have nothing else to inform your Lordship of at present.   I am,

Your Lordship's most humble and most faithful servant,

Deen, December 6th, 1726.   DAN: EATON

[**101**]   [*Wednesday*, 7 *December*, 1726.]

My Lord,
    Master Brudenell continues very well.   I have been at Oundle to day and have paid Mr. Whitwell. He desired me to return your Lordship many thanks.   I have receiv'd a message from Mr. Hawkins to let me know that my Lord Hatton has given him orders to continue Priors Haw Riding thro' Bangroves forthwith, and he desir'd me to appoint a day when to set it out; and I have apointed to meet him there to morrow, by cause I would have no time lost in this affair.   Will Wade has bought and kill'd three hogs which prove very well and cheap; he shall buy three more on Wednesday next, [the offall of¹] which will serve while our own little ones are fit to kill.

Philip came from Cotchmore with the horses to day, but Mr. Coniers stays there still. The hounds & spanniels and horses are all very well. The mare we had of Mr. Charles Kirkham made her exit this day in Little Deen hay barn. I find all the horses Mr. Kirkham has have got the glanders; but I believe this mare has done us no harm as to the distemper, by cause she was with the horses but only the first day she came, and then only in the field, and they did not find a fox.¹ Ever since she has been kept by her self and has done nothing.

I have nothing else to inform your Lordship of at present.   I am,

Your Lordship's most humble and most faithful servant,

Deen, December 7th, 1726.   DAN: EATON

[**102**]   [*Sunday*, 18 *December*, 1726.]

My Lord,
    Master Brudenell continues very well.   I can't tell whither this will find your Lordship at Bath or not, but if the roads are as bad there as here, I think it impossible for your Lordship to remove. I carried the 500£. to Mr. Denshire on Thursday, and the road from Deen to Stam-

¹ Since they did not find a fox, the horses were not galloping close together.

ford was one continued piece of ice. We have cut out Priors Haw Riding thro' Bangroves. It happens that there is to be but 5 little saplins to be cut down, worth about 35s. The hounds, spanniels and horses are all very well. I hope all distempers among them are extinct.

John Peak has serv'd all the venison your Lordship order'd except Major Creed; for your Lordship recalling your orders concerning Mr. Tryon, John Peak could not tell who should have the other half doe, if he carrye'd one half to Major Creed. He begs your Lordship would give orders very soon if you intend to have any more kill'd, for they begin to fall off. He has serv'd three warrants; he says there is not many good does left. They come very well to the foddering, and the hay proves extreamly good.

The hill before Deen gates is levelled. Deen Park Sale is at a stand, for the frost is so very much in the ground that they cannot get down the stakes. Corby labourers one and all tell me that they will be ready at a minute's warning to come to work at it, so that it will be fit to view in one week after the weather breaks. They seem to detest the ingratitude of Stanion labourers. In the meantime I have set Deen and Deenthorpe men and 6 of Bulwick to plash the hedge round Burnt Coppice, so that I hope we shall have all our sales done in good time. We have view'd Corby Sale and have appointed the 26th instant for the sale day.

I have got two pieces of sheloom,[1] one of which I shall send by the carrier to London to day; the other I intend to send to Stamford and desire Mr. Alcock to send it to Grantham. I have bespoke an other piece which is now at the fullin mills.

This week I shall state John Hinks's and Will Wades accounts and then post them. The post is very irregular here, and last Sunday Rockingham bag was intirely lost. I receiv'd the honour of your Lordship's of the 7th instant not till Wednesday last, which I should have had on Munday, but your former which orderd me to Northampton came in due time. I have nothing else to inform your Lordship of at present.

I am,

Your Lordship's most humble and most faithful servant,

Deen, December 18th, 1726.   D: EATON

[**103**]   [*Tuesday, 27 December, 1726.*]

My Lord,

Master Brudenell continues very well. Yesterday being Corby sale day I was there. It comes to 98£. 15s. 6d., all which mony I receiv'd (except a very little which I look upon as good as ready mony, for I shall have it in a few days). We shall view Stanion Sale to morrow, but shall not sell it till I return from Grantham. Thomas Bell has been with all those that owe mony for wood; he has receiv'd some of it, and says he has appointed Fryday & Saturday next to go to them all again.

My Lord Gowers butler promis'd to send an answer yesterday about the wine if he could, but we have heard nothing. If my Lord Gower will not have any of this wine, then Dan[2] thinks it would be very advise-

[1] Shalloon, presumably for the servants' liveries at Stroxton.
[2] Dan Whitworth, Lord Cardigan's butler. See Subject Index under Wine.

able to let one [of[i]] these hogsheads come up to London in the wagon, for it must be disturb'd again, it not being quite fine enough to bottle; and when it is there, he thinks your Lordship may easily get some more experienc'd person than him to manage it. The other hogshead being fine enough, he will bottle it off on Munday next, if he has no orders to the contrary.

I propose to have the wagon set forward from Deen to morrow se' night. There will be an hogshead of ale, an hogshead of small beer, half an hogshead of Mondehare's wine all in bottles; these are 22 hundred weight at least, which with venison & the other hogshead of wine, if your Lordship orders it, will be a sufficient load. Dan is very sure that the hogshead of wine will take no dammage in coming to London in the wagon, and that it may be made fit to bottle in ten days after it comes there. It is now in a very good strong vessell. Dan waited upon Mr. Brudenell yesterday, and his Honour returns your Lordship many thanks, but does not want any wine, his stay in the country will be so very short. There is Nan Wade & apples to come by the wagon, which I had almost forgot.   I am,

Your Lordship's most humble and most faithfull servant,

Deen, December 27th, 1726.   DAN: EATON

[104]   [*Thursday, 29 December, 1726.*]

My Lord,
Master Brudenell continues very well.   We view'd Stanion Sale yesterday, which, according to our valuation, comes to 80£. 3s. 0d., which I hope will be sold at the price. It is better than we expected, as Corby Sale was worse, but it is most evident that if your Lordship does not take those woods while they are younger, they will be destroy'd as my Lord Rockinghams woods are. There is some old men remember the underwood in these woods as florishing as ours, and by letting it stand to be old (for no other cause can be assign'd), it is now become not worth 30s. an acre at full growth. I can't tell what Corby Sale was sold for the last time it went, but every body that remember it agree that it is not much above half so good this year as it was then.

Pealer is mad but eats his meat as if he was well.   I have just now receiv'd the honour of your Lordship's from London. I have given Dan the particulars concerning the wine.

Master Brudenell has had a little cold, but it went off in a day or two, so I did not mention it in mine.   I should have gone to Stroxton to morrow if I had not receiv'd the honour of your Lordship's to day, but now I intend to go to Stamford to night, where if Mr. Denshire cannot return the mony, I don't doubt but I shall meet with somebody else that can.   I have nothing else to inform your Lordship of.

I am your Lordship's
Most humble and most faithful servant,

DAN: EATON

P.S.   Dan is of opinion that if the two unbottled hogsheads of wine are not drank this spring, they will be as bad as those that are bottled.

Deen, December 29th, 1726.

[**105**]

[*Saturday, Sunday*, 31 *December*, 1 *January*, 1726-/7.]

Grantham, December 31th, 1726.

My Lord,

I came to Stamford on Thursday, where I got returns for 500£. to be paid in London in a fortnight, viz: by Mr. Denshire to Mr. Child,[1] 400£., and by an other person, who will have mony in town for hogs, &c., to Mr. Gibson, 100£., which mony I shall lodge in Mr. Denshires hands till Mr. Gibson's bill comes down. The two inclosed bills I got in Grantham, for I could not hear of any other. So soon as I had spoke with Newball about them I went to Mr. Stafford & Mr. Doughty to enquire of his creadit, and they assur'd me that his bill were [*sic*] always good; but I was forc'd to pay the usual price for returns, viz: 10s. in the hundred; but that at Stamford cost me nothing. If your Lordship had given me timely notice, I could have had all the mony return'd without cost, but now this cannot be help'd.

The tenants paid very well; the only person in arrear is Will Ward, 10£. 14s. 0d.; and as he could not promise to pay before April, I thought it the safest way to let him remain in arrear rather than to take his note, for as it is an arrear of rent, it will be safer and more easily got than a debt upon a note may. I have paid all the tradesmen according to your Lordship's command, who return your Lordship many thanks, but Mr. Ellis was not at home. Young Blythe met me here (his father has got a swelling on one side of his face, so he could not come), but we could not get the account, so I have order'd young Blythe to bring it to Deen, and I will pay it there.

I am sorry I have promis'd to be at Stamford on Munday, for I think I should have gone to Hougham and Marston. I belive there is some affairs there about some cottages, &c., that should be inspected. I think the Scotch cattell were dearer than if they had been bought in our country. I mean cattel of their size might have been bought in our markets for less mony.

In my last I think I should have been more particular about the hounds than I was, for which I beg your Lordship's pardon. But the case is as followeth; that Fryday they hunted on last and had the fine chase I describ'd to your Lordship [in¹] one of my former letters, Pealer was with them, tho' he appeared a little out of his order the Thursday before, but since he eat his meat at night, they unthinkingly took him out next day. And there being a bitch going proud, the hounds were frequently quarrelling and Pealer always in the thickest of them; but they ne'er recollected his former disorder but let him go loose still. They tied him in his place in deed when he came home, but he that night eat but little. The next morning he fill'd himself, and Jack Kingston let him loose, and he [run¹] directly to a tarrier bitch and fell upon her furiously. Then he took him up again; but the next morning, which was Sunday, he came and told me of the chase & that Pealer was very well again. On Tuesday he told me he was afraid the dog was mad, which made me say nothing 'till I saw the event.

On Wednesday Jack went to Cotchmore, so on Thursday morning

¹ The banker of No. 1 Fleet Street. The firm (Child and Co.) is still there, but in 1924 was swallowed up by Glyn, Mills and Co. Nearly all the early records of Child and Co. were destroyed in the paper shortage during World War II; they no doubt included the record of this transaction.

I sent for John Fardell, who told me he did not doubt but the dog would recover, for he had eaten that morning very heartily. Then I had the curiosity to go and see him my self, and I found him as mad as it was possible for any living creature to be. [I had this as^d] John Satchell tells me he is sure most of the hounds were bit by this dog, and I fear he speaks truth. I saw my Lord Gower at Stamford and told him the whole affair, and his Lordship has order'd them to go to the salt water.

Mr. Stafford receiv'd your Lordships letter this morning. He desires me to present his duty to your Lordship and to let you know that the Duke of Rutland, my Lord Gower, &c., hunt here[1] on Munday, and that he will attend them, and by Tuesdays post let your Lordship have a particular of the days sport.

January the first.   I could not get my business done soon enough to leave this place last night, but am now going to Stroxton, wh[ere] I intend to lye to night.
  I am your Lordship's
    Most humble and most faithful servant,

                                             D: EATON

[*Direction endorsed:—*]
    To the Right Honble. the Earl of Cardigan in Clifford Street, Burlington Buildings, London.

[*The* JB *monogram across endorsement as* **86**, *etc.*   Seal.   Date of post-mark, 2 January.]

        [**106**]   [*Wednesday, Thursday, 4, 5 January, 1726/7.*]

My Lord,
    January 4th, 1726.   Master Brudenell is very well.   I saw Mr. Stafford in the morning before I left Lincolnshire, and he told me your Lordship would have the Beeson[2] mare sent to Stroxton; but when I came to Deen I found her a little lame, so I did not think it proper to send her. She is better and I think very near well, but it will not be right for her to travell too soon; as soon as she may go with safety she shall.   I have receiv'd the honour of a letter from Mr. Brudenell, wherein he tells me that the marble is come safe to Stamford, and that I must meet the stone cutter there on Fryday with a cart to bring them home, which I shall doe; and as I don't suppose that there is a full load of marble, so they shall make the rest up with malt.

Stanion Sale is all sold at the view except 7 little parcells which are not sold, and I have receiv'd almost all the mony. Deen Park Sale is entirely fenc'd and it will be finish'd to morrow, I mean the trenching; so that on Fryday & Saturday they shall mark all the trees & pollards that ought to stand, and on Munday we shall view it. Deenthorpe Sale

---

[1] "Here" means not Deene but Lincolnshire, since Dan is still writing from Grantham.
    [2] This is probably Beeston near Leeds and close to Cardigan's Yorkshire estate.

will likewise be fit to view about the middle of next week.   The wagon can not set forward before Tuesday next, but then I believe it will.

January 5, 1726.   The postman is now here and has brought your Lordship's letter to Dan Whitworth which he will answer particularly by the next post. He has likewise brought me mine that I wrote to your Lordship by the last post,[1] wherein there is two bank bills which come to 170£.; so he takes it back with him, and your Lordship ought to receive this and that by the same post. The reason why it did not go was by cause the post came into Rockingham that morning sooner by three houres than usual. He did not stay at Deen for it. Dan thinks that if your Lordship can get an hogshead of right good strong port to mix with one of the hogsheads unbottled, it will do very well, & this may come by the wagon [but it^d].

I have nothing else to inform your Lordship of at present but that Mrs. Bradshaw is almost well again.

I am your Lordships
Most humble and most faithfull servant,

Deen, January 5th, 1726.   D: EATON

[**107**]   [*Saturday, 7 January,* 1726/7.]

My Lord,
Master Brudenell is very well and as merry as possible. But Mrs. Bradshaw is not well yet; the feavour hangs upon her still, but not in a violent manner. I cannot perswade her to let me send for Mr. Baker. It has made her very weak, tho' she will go about the house.

I have receiv'd the honour of your Lordship's of the 5th inst. Your Lordship will find by mine of the 3rd where the 100£. will be paid.[2] I find the fault was not in Walker that that letter mist a post, for both Mr. Huddlestone & Mr. Bradshaw, who live in the town, were serv'd after the same manner, the post coming in that morning sooner by 3 hours than usual.   We have appointed Munday for viewing Deen Park Sale, and on Wednesday we shall view at Spencer's. I have been there to day, and I find it will certainly be ready to view at that time. Then I shall be able to tell your Lordship how much mony I can return, and if you please I can order it all into your hands. I have receiv'd J. Parsons's mony and all Pywells, & have reduc'd the arrear very much, but cannot clear it.

I have got Mr. Kirk again, who has transcrib'd my accounts to Christmas Day; and he shall transcribe all my Ladys accounts into the same book, which will fill it, and make it compleat.   Will Symson has been in the country almost ever since he sold the sheep, but went thro' Stamford for London on Fryday last, so this bill will be paid at sight. I am very glad the 300£. was duly paid.   I will make a computation about Will Wades house as soon as I can.[3] I have ask'd Mr. J. Lynwood for the mony several times, and he told me he would pay it to your Lordship.

¹ Letter **105.**
² See **105.**
³ See **121.**

Thomas Bell has been hinder'd very much of late in laying out the
sales in Deen Park and at Corby & Deenthorpe, so that for this fortnight
he has [been hi[?]^d] not had much time to spare. He has brought me
36£. 10s. 0d., and says he has been with all the chapmen and they promise
to pay in a short time. I tell him that he must threaten to enter them in
the court if they don't pay. When the sales are over he will have nothing
to do but clear his account.

I was at Stamford yesterday and have brought the marble safe, but
Mr. Falkener thinks it will be better to put it up when the rooms are
nearer finish'd for fear of accidents, and I think so too. I bought the
brushwood that was to be cut down in Bangroves Riding, and this morning I sett four labourers to cut it down, for wee could not spare them
before. I think they will finish it on Munday.

I have not paid Haimes's bill for carriage, but I paid Gretton carrier.
I took in Haims's bill at Michaelmas, and I expect to morrow to have it
to Xmas. I can't think it would make any difference to pay weekly, only
it would be more trouble.

I am sorry I could not get the shaloom sooner. I sent twice to the
mills before I had it, and got it but on Thursday last; but as it is the
very best we ever had, it will do very well for the best livery's next year.
Mark Durham wants no more.

The brick maker as soon as he had contracted with me fell to work
with some labourers, and has done casting & picking the clay, and I
expect to see better bricks of his making than any we had before.

I can't tell what remains due to Grantham tradesmen, but I believe
there is the most due to Mr. Stafford; there is but little to Mr. Grant.
I wish your Lordship had orderd Mr. Woodward to have been paid in full.

I have the small plan of Little Deen that I drew which I am sure
is correct, but I will send for Mr. Lettin, and by that without further
trouble he may draw any other at his pleasure.

The hounds are return'd from the sea, but they drounded two and
lost a third. If the wagon can come on Tuesday next I will let your
Lordship know by the next post.

I am your Lordship's
Most humble and most faithfull servant,

Deen, January 7th, 1726.   D: EATON

[108]   [*Thursday*, 12 *January*, 1726/7.]

My Lord,
Master Brudenell is very well and Mrs. Bradshaw is a little better.
We were prevented sending the wagon by the excessive rains &
floods, but now we have fix'd Monday next for the day of its setting
forwards. It must go by Northampton, for a[s] your Lordship's is a very
indifferent team, it will not be able to get thro the other roads.

We have view'd Dibbins, which comes to £84. 7s. 6d., including
what your Lordship must have for your own use. The brick maker
told me that he thinks there is wood enough before the kill to burn
100,000 Li. [*sic*] of bricks, so I shall take care for as much more. We
have likewise view'd Deenthorpe Sale, that part of it that goes this year,
which comes to 66£. 17s. 0d.; we have appointed the sale days on Mun-

day & Tuesday next.   I need say nothing about the wine, for Dan shew'd me his letter.   Kitty Parson's gives your Lordship many thanks.

Philip is come for the Beeson mare and she is sound again, so he takes her to morrow to Stroxton.

I receiv'd the honour of your Lordship's of the 7th instant. The hounds, spanniells & horses are very well. I have nothing else to inform your Lordship of at present.

I am your Lordship's
Most humble and most faithful servant,

Deen, January 12th, 1726.   D: EATON

[109]   [*Tuesday, 17 January, 1726/7.*]

My Lord,

Will Dunmore has been with me and has paid me all the Leicester-shire arrears, but there is not 30£. of that wood mony receiv'd. I can't understan'd the meaning of it, but as soon as the business of the sales are over (which has layn entirely upon me), I will appoint a day and go into Leicestershire to receive the mony myself.

Brightman came with Will Dunmore to make proposals about the plowing part of his Great Ground, which are as followeth: that he will part the Ground with a good quick fence and preserve the same, if your Lordship will let him plow 15 acres of it for 3 years, and when that is laid down, then to plow fifteen acres more for 3 years. The dividing the Ground will cost him 35£. at least if it is well done, and to fence the quick a second time will cost him 15£. more, besides weeding, &c. If your Lordship concludes anything in favour of his proposal, I have promised to let him know, that he may come and sign a particular agreement concerning it.

The inclosed[1] I believe will be paid when due; I know the person that drew it to be of good credit, and he tells me that he has given due advice upon it. When your Lordship has receiv'd the mony, I beg you would pay Mr. Leaver 16£., and I shall place 80£. to the Lincolnshire account.

All Dibbins wood is sold at the view, except what I reserv'd for the brick-kiln, but I could get but 45£. of the mony. It is sold into good hands, but had I insisted upon all the mony, I might have had the wood myself. I am going to Deenthorpe Sale to day.

The wagon set forward this morning but they were forc'd to leave several things behind for fear of overloading. The carter has a particular of the loading.   Mrs. Bradshaw is pritty well again.   I have nothing else to inform your Lordship of at present.   I am,

Your Lordship's most humble and most faithfull servant,

Deen, January 17th, 1726.   DAN: EAT[ON][2]

P.S. The hounds and horses are all well, but the spanniel Dutchess is chap-fallen.

---

[1] Presumably a bill of exchange.
[2] Paper torn.

[**110**]   [*Saturday, Sunday*, 21, 22 *January*, 1726/7.]

My Lord,
          January 21th, 1726.   Master Brudenell continues very well.
          As to particulars of things to be done by the labourers. In the first
place I think to cause a cock hedge to be made on each side of the new
road on the outside of the little ditches, and then to plant quick on each
side of the great bank, which may be clip'd when it is high enough,
and trees may be planted beside the quick as you please, and the roots
of the quick will preserve the brinks of the ditches from falling in.
          In the next place the hedge that parts Deenthorp Meadow from the
lane ought to be plash'd and the ditch scowr'd and a cock hedge made;
and the double hedge round Newlands ought to be cut this year,—most
of it has stood too long by seven years already. This will afford a great
quantity of wood that will not serve for hedging, but will serve for the
brick-kill. And some of those parcels of wood in Deenthorp sale which
I cannot sell will furnish hedging wood & stakes for all these things.
          There is one of the hedges in Langly is too old and ought to be
cut, but I fear what I have propos'd already, with the sales, will employ
all the labourers I can get till the season is over.
          We are now enlarging the plantation in the paddock and taking in
those hills and pitts where the charcoal us'd to be burnt, for the quick
and young ashes must be transplanted this season or two thirds of it at
least will dye, and I could not find a more proper bitt of ground for the
purpose anywhere than this. Without the plashing of these hedges I have
hardly reserv'd wood enough in the park for [the*] brick-kiln, for I had
these hedges in my thoughts when I sold the sale.
          Your Lordship once proposd to sow the new road with oats, but I
think it will not be worth the while for it is level enough without plowing, so if I have not your Lordship's possitive commands for it, I shall
provide some ray grass seed to sow upon it, which will be a strong
sword [*sic*] in one year.
          John Peak has kill'd the best doe in Deen Park to day, but he thinks
she is not warrantable, so has sent her directed to your Lordship; & if
your Lordship thinks her worth the gentlemans acceptance, you may
send her to him. He has been every day this week amongst the herd, but
could see none eatable but her. This last three weeks of wet weather
has drench'd them so, he begs your Lordship would order no more to
be killd.
          There is a great deal more of the garden wall at Little Deen fallen
down in several places.   I have not yet bought any dales, for if I had,
the roads from Peterborough are not passable with a wagon.   Mr. Hull
tells me that he has a large quantity of right good black oats; and I intend
to go and see them on Munday, and if I can bargain with him, I will,
for as many as will sow all the land at the Common; for I am sure they
will suit that cold land better than white ones.
          I am uneasy that I had no letter to day to let me know whither
your Lordship and my Lady receiv'd your bills or not; I hope they
could not miscarry, but I have proper memorandums and always take
witnesses when I deliver bills to the post.

Jan. 22th.   I sent to Mr. Lettin of Lowick but I find he is in London.
I will enquire when he returnes and then he shall draw the plan of
Little Deen, &c.   Wee should now be getting materials together for

altering the small beer cellar, for in a months time men will work from six to six. Dan Whitworth intends to set forward for London on Wednesday next. I have nothing else to inform your Lordship of at present. I am,

Your Lordship's most humble and most faithful servant,

DAN: EATON

[111]   [*Saturday, 28 January*, 1726/7.][1]

My Lord,

Saturday, Jan. 28th. Master Brudenell is very well. The boy with the two mares came safe to Deen on Wednesday night, and the wagon with all the goods came safe on Thursday. I have bought 30 quarter of black oats of Mr. Hull at 11s. per quarter. They are very good ones and I don't doubt but they will suit the land.

Old Grange is dead, and Mrs. Chambers;[2] there is an arrear of her rent due to your Lordship of 5£. 17s. 0d. She had some goods which are now in the house, but when her funeral charges are paid and her debts, there will be very little left for the poor children, and nothing if I seiz for the arrear. If your Lordship will be pleas'd to remit all or any part of the arrear it will be very great charity; but your Lordships directions shall be particularly follow'd.

The limes in the hedgerows at Little Deen ought now to be remov'd if your Lordship intends to plant yews in their stead.

Mr. Peach the tanner begs your Lordship would be pleas'd to order him the 40£. 8s. 0d. that is due to his kinsman for two hogsheads of port wine that was deliverd to your Lordship's use in 1721. I remember when he shew'd your Lordship the bill in the liberary, you told him it should be deducted out of the bark mony; but your Lordship not being in the country when the bark mony ought to be paid, he paid me the full without any deduction, and rather chose to wait upon you himself for this mony, since your coming into the country was dayly expected. His mony has ever since layn dead in his kinsmans hands, and now he says he wants it very much, and if your Lordship will be pleas'd to order it for him, it will be a singular favour, and of very great service to him.

Philips of Weldon that rented the Lawn of Lord Hatton will give ten shillings an acre for John Winsalls close if your Lordship pleases to let him have it; I cannot hear of any body that will give more.

Saturday night, 6 o'clock. I have just now receiv'd the honour of your Lordship's. I can't tell the meaning of the post's keeping it so long. Thomas Bell is to be with me to morrow morning, and by Tuesdays post I will send your Lordship a particular account of the cash and every thing else that you desire. Your Lordship's commands shall be exactly follow'd. I never knew the wood mony so hard to be got as it is this year. I have Will Ingram's accounts and on Tuesday next I will go to Stroxton and execute your Lordship's commands. When I

[1] The year determined from internal evidence, by calendar; and see **112-117**.
[2] Widow of Charles Chambers, clockmaker. See **29, 36**.

was at Stroxton John Black told me the boys were very good, & I gave them a shilling a piece for their encouragement.[1]

I am glad your Lordship & my Lady has receiv'd the bills. I don't doubt but the 96£. will be duly paid. If your Lordship in any of your letters order'd me to send the names of the youn[g] and old hounds and of those that were drown'd, I never had that letter. I have set the billiar'd table in the room before the chappell. Mrs. Bradshaw is pritty well recover'd. But I have got an extream bad cold my self which has been upon me ten days.

I hope your Lordship will not be disappointed of this house for want of money. I wish it may prove for [your sat]isfaction. I fear the timber in the sales this year will not raise so much [mon]y as usual, for Corby Sale seems to be very thin of oak. In Old Dibbins in Deen Park there is about 60 old trees that are mere headless truncks, and no ornament to the park, that if they were cut down would raise about 200£., and if they stand 20 years longer they will not be worth so much by 50£. at least. I need not tell your Lordship the mony that will be lost by their standing considering the interest, but if I thought them ornamental I should be unwilling to have the beauty of the park defac'd at any rate.

I was at Weldon on Thursday, where I saw Mr. Baker as he came from Mr. Goode. I ask'd him how he was, and he told me that he was in a very wasting condition, & he thought he could not hold out long, and that his recovery could not be expected.

There can no great charge attend the billiard room, but I will compute it on Munday as near as I can. As to dividing of Newlands, I think it will be done as well another year, for I think your Lordship's quick is most of it too small to plant out. I believe I can buy good oats for provender for about half a guinea a quarter and have them brought in. I must refer the rest to the next post. I am,

Your Lordship's most humble and most faithful servant,

D: EATON

[112]   [*Tuesday*, 31 *January*, 1726/7.]

My Lord,

Master Brudenell continues very well. I stated my account of the rents upon December 24th last, which with all my Lady's accounts are very neatly and correctly transcrib'd. The ballance due to your Lordship was 45£. 17s. 5½d. and the arrear was 60£. 19s. 10½d., whereof 30£. 10s. 0d. was John Radoffs, 13£. 9s. 0d. John Peak's, 5£. 10s. 0d. Widow Harrisson's and 5£. 17s. 0d. Mrs. Chambers's; & since December 24th I have in a new account in 42 articles disburs'd 265£. 0s. 0d., and I have now in cash 240£. Thomas Bell was with me, and I have orderd him to let all the people know that they must be sued unless they forthwith pay the mony. There is 36 of them that have not paid, and a great many of them are people which we have always look'd upon to be our best chaps, but I have told Thomas Bell that I will not favour one of them.

---

[1] On 3 July, 1727, Dan gave to John Black's five boys "for their encouragement, 2s./6d." (ASR, 252).

I hope your Lordship will not be disappointed for want of mony. There is about 240£. of the last years wood mony still to receive, but how to get it immediately [sic] I cannot tell. But if your Lordship shall approve of this method, I believe I may venter to promise to return to your Lordship in five weeks time at the furthest a thousand pound at least, without any difficulty, which is to receive it of the best of the tenants in Northamptonshire & Leicestershire. I have already pay'd my Lady 90£. in part of Michaelmas rent, and have receiv'd very near that sum of the tenants, and I don't think I have put them under any difficulties thereby; so likewise among the rest of your Lordship's tenants, it is not to be supposd but that tho' we seldome ask them for Michaelmas rent till April, yet all the prudent ones are laying up there mony for several months before, and I know a great many of them that are able to advance half a years rent almost any time. If your Lordship approves of this proposal I believe I can easily & certainly execute it, without saying any more upon it at present; and I am not able to describe an easyer method for preventing your Lordship's disappointment than this.

The charge of making the summer house into a compleat billiard room as near as I can compute will come to near 30£. in everything; and I think the chimney must of necessity be on the outside, and not into the liberary chimny.

I am going to Stroxton to day, but my cold continues as it was.

I am your Lordship's

Most humble and most faithful servant,

Deen, January [31st],[1] 1726.　　　　　　　　DAN: EATON

[113]　　　　　　[Wednesday, Thursday, 1, 2 February, 1726/7.]

My Lord,

February the first, 1726. Master Brudenell is very well. I have been at Stroxton and have done every thing as your Lordship commanded me, and have deliver'd all the horse cloths, &c., to John Black. The horses are all well, both the racers and hunters.

The computation that I sent your Lordship concerning the billiard room was made upon this foundation: that the arch at the east end should be made into one entire compass sash (which with the frame, seat, &c., will cost 10£.); the arch over the steps into the garden, to be made up with a large sash door in the middle of it, which with the door case, door frame, wainscot door jaums, stone, brick, lime, workmanship (that is masons work), lock, bolt & hinges will cost 8£., or be worth that sum if the materials are your Lordships; the other arch to be made up with stone, brick & lime, with a chimny close by the side of the peer that supports the two arches, which chimny must be carry'd up with a free ston tunnell above the leads on the out side, which with the chimny piece, harth p[l]ace and other materials, out and masons work, will come to 9£.

One reason why I think the arch at the east end ought to be made into a large compass sash is that when it is so made, it will cast the same light upon the old staircase as it now does; but was it to be made with a single sash, those old windows in the passage would become useless;

[1] A hole in paper here. Date confirmed by 111 and 113.

but this would save about 4£. of the charge. I find there may be a chimny made on the other side in the corner by making the tunnell thro' the closet in Mr. Brudenell's room and thro' the other little closet in the blew damask room, and so into that room chimny; but I think the other will be better. I could not get a work man to assist me in this, but I believe I am pritty near the mark.

The inclos'd is a list of all the hounds at Deen, which I got John Abbay to make while I was at Stroxton. They are all well but Countess & Abbigale, who' are lame.[1]   I have nothing else to inform your Lordship of at present.   I am,

Your Lordship's most humble and most faithful servant,

Deen, February 2d, 1726.   DAN: EATON

I have receiv'd Master Brudenells gloves, which fit very well.

[114]   [*Saturday, 4 February,* 1726/7.][2]

My Lord,

Master Brudenell continues very well.   I return your Lordship many thanks for the favour of a receipt for my cough, which Mr. Leaver tells me your Lordship orderd him to send me. I am very little better, and intend to make use of it on Munday. I have a calf of my own which I will cause to be kil'd for that purpose.

I have receiv'd certain information from Slawston that Christopher Bassett has declar'd openly that he finds it impossible to hold his farm any longer, and that he intends to quit the fallows at Lady Day and sell all his crops upon the ground. Tho' he could not live upon it, yet I belive the farm will bear some advancement, notwithstanding the land is very much out of heart.

I hear from Mr. Christopher Jackson that Mr. Roberts has obtain'd a commission from his Honour to sell all the timber that is saleable in Thistleton, Stockin and else where. I cannot tell whither this gentleman intends to do his Honour truer service than formerly or not, but I dare venture to say that he may now act more securely than ever he did, for sure no one hereafter will endeavour to discover any indirect practices, since those who have already attempted to do his Honour justice are so manifestly slighted.

Will Hawksby desires me to ask your Lordship whither he may plow the neither part of the pasture one year longer or not, and the last year at 12s. per acre. If not he must provide some grass seeds to sow upon it this spring. He is in hopes your Lordship will grant this favour bycause he has had but poor crops these two years.

Thursday and yesterday I was in the sales. They go on very well, and I hope the wood will be all down in proper time.

Mr. Good declines very fast. He is seldom sensible and cannot stand without assistance, but says (in his intervals) that he feels no pain, and has not been sick all this time.—His legs swell now.

I have nothing else to inform your Lordship of at present. I

---

[1] This list has not survived, but see **96** and Index of Subjects under Hounds.
[2] Date corrected by internal evidence. See **111-119.**

intend to stay at home this next week if I can to see if I can get my cold off.   I am,

Your Lordship's most humble and most faithful servant,

Deen, January [*sic*] 4th, 1726.   DAN: EATON

[**115**]   [*Tuesday, 7 February, 1726/7.*]

My Lord,

Master Brudenell continues very well.   I have receiv'd the honour of your Lordship's of the 4th instant. I am very sorry that your Lordships eyes are not well, and that your Lordship is disapointed in the purchase of the house.   I think I am something better of my hoarsness; I return your Lordship many thanks for your goodness concerning it; I hope this water will cure me.   I will execute your Lordships commands concerning the wood arrear, and will go to Stamford as soon as I get off my cold.   I can say nothing further concerning Mr. Goode but that he continues languishing as I mention'd in my last.   The brawn was sent by the carrier on Sunday; there is three collers.

Notwithstanding the season is and has been so very wett, yet I never saw the wheat so prosperous as it is in all the country's hearabouts.   I have nothing else to inform your Lordship of at present.

I am,

Your Lordship's most humble and most faithful servant,

Deen, February 7th, 1726.   DAN: EATON

[**116**]   [*Thursday, 9 February, 1726/7.*]

My Lord,

Master Brudenell continues very well, and my cold is better.   I intend to appoint a day at the lattar [*sic*] end of next week to receive the arrears of Leicestershire wood. Mr. Elliot bought a great deal of old ash, and there is an account not stated of mony due to him for his son's board, &c.,[1] before your Lordship withdrew your bounty. I beg your Lordship would give me instructions about this affair, whither to state and allow the account or to let it remain as it now is.

The hounds, spaniels and horses are all very well. The deer are very well and don't dye, but the wet season has made them very poor.

I am,

Your Lordship's most humble and most faithful servant,

February 9th, 1726.   DAN: EATON

[*Direction endorsed*:—]

To the Right Honble. the Earl of Cardigan in Clifford Street, Burlington Buildings, London.

[*The* JB *monogram across endorsement as* **86**, *etc. The MS. also bears a pencil endorsement, in another and shaky hand*:—] Vouchers in Suffolk Street. [*Seal.   Date of postmark,* 10 *February.*]

[1] Lord Cardigan sent the Rev. J. Elliot's son to Oundle School for six years. B.D. p. 216.

[**117**]   [*Sunday, 12 February, 1726/7.*]

My Lord,
      Master Brudenell continues very well and my cold is much better;
I believe the pluck water has done me a great deal of good.
      The inclosed bills are drawn by a gentleman that I know very well.
I don't doubt but they will be duly paid, tho' they are but badly writ;
yet his agent knows the hand, for all his bills are drawn after the same
manner, which is not easily counterfeited. But least your Lordship
should be puzled to find out the person they are drawn upon, it is Mr.
Robert Rogers in Hudsons Court on Great Tower Hill.—The 60£. 11s. 9d.
I intend for the ballance of the old account of wood sold in winter, 1724,
and in the spring, 1725;[1] and the other bill of 14£. 12s. 6d. I intend is
to discharge the summes which I have inclos'd a particular of, which I
could not conveniently introduce into my accounts. Your Lordship may
remember that the old account of wood was posted (or book'd) and the
arrear plac'd before you left the country, but the account was not clos'd.
      I think Thomas Ayer of Little Oakly, who rents a close of your
Lordship in Stanion lordship, is a very bad tenant, for he destroys the
fences by cutting them wrong, and scowers no ditches, and continually
sells the hay and mowes it every year, by which he has impoverish'd
the land very much. He has no cattell, and generally pays his rent with
the mony that he receives for hay before it is grown. I saw the fences
very much abus'd; which made me enquire into these things. There are
several of your Lordships tenants of Stanion that want inclosure which
I believe this close would be of service to, and sure it would be more
for your Lordship's advantage to have the product of it expended upon
your own land.
      Mrs. Bradshaw desires to know whither any flaxen cloth must be
bought this spring or not, bycause the season for whitening is at hand.
      Alise Lightfoot desires leave to quit your Lordship's service.[2] She
hopes your Lordship nor my Lady can't take ill: she does not go away
out of any dislike, but out of a necessity of taking care of her very old
mother. [I believe she intends to go on Thursday next.[d]] There was a
messenger came from Grantham for her. My sister Theo shall assist my
mother, while your Lordship and my Lady are provided, if you think
proper.
      The hounds, spaniells & horses are all well.
            I am your Lordship's
                  Most humble and most faithful servant,

Deen, February 12th, 1726.   DAN: EATON

[**118**]   [*Sunday, 19 February, 1726/7.*]

My Lord,
      Master Brudenell is very well, and my cold is almost well.   I have
paid Mr. Richards forty pounds, and there is eleven more due.[3] When

---

[1] This may be 1725/6.
[2] See **135**.
[3] This payment was for Lady Exeter's goods bought at the Wothorpe sale. See
39, **41**.

I was at Glapthorne to receive my Lady's mony, I told the tenants what your Lordship had heard concerning the hounds. I see most of the hounds my self, & I did not see any that wanted meat, nor could I hear of any that had been abus'd, so that I hope this was a wrong information. But there is one or two of the tenants of Corby who' did not do the dogs justice, & I threatned them, telling them that your Lordship would certainly sue them for a breach of covenants, since it was a clause in their leases that they should take care of a hound; and I hear that they have taken better care since.

The small pox are so very much at Uppingham that we durst not send thither for cloth. So we must defer the buying of any till Brigstock Fare.   I have sent the boy to Stroxton and have order'd Philip to be here today with the little mare the boy rid upon; so he will be ready when your Lordship wants your pad mare.   The hounds, spanniels & horses here are all very well, and very great care is always taken at every full & change of the moon.

There are several of the tenants of Stanion that would be glad of John Ayre's close (I have discharg'd him), but I think none really wants it so much nor would make a better tenant than Will Bell. Thomas Meadows & John Winsal give 11s. per acre for their close; the reason why Thomas Meadows will not give the price for John Winsal's is by-cause he thinks it too dear, for it is rather worse than his part. I have nothing else to inform your Lordship of at present.   I am,
Your Lordship's most humble and most faithful servant,

Deen, February 19th, 1726.   DAN: EATON

[119]   [*Wednesday, Thursday, 22, 23 February, 1726/7*]

My Lord,
       Deen, Feb. 22th, 1726.   Master Brudenell continues very well. Mr. Goode dyed last night.

John Ayre of Oakly was with me on Sunday; he brought his Michaelmas rent, and begs very hard to be continued tenant to the close. (He was not at home, so I left a discharge in writing at his house.)   He promises that he will scower the ditches and make cock hedges ·against every part of the fence that has been lately cut, before Lady Day next, or he will then take a discharge peacably, and that he never will here-after suffer one load of hay to be carryed out of the close without your Lordship's consent. He says that he has been tenant to the close thirty years, and formerly has carryed more loads of stuff to it than ever he has let be carryed away. I hope this check will make him a better husband if your Lordship pleases to continue him, but I gave him very little encouragement. He has, I hear by further enquiry, four beasts & twelve sheep which were in a little close he rents at Oakly, when I was in his close at Stanion.

I was in Leicestershire on Munday, but did not receive three pounds.   There is more due to Mr. Elliot for his sons board & the arrears of your Lordship's charitable subscription to clergimens poor widows[1] than his wood comes to, and he desir'd I would not insist upon

---

[1] This is The Corporation of the Sons of the Clergy, for the relief of the poor

the wood mony, bycause he was going yesterday in pursuit of a very good living,[1] wherein he was likely to succeed, and if so he should want his mony. Will Worth had a large quantity of the wood, but paid no mony; he has promis'd to bring it on Munday next. Thomas Woodcock had as much as comes to 10£. 6s. 6d., but has not paid a farthing. I order'd Will Dunmore to enter all those that are under forty shillings in Gartry Court,[2] but I fear we must be forc'd to arrest T. Woodcock.

The continual rains have made all the roads hereabouts extreamly bad, and the green sword [sic] in most places cuts in very deep. The waters are very much out now in all our brooks. Christopher Basset says that he intends to hold his farm on, and hopes he shall continue to pay his rent by the assistance of his brother; he is not in arrear.

Feb. 23th, 1726. I have receiv'd the honour of your Lordship's of the 21th instant. I will let Thomas Meadows know the contents of it to day. The postman tells me that there has not been such a flood in the meadows these forty years as there is now. Here was snow fell here [sic] last night which lies ankle deep in the park, but I don't think it reach'd London.

If your Lordship intends to let J. Ayre continue, I beg you would let me know, that I may order him to go on with what he proposes concerning his fences. I have nothing else to inform your Lordship of at present. I am,
Your Lordship's most humble and most faithful servant,

DAN: EATON

The hounds, spaniels & horses are all well except your Lordships pad mare, who has got a very bad cold.

[**120**]   [*Sunday*, 26 *February*, 1726/7.]

My Lord,
Master Brudenell continues very well. I told Thomas Meadows on Thursday morning last what your Lordship commanded me. And he says he is very much surpris'd that your Lordship should proceed after this maner, since he had very good assurances from your Lordship that his part should not be taken away from him, paying his rent; which has made him put himself to near 3£. charge in draining, dividing and quick-setting the old gaps.

He says that he did not choose this part, but it fell to him by lot; and that if it had been his chance to have had Winsals part he would not have quitted it, since your Lordship was so kind as to let him have it, tho' he had lost by it. But since he has had two years experience upon this part, and confesses & knows that it is better than the other, and

widows and children of clergymen; it received a charter from Charles II in 1678. (E. H. Pearce, *The Sons of the Clergy*, 1904). Cardigan's subscription was three guineas (B.D. p. 216).
    [1] Perhaps the Rectory of Langton, Leics.
    [2] Gartree Hundred Court, Leic. By the 18th century hundred courts had come to be for the most part courts for the collection of petty debts. From Edward I's time the competence of the courts was limited to 40s. (Potter, *Historical Introduction to English Law*, 91, 94).

yet has not got a shilling by it, therefore he is resolvd rather to lose the mony he has already laid out upon it and run the hazard of loseing as much more by parting with his stock at so short a warning, than to hold the whole at the rent if your Lordship's resolution is immutable. But if your Lordship will be pleas'd to let him hold his part but one year longer, that he may have an oppertunity to make the best of his stock, he shall be very thankful, and will then most willingly quit it.

After I had been with T. Meadows on Thursday morning I saw John Peak, and he told me your Lordship wrote to him some time since about Winsal's part, and that he did not answer your letter bycause your Lordship was continually expected here. He told me he intended to have the close for one year at the rent rather than your Lordship should be disappointed of a tenant. I went that day to Weldon Court, where I saw Philips, & he told me that he would give your Lordship the rent for the close for one year if you please, & will graze it. But J. Peak propos'd to mow it to serve him with hay for his other ground.

The weather continues here extreamly wet, which makes our seeding very backward. The hounds, spaniels, & horses are all well (except the pad mare & her could is no better). I have nothing else to inform your Lordship of at present.

I am your Lordship's
Most humble and most faithful servant,

Deen, February 26th, 1726.   DAN: EATON

[**121**]   [*Saturday, 4 March, 1726/7.*]

My Lord,
Master Brudenell is very well and very merry. His Honour makes use of his tongue now to declare his resolutions, for he says Yes and No very plainly.

I receiv'd the honour of your Lordships letter of 28th ult. I was the begining of this week in all the sales, and Stanion Sale is all down but two or three parcels. Corby Sale has very little standing, so I brought 16 of Corby men to work in Deen Park Sale for this is the most backward, the work being so very tedious. But these men with our own will finish it in good time. Deenthorpe Sale goes on very well, and there is five men constantly cutting up the old hedge in Newlands and quicksetting the dead gaps, &c., as they ought to be. Deenthorpe Meadow hedge is plashd and when the ditch is scower'd it will help that road very much.

I was at Peterboroug yesterday & bought four hundred dales, half an hundred of fine dry ones and three hundred & an half of a courser sort, which will finish Little Deen. I bought them at the same price we had the last, with some difficulty, by cause the prospect of the approaching war[1] has raisd the price of them, for people apprehend that then their passage will be retarded. Mr. Delarue has a very great quantity by him, and if your Lordship thinks the warr is inevitable, there might be some mony sav'd if you was to lay in a stock against the time you intend to finish Deen Church.

[1] In February, 1727, Spain had laid siege to Gibraltar but war was averted, and England, France and Holland concluded an armistice with the Emperor on 31 May 1727.

The lanes continue very bad, but this week's dry weather has dry'd the fields finely, so that people are got to seeding and I hope we shall begin upon the Common about Tuesday.

All the dales that I have bought are right good red wood, and the courser sort have been stock'd ever since Midsummer last, but the fine ones are kept in a barn. I intend to get a load of them home this week if the weather continues dry, that the joyners may get to work as soon as your Lordship comes.

I am sorry Thomas Woodcock proves so bad a pay master; but if he would have bought as much more wood of us at that time, we should have sold it him, for it was impossible that we could foresee what difficulty we should have in getting the mony; but this mony will not be lost. I wish I could say so by one of Corby who has bought a great deal of wood every year of your Lordship, and has always pay'd very well till this year, and now he is run away. I hope we shall not lose a great deal by him, but these things will some times happen, notwithstanding all our care, where capmen[1] are so numerous.

Will Worth has not been with me according to promise.   Your Lordship's mare is much better; Philip has blooded & drench'd her, but she coughs a little still.   Joseph Lynwood is not at home today. I believe his mare will please your Lordship for the road; I have rid along with him several times, and I think she moves very well, but Philip shall try her this week.   The hounds and spaniels are all well, and I hope now they will continue so.

I remember very well that I promis'd your Lordship a draught of Little Deen and likewise an estimate of the charge of removing Will Wade's house. I waited for both till I could see Mr. Lettin, and he has now promis'd to be with me on Tuesday next.

I have been at Deen Parsonage house today to see the delapidations, which I think will not amount to a great deal. The church yard and garden wall is in very good repair. There is some little that ought to be done at the house, but in obedience to your Lordship's commands I have order'd Will Hawksby, Da[n] Smith, Robert Hibbins, & John Radoff to attend on Munday and make an estima[te.]

I hope your Lordship's goodness to Lummis will enable him in a short tim[e][2] to do your Lordship justice about the Corby affair,—I mean as to the house. I think the[re] is no danger but that he will please the Dutchess[3] and do her good service, to his own very great advantage, and that your Lordship will lose no creadit by recommending him, provided this new preferment does not put him upon new extravagancies.   I know nothing of your Lordship's Yorkshire affairs, but I believe the measures Lummis & I took at Hougham & Marston have been a considerable check upon the tenants, and I don't know but that if the same method was taken in Yorkshire, it might be equally advantageous to your Lordship.

I am your Lordship's
        Most humble and most faithful servant,

Deen, March 4th, 1726.   DAN: EATON

---

[1] i.e. chapmen. cf. "chaps" in **112**.

[2] ASR 253 records payments to George Denshire in October 1729 for principal and interest due on mortgage of Lummis's house in Corby.

[3] The Duchess of Montagu.

[**122**]   [*Wednesday, 8 March,* 1726/7.]

My Lord,

Master Brudenell is very well.   Mr. Lettin was here yesterday, and I shew'd him the plan of Little Deen which I drew, and went with him to the place, and by my stationary lines I let him see after what manner I proceeded. And he approv'd of it entirely, and told me very franckly that he could not pursue a better method, and that he believ'd this plan as correct as any he could draw or any other man; and whereas he could not possibly spare so much time as to do it this week, he advis'd me to transfer it my self upon a larger paper; for since I had finis'd the mathimatical and most troublesom part, he thought it pitty the transferring part should be taken out of my hands. I have begun it and will send it in a case by the carrier on Sunday next.

The inclosed is an estimate of what ought to be done at the Parsonage house. I screw'd it up as high as possible and gave them a method to write it in, which I thought would be better than if I writ it my self ; but as several of the things are not already delapidated, I fear they will not all be allow'd by the Court.

Edward Philips accepts the close at the rent; and I don't doubt but Will Bell will comply with what your Lordship requires, but he is now in Essex.   Mr. W. Goode was at the Parsonage to day and I hear intends to set workmen fourthwith about repairing it; but I believe it will be better for Mr. Foden to have mony allow'd.

Your Lordship's mare is much better of her cold, but she is putting out a splint, which Philip hopes he shall stop with oiles.   The hounds & spaniels continue very well, and now I hope they are out of danger.

I am,

Your Lordship's most humble and most faithful servant,

Deen, March 8th, 1726.   DAN: EATON

[**123**]   [*Monday, 13 March,* 1726/7.]

My Lord,

Master Brudenell continues very well.   I receiv'd the honour of your Lordship's of 11th last, and likewise of Mr. Leavers. Dan Smith was going to mend the slates upon the Parsonage on Saturday, but I stop'd him, for I knew such proceedings were not usual. I intend to see Mr. Goode tomorrow.   I sent your Lordship by the last post three bills for 98£. 17s. 0d., and I believe I may venture to promise your Lordship to send by next Saturdays post bills to make that sum up 200£. I shall go to Stamford Fare on Thursday, and if I can't meet with returns there, I don't much fear but that I shall meet with success amongst my acquaintance at Kettering on Fryday. I will get the bills payable as soon after date as I can.

I have sent a plan of Little Deen by Gretton carrier, for Haimes's man came and went a way again while I was gone to get Hawksby fix it in the case, notwithstanding he was told by two or three people to stay while I came again. I have transferr'd it by the same scale I plotted it by, and I took my instruments to the place and found the position of the

pond head, back brook, &c., which I thought very material to know if
your Lordship intends to make any alterations there; and I could not
have plac'd these upon the same scale had I transferr'd the plan by a
larger scale. My needle[1] is not worth one farthing, so I send it by this
post to your Lordship and beg you would desire Mr. Webber to get
another, which the person he bought my instruments of will let him have
for nothing if he is an honest man, since he is paid for this. It must be
of the same length with this exactly.

Inclosed is Mr. Child's note for 400£., and Worth's bond: I made
it absolute to us, the trustees, for we shall always keep it, and we shall
declare the uses in a defeasance, which will be in the custody of Will
Worth for his security. I have likewise inclosd Mr. Childs other note
for 100£. that was paid him at the same time.

Your Lordship's mare goes pritty sound again. Jewel the spanniel
goes proud; she is taken care of 'till your Lordship shall order what
dog she must have. The hounds are all well.

I am your Lordship's
    Most humble and most faithful servant,

Deen, March 13th, 1726.   DAN: EATON

[124]   [*Saturday*, 18 *March*, 1726/7.]

My Lord,
    Master Brudenell is very well.   I receiv'd the honour of your
Lordship's letter of the 16th with the bond.   I am sorry I did not
make a scale upon the plan, but your Lordship may know the distances
by a common foot rule, for it is 22 yards in an inch.   Here has been
Eberill the joyner here to day. The prices he proposes to work at are
the same which are usual here, but as I never had your Lordship's resolutions after what manner the work should be done, I could not contract
with him.   We have not gott any of the dales home yet, for the oats
go into the ground very well & I think it pity to lose a day seeding.
I think that nothing can hinder a plentifull crop.   I have directions
where to write to the joyner when your Lordship has resolv'd upon the
manner how the work shall be done. I think it will be best to have the
dining room floor'd with Norway oak, and the staircase, for the workmanship is the same, and the difference in the price of the stuff will
not be above three pounds ten shillings as I have computed it.

I could get no bills at Kettering but the inclosed, except some
payable a month after date, and Mr. Denshire told me that he could
return the mony in less than three weeks. John Parson's bill is for mony
he ow'd me for malt, &c.; the other seventy pound shall be paid to
Mr. Child.   The hounds & horses are very well. I wonder your Lordship did not take notice what dog should be put to Jewell.   Next
Saturday being Lady Day I shall write to James Ashly to get his dogkenell account ready & we will state it to that day.   I receiv'd Mr.
Staffords letter, and my mother thinks that Master Brudenells old coat
skirt may serve again with a new bodice if my Lady pleases.   I'll

---

[1] Part of Dan's surveying instrument (theodolite).

write to Mr. Denshire & order him to sue the carrier.[1] I have nothing else to inform your Lordship of at present.   I am,
      Your Lordship's most humble and most faithfull servant,

Deen, March 18th, 1726.   DAN: EATON

Mrs. Bradshaw desires to know if she must send more pickles.

[125]   [*Saturday, 25 March*, 1727.]

My Lord,
      Master Brudenell is very well.   I was in Leicestershire on Thursday and have received T. Woodcocks mony. I believe he borrow'd it, but I could not prevail with him to say he would quit either your Lordship's land or the gleebe; he says he hopes he is able to hold both. I receiv'd some more of the wood mony, and I hope there is none in danger of being lost, but neither Will Worth nor Mr. Elliot could pay any. I receiv'd 30£. of Mr. Brightman & 10£. 10s. 0d. of Will Dunmore in part of their rent, & I pay'd 70£. into Mr. Denshires hands yesterday, which he promises to return to Mr. Child, which makes up the 200Li.   The tenants of Cranoe make very great complaint against Mr. Edwards for cutting their sla[t^d]des with his carriages in fetching of sand, and I think they have a good deal of reason for it, for he has carted at a very unseasonable time when the ground was tender. If your Lordship pleases to tell him of it now he is in town, it may be of service. The damage he does by diging it in your Lordship's ground is trifling, and could he be prevail'd upon to fetch it only in summer time and lay it up against he should want it in winter, the tenants would not suffer much.   The hounds have done a great deal of damage among the lambs, and several of the tenants have clog'd their hounds. I told them this way of proceeding would certainly incur your Lordship's displeasure, but they are so troublesome they don't know what to do with them. They are all of them very well kept, and fine hounds. The hounds here are all well, and the spanniels. Jewell is loyn'd by the dog your Lordship orderd, and Janny is going proud. The red horse had no hurt of his eye, but it is an humour that attends it; it is still very bad.
      I received the honour of your Lordship's both of the 21th and 18th instant, for I did not receive that of the 18th till this morning. The hounds have not had a chase lately worth describing, for they have been out so seldom, being forc'd to stay at home three days before the full and change of the moon and three days afterwards, which takes up half there time, and being confind keeps them out of breath.
      The dining room floor at Little Deen will take 400 foot of board and the staircase 450 foot, which of the finest dales will cost 2d.$\frac{3}{4}$ per foot or thereabouts, and of Norway oak it will be bought somthing under 4d. per foot. The difference will be about 3£. 10s. 0d. or very little more; so that if your Lordship pleases, I will go to Peterborough and buy as much oak as will suffice, which I shall take care may be all of a colour.

---

[1] Possibly the Oundle carrier. See **84**.

The brickmaker is now here.[1] We are repairing the kill, and he is levelling the bed to lay the green bricks upon, prepairing his molds, &c.

I spoke to Mr. Joseph Lynwood about his mare; he says that 14£. is the lowest price. She is five years old this grass.

The dales may be ready soon for the alcove room, but the lime cannot be ready yet, for I think it ought to lye in the bead a long time after it is slak'd, to prevent its blistering as the greenhouse does. I'll get the kill mended as soon as I can, and a killfull burnt for that purpose. I'll get the wood in the alcove room taken down, but none of it will serve for Little Deen, for the architraves for those doors have been all ready to put up a great while ago.

I think it would be as well to begin the billiard room first & finish that; then your Lordship will not lose that diversion whilst Little Deen is prepairing.

The oats prove very good, and I don't fear but there will be a better crop this year upon the Common than ever there has been yet, for by the method I have take[n] I dare answer for it the grubbs are all destroyd.

Philip desires to know what saddle he must bring to New Market for your self. The horses are come safe from Stroxton. Philip will set out for New Market on Saturday and be there on Sunday.

Will Hawksby, upon hearing that Eberill has been with me about the work at Little Deen, says that rather than lose the work, he and Thomas Nichols will undertake it at an under price. I don't remember that I have seen a better workman than Thomas Nichols, so that this proposal may be advantagious to your Lordship, and I think the work may be well done. If your Lordship is in hast of it, they will get good hands to help them and be as expeditious as you shall require.

Your Lordship's pad mare is now lame again, and as she has been lame and well again so often lately, Philip is afraid she will not be fit to come to New Market.   I am,

Your Lordship's most humble and most faithful servant,

DAN: EATON

P.S. I have amongst my vouchers Mr. An. Keck's bill for 200£. paid into his hands Feb. 25th, 1725, which your Lordship may perhaps have forgot. If you want it I will send it by the post.

Deen, March 25th, 1727.

[**126**]   [*Wednesday, Thursday*, 29, 30 *March*, 1727.]

My Lord,

Mar. 29th, 1727.   Master Brudenell is very well.   Mr. Foden came hither last night and was inducted this morning.[2] I had been with Mrs. Goode before he came, & I told him what shee said. Mr. Foden has appointed Munday fortnight for valuing the delapidations of the Parsonage.

March 30th.   I have receiv'd the honour of your Lordship's. I will

---

[1] This is Jonathan Lewtener.
[2] As Rector of Deene.

take particular care about sending the horses to New Market, but I durst not buy Mr. Joseph Lynwoods mare upon my own judgement. He has lately rid her very much, having no other, and she is poor. I will prevail with him to send her to Newmarket if I can; then your Lordship will be a judge of her.   I made no proceedings with Eberil, but since he has had the expence & trouble of two journeys, I think he ought to have something allow'd him. But I hope Hawksby & Nichols will do the work as well, and I shall be very particular in describing the method they shall proceed in if I contract with them.

I have spoke to the glazier to prepare lead ready for the little tower as soon as possible; then I will cause it to be taken down and cover'd again forth with, and the stone will serve for the billiard room. Your Lordship did not say whither you would have a compass sash for the east arch or a common sash window.

Your Lordship says nothing about your spanniel Janny, what dog she is to have. I have receiv'd Dan Whitworths and I will send up the ale as soon as I can.

I am your Lordship's
Most humble and most faithful servant,

Dee [sic], March 30th.   DAN: EATON

[**127**]   [*Sunday, 9 April, 1727.*]

[My Lo]rd,
Master Brudenell is very well.   I was yesterday at Stonton at Mr. Staffords induction. The tenants of Glooston and Cranoe complain very much about the continual damage they receive by Mr. Edwards's fetching of sand, as I mentioned to your Lordship in a former letter; he has carted all these last rains.

I have order'd the hounds to be brought in on Tuesday next. The kenell is now fit for them, and I hope there can be no danger in it, for there has not been a dog there these seven months.

We have been hinder'd by rains this week, but I think we shall finish sowing the oats on Tuesday; then the team shall fetch the dales, &c., for finishing Little Deen. I intend to go to Peterborough on Wednesday to buy the oak, and if I don't receive objections from your Lordship against the method I propose to proceed in, I shall contract with the joiners the lattar end of the week, & they shall begin to work on Munday at the farthest.

John Black[1] has been here and I have stated his account to Christmas last, & there is due to him upon the ballance 148£. 19s. 7½d.

James Ashly[1] has been here, but we have not stated the account. He says he could not get in his bills without mony to pay them. He left a receipt for forty pounds, which I must send him as soon as I can get the mony; which mony, with a bill of 119£. 18s. 6d. for several things paid for by John Black, included in his account, which is upon your Lordships and Lord Gowers joint account, and mony paid by me to clear the dogkenell expence at Deen to Lady [Day] last, &c., I believe will partly clear the account on your Lordship's side.

[1] Black's and Ashly's accounts are for expenditure at Stroxton and Cottesmore respectively.

The hounds and spanniels are all well, and the horses, but the red horse's eye is very little better.

I have nothing else to inform your Lordship of at present. I am, Your Lordship's most humble and most faithful servant,

Deen, April 9th, 1727.   DAN: EATON

[**128**]   [*Thursday*, 13 *April*, 1727.]

My Lord,

Master Brudenell is very well. I have not been at Peterborough as I propos'd in my last, but I writ to know if there was such sort of Norway oak there and such a quantity as we shall want, and I find there is not, so I have desir'd Mr. Delarue to procure it, and then I shall go to Peterborough and buy it. Mr. Joseph Lynwood some time since gave me a particular of the prices of the several sorts of Norway oak at Lyn, which will enable me to bargain with Mr. Delarue when he has brought it to Peterborough.

We have finish'd sowing the oats, and there is the finest prospect of a good crop imaginable. I dare answer for it there will be more oats in that 20 acres that is next to Langly than there was upon the sixty acres last year.

We have laid Newlands, Langly and Sheepclose; we reserve the meadow and Halbanks to keep those cattell in that are fat, till your Lordship comes to Deen. The wall of both the paddocks is so delapidated that the deer cannot be kept out. We have laid Presto and Lammas Close for the use of the park.

I am going to day to measure the rooms at Little Deen, in order to contract with the joiners.

I have caus'd the clock to be remov'd out of the little tower into one of the closets below, and have contriv'd the waits to hang in such a manner that tho' their fall is shorter by twelve foot than it was, yet the clock will go longer by twelve hours without winding up than it did before. The lead is now ready, and I have orderd Robert Hibbins to begin to take down the tower on Munday next; and I will have help enough that in three days the place shall be cover'd again for fear of wet, which would damage the ceilings in the rooms below.

Thomas Watsons gray mare, Mrs. O. Bryons[1] mare, and your Lordships brown mare are very well; they have not any of them fol'd yet, but I expect every day when they will.

There is a great many grubbs in Mr. John Lynwoods plow'd ground, but I cannot find any in your Lordships land.

I took Mr. Joseph and Mr. John Lynwoods bond for the 50£. due to the poor of Deenthorpe instead of their note. They are bound to your Lordship in trust. But Mr. Joseph came to me the other day and told me that your Lordship was pleasd to promise his brother when he was last in Town that you would exonerate them of that bond, and take the payment of the mony upon yourself, which rejoices the parishioners very much, for they dreaded some difficulties concerning this affair.

[1] Mrs. O'Brien of Blatherwick.

Mr. Foden comes to Deen on Saturday in order to read the Articles[1] on Sunday, and have the delapidations of the Parsonage valued on Munday.

I never saw a more forward spring in my life, and all sorts of grain here are very promising.   I am,

Your Lordship's most humble and most faithful servant,

DAN: EATON

The hounds are all well, and the young hounds are come safe home.

April 13th, 1727.

[**129**]   [*Tuesday*, 18 *April*, 1727.]

My Lord,

Master Brudenell is very well.   I receiv'd the honour of your Lordship's of 13th. We are all extreamly rejoic'd that the small pox are likely to be so favourable to dear Lord Brudenell.   I have enclosd the abstract of John Black's account. The mony that your Lordship has paid for his rent was not introduc'd; he told me he could not tell certainly how that affair stood, so he left it to your Lordship to charge upon him. I have all the bills in my custody.

We have taken down the tower, & I hope to morrow it will be cover'd again.

I think I forgot in my last to tell your Lordship that Philip was come safe with the horses to Deen.

Mr. Forden [*sic*] is still here, but goes away to day. Mr. Goode after a very long debate yesterday paid him 20£. for the delapidations, which Mr. Forden accepted.

I have enclos'd a copy of the bargain I made with T. Nichols.[2] I let the time be so long before the rooms are intirely finish'd by cause of the floors; but I have told him that if he does not contrive his business so as to have finishd all the [rooms*d*] wainscot and everything else except the floors before July, I will procure other hands to work the staircase, for I am resolv'd to have the house compleatly finis'd before Michaelmas.   I am,

Your Lordship's most humble and most faithful servant,

Deen, April 18th, 1727.   D: EATON

[**130**]   [*Thursday*, 20 *April*, 1727.]

My Lord,

Master Brudenell is extreamly well.   I have receiv'd the honour of your Lordship's of the 18th inst. which brought me the joyful news of dear Lord Brudenell's being out of danger, but I am very sorry to here of Lady Frances's illness. I hope change of air will relieve her Ladyship.

---

[1] The Thirty-nine Articles of Religion in the Book of Common Prayer, read by the clergy on their institution to a benefice.
[2] For this bargain, see Appendix II.

I'll take care to have the Lodge[1] in order to receive Lord Brudenell according to your Lordship's command. I believe all John Peaks family have had the small pox except their two children, which they may send to Lutton to their grandmother unless your Lordship has an objection to their living in the Lodge while Lord Brudenell is there. Thomas Meadows cannot live their by cause his wife has a very young child that sucks.   And the joiners must work in the old rooms at Little Deen for fear in turning their boards, &c., they should hit the stuco-work cornices.

I will be very particular when I state James Ashleys account. I know the payment your Lordship made for oats at Stroxton; the man came to Deen for the mony, and you gave it to me to pay him.

Mr. Pearsy was here yesterday and likes all the hounds that came from Leicestershire very well, except one. The tenants of Corby and Glapthorne have made no great complaints, so I have not order'd their hounds home.

I am sorry that J. Lynwood has impos'd upon his brother. I believe he told him what I writ your Lordship word of, but Mr. Joseph seem'd to doubt the veracity of it; but I cannot see Mr. John, bycause, poor unfortunate man, he has been forc'd to remove from Benefield incog. for better air.[2]

Your Lordship's pad mare will certainly fole soon.

I don't doubt but Hawksby will do his work well, and likewise T. Nichols, for they will one strive to exceed the other.

The size of the bricks as near as may be are the same with those made by Horn, and I believe will be full as good; but the brickmaker[3] still visits his whore at Bulwick.

The roads in all our lanes hereabouts are very bad, and the slows are as deep as in winter, but the fields are padded.

Master Brudenell lies in a cradle, but my mother intends to have a little bed for him in a day or two. She spoke to me above a week ago about it.

I was yesterday in most of the pour'lles, and I find there is a great many deer in them; and Thomas Bell says that there is several very fine bucks, but I see but one, which was a pollard.

The post stays. I will be more particular in my next.   I am,
Your Lordship's most humble and most faithful servant,

April 20th, 1727.   DAN: EATON

I beg your Lordship would let the inclosed go to the post with your letters; 'tis to him that married my sister.[4]

[131]   [*Sunday, 23 April,* 1727.]

My Lord,
Master Brudenell is extreamly well.   I have receiv'd the honour of your Lordships of the 20th. I have sent by this post in another packet

¹ This was where John Peak, Cardigan's park keeper, lived.
² See **128**.
³ Jonathan Lewtener.
⁴ No doubt the trooper mentioned in **9**.

an exact copy of John Blacks bill of expences upon your Lordship's and Lord Gowers joint account.[1] The bill of board wages is the same your Lordship saw when at Hamby.

I forgot to tell your Lordship in my last that Lord Hatton is in the country and that his Lordship has call'd here several times to see Master Brudenell. I here that his Lordship intends to set forward for London on Tuesday next, but intends to return soon with my Lady Hatton and live at Kirby all the summer.

I did not go to Wellom as your Lordship order'd me; for I have never been in Mr. Elliots company but we have made the affair of Slawston part of our discourse. From which I gather that your Lordship will find more difficulty to agree with Mr. Edwards, as well about a division for his share of the impropriate tyths as for his real estate, than with all the rest of the free holders, for he is a subtile avaritious man, and will over reach any man when it is in his power. I remember he once propos'd to fence out his own ground if your Lordship would give him the breadth of a ditch out of your land; this he would do for the sake of the wood that may hereafter grow in the fences. If he continues in this mind, or proposes any thing near it, I would advise your Lordship to agree to it, for I am very sure that no fences in Slawston will ever produce wood enough to defray the charge of plashing, &c., and the want of juditious labourers to cut them must of course in a term of years destroy them. I never yet saw an hedge in Leicestershire cut in a proper manner. If Mr. Edwards is not so hot upon the fences as he was, I think the method propos'd, which is to enclose the fields at your Lordships and Mr. Edwards's proportionable charge without laying any expence upon the free holders, will make it very easy for them to come into the agreement.

I shall be very careful that my future actions may never lessen the good opinion your Lordship has of me, and I do assure your Lordship that I read that clause with the greatest joy immaginable.

I expect that Lummis came to Corby last night, so that to morrow we shall begin to view the timber.

I most heartily congratulate your Lordship upon Lord Brudenells recovery. I receiv'd a letter from Mr. Billinge yesterday which confirms it.   I am,

Your Lordship's most humble and most faithful servant,

Deen, April 23th, 1727.   DAN: EATON

Your Lordship will have the draughts on Wednesday evening.

[**132**]   [*Tuesday, 25 April*, 1727.]

My Lord,
    Master Brudenell is very well.   I have receiv'd the honour of your Lordship's of 22th instant.   I went to Lummis to Corby on Sunday in the afternoon, hearing he was there, and he tells me that your Lordship would have had me gone to Wellom to have made a computation concerning the value of the impropriate tyths of Slawston; and I am

---

[1] For hunting expenses at Stroxton.

sorry I did not go according to your Lordships former directions. If Mr. Elliot while he is in Town sends me the case stated, I will by the next post send a calculation upon it.

Jonathan Lewtener the brickmaker came to me on Thursday last to have got some more mony of me. But I told him that I did not care to part with any till I saw his debts and workmen paid, for I heard that he had not paid his debts with the mony I had let him have before (which was in all 10£., but I would never let him have a shilling since he brought this whore with him). Nor should I have been so credulous before as to have paid the mony as fast as he earn'd it had I not been deceiv'd by the extraordinary good caractar which my Lord Gowers footman, John Bruff, and the butler gave me of him when they came here to tast the wine. He had very little to say for himself, but on Fryday thought fit to march off, and has left about 50 shillings to pay in the town. I am not at all sorry that he is gone, but only that the people are likely to lose by him. I hope justice may pursue him. He lives at Henly Green near Newcastle Under Line in Staffordshire.

I have secur'd your Lordship from damage by him by letting his bargain to a poor laborious fellow[1] who he employ'd in helping him to mold the bricks, who is willing that I should pay his debts & workmen that he employs, and give him the over plus if any be. This fellow is not to have his victuals in the house, as Jonathan was to have had, but only a bottle of small beer every night they burn. He is very handy at molding the bricks, and enters at a disadvantage now, that he may be employ'd for the future, which he will do at the same price that Horn had, without the advantage of eating in the family. As soon as he gets a kill full burnt, I will let your Lordship know how they proove. There is about 25,000 molded.

Yesterday we view'd Corby timber, which comes to 111£.   And yesterday after noon poor Christopher Dexter sent to me to desire me to come to Gretton. He wanted to alter his will, which I had in my custody. He could not write his name; he is very sensible, but will certainly dye in a very few days. So I could not measure the things at Little Deen as your Lordship orderd me, but will send a particular by the next post.

The lesser new bedchamber is to be wainscotted throughout, and the hall surbase high, by Hawksby; and by Sundays carrier I will send your Lordship a draught of the pannells, &c.

We are going to day to view Deenthorpe timber, and if I can I will meet Master Robert at Lilford in the afternoon.

Tomorrow we shall view at Stanion, and Thursday and Saturday are our sale days.

We are all extreamly concern'd for Lady Frances and Lady Mary's being ill. I wish Little Deen was finish'd for their sakes, for I believe that is a wholesome aire.   I am,

Your Lordship's most humble and most faithfull servant,

Deen, April 25th, 1727.   D: EATON

---

[1] Will Newdall.

[**133**]   [*Wednesday, Thursday, 26, 27 April, 1727.*]

My Lord,

April 26th.   Ma[s]ter Robert arriv'd safe at Deen last night before eight, and now I think we have two the finest [*sic*] young noblemen at Deen that England can afford.[1]

Your Lordships bedchamber at Little Deen is eleven foot high. The end of the room fronting the chimny has a vacancy for hangings 13 foot long and seven foot high (I take it that the bed will hide part of this, so it need not be all hung). The other side fronting the windows has a vacancy for hangings 16ft. 3in. long and seven foot high.

Daniel White of Corby is dead. The land which he rented of your Lordship was under lease to one Francis Cliffton and given by will to Dan White for life, or till the lease expir'd; and if Dan White should not live to the end of the lease, then he gave the remainder of the term to John Lee, who now claims it, but has neither horse nor cow to mannage it. Nevertheless he is very desirous of holding it. I think it would be better for him to assign it over to some person that is able to mannage it, and will give him something for the advantage of it; for he must hire it plow'd, and that will in a short time impoverish the land.

April 27th.   Your Lordships pad mare has got a most fine horse fole; it is brown with a large star and snip, with four white feet.

The hounds are all well except Fidler, who has been out of order these three days, but has eaten his meat very well, even this morning, but I fear he will be mad. The horses are all well, but I fear the red horse's eye will not be recover'd.

I have stone and seacole ready at the kill, and they are mending it to day, and about Munday they shall begin to burn.   I believe the poor fellow that is now making the bricks will do them very well.   I am going to Corby Sale today, and will be more particular by the next post.

I am,

Your Lordship's most humble and most faithful servant,

Deen, April 27th, 1727.   DAN: EATON

[**134**]   [*Sunday, 30 April, 1727.*]

My Lord,

Master James and Master Robert are extreamly well. The inclos'd is the result of three days labour.[2] Tho' when Jonah Chapman had sign'd, the rest follow'd without much difficultie, there is some that are still obstinate, but I don't doubt but they will all comply except two. I think I can answer for about 5 more that will sign to morrow, that we could not see yesterday. I am very glad that there is now a probability of your Lordship's becoming intirely master of that fine tract of land. I have no occasion to describe the method we took nor the reasons why, but we saw very plainly that if we did not make use of this oppertunity, we should not have such another these three or four years. We have not

---

[1] The other being James, now two years old.
[2] This refers to common rights in woods at Corby. See **135** and **139**. For the names of the commoners see **135** and also Bru.MSS.O.vi.4.

sold the timber, but have as many chapmen as trees, and to morrow is the day.

I was at Kettering to have got a bill for my Lady on Fryday, but could not meet with any that would be paid within these three weeks, and I hope to return her Ladyship's mony in a shorter time.

I could not finish the draughts of the wainscot as I promised, which I hope your Lordship will excuse.

Fidler is mad. He did not refuse his meat till yesterday morning. He has been tied in the hay barn at Little Deen this half year, but on Tuesday morning he broke his chain and got out of the window and came to the dogkenell and bitt Mistris, who had whelps in the stable, and then he was secur'd without doing further damage.   I am,

Your Lordship's most humble and most faithful servant,

Deen, April 30th, 1727.   DAN: EATON

[**135**]   [*Tuesday, 2 May, 1727.*][1]

My Lord,

Master James & Master Robert are very well. I receiv'd the honour of your Lordships of the 29th. We are very sorry that Lady Frances is no better.

I don't know whither Mr. Denshire has paid the 70£. to Mr. Child or not.

Alice[2] left Deen about six weeks since, when her year was up. So she was here just nine years. And my sister Theo is in her stead.

The reason why Corby Sale came to no more was bycause I would not let several trees be view'd. Tho' they were very old, yet as they were not decaying, I thought it better to let them stand unview'd till we saw how we could sell the very worst; which prov'd a good method, and we view'd fourteen trees more yesterday, which we sold after the rest were all gone. I think it is a great deal of pitty that there is not in this fine wood any oaks that are less than seventy years growth. If your Lordship does not take the method I formerly proposd of planting acorns in the vacancies, in two sales more there will not be an oak left. There is now forty trees more than we have taken which are full grown and will not improve by standing, but as there is no young ones, I thought it would be wrong to take the beauty of the wood all away at once.

We sold the bark to Mr. Peach at 2s. 6d. without any allowance for dodderels. Wee have likewise sold Stanion saplins, and the bark to Mr. Peach at 6.6 p. Li. And we came from Corby to Deenthorpe, where we sold all the timber we view'd in Burnt Coppice and the bark to Mr. Mun & Mr. Eddins at 4s. p. Li. And last night I set out ten of the most decay'd oak trees in Dibbins in Deen Park to be cut down for your Lordship's use, and the labourers are about them today. The bark we sold to Mr. Eddins & Mr. Mun at five guineas a scoe. I have not yet cast up the books, but as soon as I possibly can, I will send your Lordship an abstract of the whole account.

There may be but six pannells of wainscot of that side, or as many

---

[1] Dated from internal evidence. See **134**, and **136**.
[2] Alice Lightfoot. See **117**.

or as few as your Lordship pleases. If you please to name the number, the joiner shall make them accordingly, which will make no alteration in his bargain.

I saw Mr. Hawkins about a fortnight since, and he told me that he had bargained with two men to grub the riding in Bangroves, but they have not yet begun it.

I don't think John Black has any ill view in keeping his accounts after that manner; I belive it is owing to his bad memory, for he certainly forgets the method which your Lordship prescrib'd.

I never saw Deen Park so good a pasture as it is now, and the deer thrive very fast.

Edward Bullivant, Will Risbee, Junior, Widow Burrow, & Will Streadore have sign'd the agreement, so there is 27 have signd this and sixteen the other. There is eight to sign, three of which I believe I can answer for, but I doubt the other four will be inflexible.

I am glad my Lady has drawn a bill upon me.

I will set labourers about Priors Haw to morrow. Fidler died on Sunday; all the rest of the hounds are well.

I am your Lordships
   Most humble and most faithful servant,

Deen, May the second.   DAN: EATON

Lummis set forward for London last night; he is to stay by the way about the Dutchess's[1] business, but proposes to be with your Lordship on Fryday next.

[136]   [*Thursday, 4 May*, 1727.]

My Lord,

I have reieivd [*sic*] the honour of your Lordship's of the second. Master James and Master Robert Brudenell are very well, and Master Roberts ears run as they ought to do. We are very glad to find by a letter from Dan[2] that Lady Frances is much better. I causd the whelps to be drown'd and the bitch to be secur'd so soon as I knew that Fidler was mad. I did not send the ale as I proposd, for a jocky wagoner promis'd me to fetch it on Tuesday last, but he did not come. I had two jocky wagoners with me yesterday to let me know that they were ready to go to London when I should order them, so according to Dan's letter I will send to one of them to day that he shall set out either to morrow or Saturday.

Lummis will tell your Lordship more particularly of things than I can write; only the brick maker began to burn to day, and I hope to let your Lordship know by next Tuesdays post that there is a good kill full of bricks burnt.

The dales are all come from Peterborough, but I fear I must either go or send to Lin for Norway oak, for their is not enough of a sort at Peterborough to floor the dining room.

Philip Day has work'd a case for the sash door for the billiard room, and is going about the chimney. I wish your Lordship wou'd say

[1] The Duchess of Montagu.   [2] Dan Whitworth, the butler.

whither you would have a single sash or a large compass sash for the arch at the east end.

The horse breaker has the two colts in hand & says they will be very gentle soon.

We have not begun to burn lime yet, for the fore part of the kill fell down which we have been building and it is partly finish'd.

I have nothing else to inform your Lordship of at present.   I am,
        Your Lordship's most humble and most faithful servant,

Deen, May 4th, 1727.   DAN: EATON

[**137**]   [*Sunday,* 7 *May,* 1727.]

My Lord,
        Master James Brudenell & Master Robert are very well.

The grey mare has got a marefole with a star & blaze; it is a bay one.

The brick maker goes on very well. I believe the bricks are well burnt, but cannot tell certainly till they are cool enough to open.

To morrow is the rent day in Leicestershire; I hope the tenants will pay their rent well.

I have got a jocky wagon which will be in Town on Wednesday next to load the things that day; I have sent the ale by it.

About three months ago I was inrol'd as an attorney of the Court of Common Pleas. An attorney of credit, making a certificate of my capacity, and producing one of my letters in the Court, got it done without any manner of difficulty and with very little charge.   Your Lordship may probably think that I have some strange views by this proceeding; but I do assure your Lordship that [the^i] chiefest inducement to it was, that whereas I have for these seven years last past dispos'd of a great deal of mony upon mortgages, &c., to the general satisfaction and security of all my friends who have intrusted me, as well as my own advantage, my just fees have sometimes been denied me; and I, having no authority to practice, could not redeem them by law. Now that case is alter'd, for I have an attachment of privilege sign'd and seal'd; and I hope this may some time or other be of conveniency to your Lordship.   But I shall not endeavour to practice in any other way; for as your Lordship's house being pester'd with my clyents, which might probably be very numerous, must certainly be irksome to you, so consiquently I could never propose any such thing to my self.

I shall send the plans of the wainscot of the hall and chamber above it by the carrier to day.

Lummis's child that he had by Fell's daughter is dead.

I intend to send Will Wade to Grantham Holy-Thursday-Fare[1] to buy about 80 sheep, for I believe the Common will keep them. We have a most fine spring, and all sorts of grain very prosperous.

The hounds, spanniels & horses are all well.   I am,
        Your Lordship's most humble and most faithful servant,

Deen, May 7th, 1727.   DAN: EATON

---

[1] On Ascension Day, 11 May, 1727

[**138**]   [*Monday, 8 May, 1727.*][1]

My Lord,

    Munday morning. Master James & Master Robert Brudenell are very well; but yesterday about 3 o'clock the poor nurse[2] fell down in the stone court, it being wet and slippery, and broke both the bones of her arm about 3 inches above her right hand. I sent immediately for Mr. Fryer, who came and set it before eight. We do not suffer Master Robert to suck for these five or six days, for these things are always attended with a feaver. My mother and Mrs. Bradshaw will take care of the child, and the nurses sister is with her.

    Had it not been for this accident I had gone into Leicestershire last night, but now I am going this morning. I leave the two draughts[3] with this letter to come by the post to morrow morning. If your Lordship would have any alterations in the draughts, be pleasd to make them and send them down by the post again, for I have not an exact coppy of these two last. I am,

    Your Lordship's most humble and most faithful servant,

Deen, May 8th.

                             D: EATON

[**139**]   [*Thursday, 11 May, 1727.*]

My Lord,

    Master James & Master Robert are very well; and the nurse is intirely free from pain, and has not been at all feavourish as we could perceive, so that in a day or two the child may suck without any manner of danger. Her breasts have been very regularly drawn all this time, and Master Robert has born the loss of the pap with a great deal of patience.

    I never saw the Leicestershire tenants so backward in paying their rent as they were on Munday. There was but three of Stonton, six of Glooston, one of Cranoe, and six of Slawston tenants who paid in full. I receiv'd none of Richard Godfrey, Edward Worth, Thomas Watts, Thomas Orton, John Spencer, and Will Worth. It was Will Timson of Cranoe that clear'd his rent, and Mrs. Knight left but forty shillings unpaid. A particular bill of the arrears would be too long to trouble your Lordship with. I have promis'd the tenants a second visit upon the last day of this month, when I hope I shall bring the arrears into a narrow compass. This scarcity of mony among the farmers I believe was occasion'd by the badness of their crops of wheat & beans last year. They have no wheat to eat at Leicester but what comes out of other counties, and notwithstanding there is as fine crops upon the ground as ever were seen, yet my brother[4] sold there last Saturday for 5s. per strike, and I believe it will be no cheaper. The complaints made by the graziers are so many and so different that I think it not worth while to trouble your Lordship with them.

    The lime kill is substantially mended and fill'd, and to be fir'd this

---

[1] Dated by internal evidence. See **139-142**.
[2] Mrs. Townsend.
[3] Of wainscotting at Little Deene. See **140**.
[4] This is Stephen Eaton, Dan's brother.

morning. I had it rais'd about 20 inches higher, which will make it burn about six quarters more than it wood before.

I was last night at the brick kill, but it was so hot that the bricks could not be drawn.

We have begun to take down the small beer celler in order to secure it, for it would certainly have fallen in a short time. I have Robert Hibbins and five more, so that it will be finish'd soon.

The pavement that has layn expos'd to the weather so long in that place beside the billiard room I hope will most of it serve for paving the celler at Little Deen, and I shall cause it to be taken up for that purpose.

I have receiv'd the honour of your Lordship's of the 9th instant. Heathcock has taken nine young foxes in Jenkinson's Spinny by Lord Exeters desire, as he says; but I believe it was only by his Lordship's permission, upon his making complaints that they would destroy the game. He carried them to Burleigh, but what reward he receiv'd I can't tell.

We are very much concern'd for Lady Frances's illness. My mother fancys if her Ladyship was at Deen, her native air would prove the best phisick.

I will go to Collyweston to day as your Lordship orders me, and pay the sixty pounds and also your Lordships bill to Mr. Tryon.

I believe there will be more difficulty to make Corby people agree about choosing their refferrees, than with the refferrees when they are fix'd upon, to agree about the land to be exchang'd; for I take it that Jonah Chapman will be one of them, and he talks very reasonably about the affair.[1]

I am sorry Lummis's proceedings should be disagreeable to the Dutchess already. I don't doubt but he had your Lordship's wholsome advice as well as your assistance. What advice I was able to give him, I did it in writing as soon as I knew for whom he would be concern'd, but I found by his discourse when he was in the country that he left my letter at home.   I wish the intrepidity of his continual proceedings does not some time or other prove his overthrow; was he to be always in the right, there would not be such [a^d] [another^i] man living, but he often proposes things before he has consider'd the consequences of them.

The hounds, spaniels and horses are all well. I have nothing else to inform your Lordship of.   I am,

Your Lordship's most humble and most faithful servant,

Deen, May 11th, 1727.   DAN: EATON

[**140**]   [*Sunday*, 14 *May*, 1727.]

My Lord,

Mr. James and Mr. Robert are extreamly well, and the nurse continues free from pain and has not been at all feavourish, so that yesterday Mr. Robert began to suck again.   I receiv'd the honour of your Lordship's of the 11th instant.   We hope that Lady Frances is better, bycause your Lordship says nothing of her.

Thomas Nichols may go on with wainscotting his two rooms, for your Lordship seem'd not to dislike the manner of the wainscot, so he

[1] See **134, 135**.

has cut out the stuff. But Will Hawksby shall not go on with the other two rooms without your Lordship's particular directions. By them plans I sent last, your Lordship, whilst in London, may have other drawn to your mind as well as if you were in the country. There will be no inconveniency in staying but the prolonging of the time. I have set Hawksby and his two men to make shutters for the garret windows. The sashes are not yet painted over a second time, but Hawksby shall do them to morrow. They have taken no harm.

Your Lordship's letter did not come till after I was gone out yesterday into the sales, &c., so I could not measure the Bowling-green House,[1] but I will send the dimentions by the next post.

I went to Colliweston on Thursday last, but lost my labour, for all the family were gone to Luffenham. Mr. Burton[2] being very ill of the gout.

The bricks prove pritty well. There is about 18,000 of them, but they had not taken them all out of the kiln last night. They are not so high fired as they ought to be for outward work, but they will do very well for inward work. We shall make use of some of them for the small beer celler. The arch is taken down. I believe this poor brickmaker will prove as good as Horn was. He is very laborious and sober; and he and his wife, who works as hard as himself, lye in that hovell that is in the close, that they may be near their business, and I don't doubt but the next killfull will be well burnt, since he now knows the killn and the fuel. He is to have but 5s. a thousand for the bricks he makes of the clay the other man dug, and 6s. a thousand if he digs any fresh clay for another year.

The crops upon the Common are very hopeful, and I believe there is not one grub left alive. I never saw a finer crop than there is now likely to be where there were the most grubs last year. I causd some barly to be sown against Parkhole, and it is likely to be a very good crop.

Philip brought the two colts safe to Stroxton and seems to be highly delighted with them, especially with the grey one.

I intended to have gone to Collyweston to day, but it rains very fast and seems to be a set rain. We have not had too much rain yet, tho' the meadows last week were a little flooded. I am,

Your Lordship's most humble and most faithfull servant,

Deen, May 14th, 1727.   DAN: EATON

Wou'd your Lordship have the mares that have fold' coverd again this year? The hounds & spanniels are all well.

Wou'd your Lordship have the Kirkham mare turn'd to grass?

[**141**]   [*Tuesday*, 16 *May*, 1727.]

My Lord,

I receiv'd the honour of your Lordship's of the 13th instant. We are extreamly glad that Lady Frances is better. Master James & Master

---

[1] The measurements are given in **144**, where the building is described as the Green House.

[2] Bartholomew Burton, father-in-law of James Brudenell and of John Tryon of Collyweston.

Robert are very well, and Mr. Robert sucks again, for the nurse is very well.

The rack ways in Priors Haw are all brush'd up regularly, and the path all the way by Waterfalls side is grubb'd and leveld again nine foot wide.

Nanny Jill begs the favour of your Lordship to speak to Mr. Webber to get Dr. Purcel to pay her in[terest] due upon the 20£., and to declare in writing that the bond is good and that he acknowledges himself indebted to her 20£. upon it. For the declaration of trust which entitles her to the mony is so very much defac'd, that it is hard to know what the meaning of it is; and was the bond to be renew'd, the mony would be no longer at six per cent. If the Doctor shou'd refuse to do this, she desires that Mr. Webber would force him to pay in the mony.

We have in the gardens a very great quantity of fruit of all sorts. There was 17,500 bricks in the killn, and they are pritty good ones. Will Wade bought sixty five sheep at Grantham Fare. They seem to be such as will suit the Common very well.

I was yesterday in Priors Haw whilst Mr. Goods servant was tything the brush-wood that was cut out of the rack ways; he said he had orders to tythe the roots also, but I perswaded him to let them alone whilst I could see his master.

I went likewise to Mr. Hawkins and found him at home (I went on Fryday last but mist of him), and he assures me that he let the grubbing up of the roots in Bangr[oves] Riding to Sam Wells by the great three weeks ago. And he sent to him last night to know why he had not done them according to bargain, and the answer was that he had been very ill, which I believe was true; for I had heard before that he was sick. But I told Mr. Hawkins that there was no excuse any longer for it's not being done, for I could furnish him with six good labourers for that purpose. He [said] he would speak to Sam Wells about it. He said that he had receiv'd no orders from Lord Hatton about cutting down those five saplins that stand in the place and will spoil the prospect. I told him it was very plain that his Lordship intend[ed] all the trees to be cut down as well as the shrubs, or the riding would not answer the end, and he said he would write to his Lordship about it.

The Albermarston colt is very much fallen away in his flesh since he went to grass. [I] thought at first it was the Hornby colt's beating him that made him he did not thrive; but since there is so much grass, I fear he has got a surfeit. I have caus'd [him] to be taken up in order to have a drink or two. The Fielders colt and Lord Brudenells filly behave themselves very well, for the time. Will Abbot rides them any where; they are in good flesh.

Christopher Dexter dyed yesterday morning.   I am,
        Your Lordship's most humble and most faithful servant,

Deen, May 16th, 1727.   DAN: EATON

[**142**]   [*Thursday*, 18 *May*, 1727.]

My Lord,
    Mr. James and Mr. Robert are very well, and the nurse continues free from pain.   The goods came very safe, but I am very sorry that

your Lordship order'd me to send a wagon up when there was but 13 hundred.[1] I have paid Mr. Rowley and Mr. Tryon.

I was last night at Christopher Dexters burial, and I saw Mr. Hawkins, and he told me that to day the labourers would begin to grub the riding.

We are going forwar'd with the small beer celler as fast as possible. The lime is burnt, and I hope it is good.

I have receiv'd the honour of your Lordship's of the 16th. I believe it would be the best way for your Lordship to buy the colours ready ground in London, for I know they grind them there with a mill, and can afford them cheaper than any man can grind them by hand; and if you have different colours they may be easily mixt. Or you may pitch upon a proper colour and have it sent down thick, and some clear oil, and it may be made here fit for the brush without any trouble.

The alcove room is fit for workmen, but the lime is so hot that it cannot be drawn, so I can't tell whither it is right good or not. I believe it is, but I will let your Lordship know by the next post.

I will write to Mr. Tryon to day about returning the mony.

I have nothing material to tell your Lordship of any progress in Slawston affair. I believe an Act of Parliament will be the surest way to compleat it, but I could not hear of any thing done by Mr. Edwards since he came last into the country.

I will send for Hornby today, for I think that is better than to send the mares. We are very glad that Lady Frances is better and hope that Deen air will perfect her recovery. The post stays. I am,
Your Lordship's most humble and most faithful servant,

Deen, May 18th, 1727.   DAN: EATON

[**143**]   [*Sunday, 21 May,* 1727.]
My Lord,
I have enquir'd further about the paint and I find that what I wrote before was right, except that the clear oil may be bought as cheap here as at London, for it is made about two miles from Peterborough. But the buying of the colours in Town and making Hawksby work them up I am sure will save very near half the charge.

Hornby is come safe and has cover'd the black mare.

The lime proves very good and the kill much better than it was before, so the workmen may come as soon as they will.

They began to grub Bangroves Riding on Fryday, but yesterday they could not go on for the rain.

The inclos'd bill is the ballance of my account of Lincolnshire rents.

The hounds & spaniels are all well, and the deer in the park begin to look pritty clean.

I don't doubt but your Lordship will like Thomas Nichols's work. He goes on very well and very fast, and I believe will finish his bargain before the time limited.[2] I am,
Your Lordships most humble and most faithful servant,

Deen, May 21th, 1727.   D: EATON

---

[1] i.e. cwt.
[2] For the agreement between Dan Eaton (for Cardigan) and Thos. Nicholls, for panelling at Little Deene, see Appendix II.

[**144**]   [*Thursday, 25 May, 1727.*]

My Lord,

Mr. James Brudenell and Mr. Robert continue very well, and the nurses arm mends as fast as can be expected. I had a letter from Lummis on Munday, and he takes no notice of Lady Frances, so I hope she is recover'd.

Here is two brickmakers from Darby came to enquire for work. They seem'd to be clever fellows, so I perswaded our man to employ them under him, which he does, and one of them tempers the clay and the other molds. They do their work well, and one of them tells me that the man who run away[1] in diging up the clay did not dig deep enough, but left the best and strongest clay behind; and says that he is sure that some of the clay that is left unmov'd will make ridge tiles or pan tiles, and that he has often made these things, so he knows what he says to be right. But if that clay was mix'd with the other that they are now working up, the bricks would be abundantly harder than any of the old ones that were made by Horn; but these they make now will be partly such sort, or rather better. I cannot tell whither this will prove true or not, but I intend to make them break up as much of that strong clay as will make 1,000 bricks for a tryal.

Hornby has cover'd all the mares, and they are very well.

I should have sent your Lordship the dementions of the Green-house[2] before now, but I forgot, for which I beg your Lordship's pardon. It is 15ft. 2in. broad, 20ft. 10in. long, 13 foot to the foot of the cove, and 15 foot from the top of the ceiling to the floor.

We are going on with the celler and the billiard room. I have caus'd the pavement that lay out of doors near the billiard room, between that and the chappell, to be taken up, and there is almost enough of it to pave the celler at Little Deen.

There was thirty quarters of good lime in the kill, and better burnt than any we ever had before.

I have nothing else to inform your Lordship of at present.   I am,
     Your Lordship's most humble and most faithful servant,

Deen, May 25th, 1727.   DAN: EATON

I hope your Lordship has receiv'd mine of Sunday last wherein I sent two bills of exchange, one for 17£. 18s. 1d. for your Lordship, and the other for 25£.-0-0 for my Lady; both payable by Mr. Rogers in Hudsons Court on Great Tower Hill.

[**145**]   [*Sunday, 28 May, 1727.*]

My Lord,

Mr. James Brudenell and Mr. Robert are very well.   I have re-ceiv'd the honour of your Lordship's of 25th. It must certainly be the fault of the little boy that Will Walker sends for the letters that mine don't come to your Lordship's hands regularly. I have not mist a post

---

[1] Jonathan Lewtener. "Our man", above, is Will Newdall.
[2] Described as the Bowling Green House in **140**.

these six weeks, except Tuesday last, and he never stays for my letter unless it is on Thursdays, while I answer your Lordship's by the same post.

I sent your Lordship by the last Thursdays post the dimentions of the Greenhouse.

It will be much the best for me to send a jocky wagon for the goods, unless your Lordship has a load of something to come to Town, for the expences of the journey will come to as much as the load is worth bringing to Deen. I can send a jocky wagon to load any day your Lordship shall order it.

Philip will bring to Stamford the Kirkham mare for your Lordship, the grey mare for Mr. Billinge, the bay mare for John, and the Kirkham guelding for himself, besides which there is only the Bath guelding, & Lummis's guelding that is in the cart, that can go to London for servants.

Fielders colt and the filly are perfectly well broke. I rid the colt my self on Fryday to Corby Sale, and he behaves himself very well. So we have done with the horse-breaker. My horse's old lameness returns so often that he will hardly bare five miles riding.

My Lord Rockinghams steward gave the tenant of Corby possitive orders to turn his cattel into the youngest Southwood on Munday last, which he did, and made way for the rest of the Common cattel, which Thomas Bell had kept out till that time. 'Tis talk'd here that my Lady Sands resents your Lordship's not applying to her about this affair sooner.

The hounds are all well, and the horses. The red horse seems to have recover'd his surfeit; he lookes very well, and his eye is almost well. And the young colt that I caus'd to have two drinks is better; but I am forc'd to have him kept in Halbanks, where he rests very well with one companion, for the colt in the paddock us'd to beat him so very much, I believe that made [him*] he could not thrive.   I am,

Your Lordship's most humble and most faithful servant,

Deen, May 28th, 1727.   DAN: EATON

[**146**]   [*Tuesday, 30 May,* 1727.]

My Lord,

I receiv'd the honour of your Lordships letter of the 27th instant.

Mr. James and Mr. Robert Brudenell are very well, and the nurse as well as can be expected.

I think it will be better to send the horses to London than to lodge them at Biggleswade, so they shall be at London on Saturday.

I see very plainly that my letter of Thursday last never came to your Lordship's hands, and yet the boy denies that he was too late for the post.

I will get Mr. Childs note from Mr. Denshire and send it to your Lordship by the next post.

The table leaf that slides is six foot one inch long and four foot two inches broad, and the liberary table is six foot one inch long, four foot one inch broad, and two foot six inches high.

My Lord Brudenells old hunting saddle is at Oxford, but T. Parsons has one ready made which I think will suit his Lordship pritty well.

I have nothing else to inform your Lordship of at present.   I am,
Your Lordship's most humble and most faithful servant,

Deen, May 30th, 1727.   DAN: EATON

[**147**]   [*Thursday*, 1 *June*, 1727.]

My Lord,
Master James & Mr. Robert Brudenell are very well.
I was at Stonton yesterday according to appointment. There is still
in arrear 130£., whereof Will Worths & Thomas Watts's of Glooston
is above 60£.
I have receiv'd the honour of your Lordship's letter of the 30th last.
I intended if I had not receiv'd it to have sent Edward Vine to morrow
with three horses to London, and he may come back on foot; so they
will certainly be there on Saturday. And I hope to meet your Lordship
at Stilton on Munday morning as you order us.
It is the time that the people of Corby us'd to turn in there cattle
into the wood,[1] it being seven years old, but Thomas Bell kept the fences
good in hopes to have kept them out till your Lordship came, bycause
there were some good deer there.
One of Mrs. Walkers sons wants to come to London to stay, so he
shall help Ned with the horses.
I writ to Mr. Denshire for the bill and sent him his note, but he
says that his son had orders to deliver it to your Lordship on Munday
last.
Mr. Edwards is gone into Ireland, but made no proceedings in
Slawston affair before he went.
The continual rains have done the corn in Leicestershire a great
deal of damage, but their beans were never better. The meadows are
all flooded. I have nothing else to inform your Lordship of at present.
I am,
Your Lordship's most humble and most faithful servant,

Deen, June the first, 1727.   DAN: EATON

There is little evidence as to Cardigan's whereabouts between 2 June and
5 July. He was at Stilton for the races early in June. Elmsall sent him money to
London on the 14th and wrote to him at Deene on the 27th.
Dan's letter of 6th July shews that he himself was as busy as usual in
and about Deene, but also that he had been engaged in valuing a property at
Little Ponton in Lincolnshire, the purchase of which Cardigan had under
consideration.

---

[1] i.e. Southwood, referring to rights of common. See **145**.

[**148**]   [*Thursday, 6 July,* 1727.]

My Lord,

We have made the arch in the little room at the Bowling-green House and pav'd the celler with the square paving tile, but I think to pave the room with some of the old freestone pavement. Thomas Nichols has done as much at the two rooms as is proper to be done at present, bycause the stuff for the floors & doors ought to be as dry as possible before they are finish'd. So he is about the sash and sash door for the billiard room. The bricks in the last kiln prove as good as possible and I don't doubt but they will always be so, since the poor man knows the right method now. There was 16,800 in this last burning.

I went to Kettering last Fryday to let Mr. Remmington know that the bill was not paid by Mr. Rogers; & he told me that Mr. Rogers wrote him word as soon as the bill was drawn, in answer to his letter of advice, that he would pay it. I find that Mr. Remmington has a great deal more mony in Mr. Rogers's hands than these bills came to, but if Mr. Rogers's credit sinks, it would be very adviseable to return the bill upon Mr. Remmington. There is thirty days allow'd for it by law, which are now almost expir'd. But if the person that has the bill should threaten Mr. Rogers that if he does not immediately pay the bill he will return it, I am apt to think it will be paid.

I have James Ashleys accounts, & I find that your Lordship & John Black & myself have paid more by an hundred pounds than your Lordships share of the last years expence amounts to.[1]

We have got about two thirds of the hay in Sheep Close very well, and all the rest will be got to morrow if the weather continues good. Last week was very bad weather for it, but it has not receiv'd much damage.

Mr. Tankred & I think that our valuation of Little Ponton was to the tip top of its present value. The chiefest part of the expence of improving it will consist in making good the old fences and making several new ones. There is 1200 acres which we have not valued, at half a crown an acre, which with due management in about seven years or eight years time may be made worth ten shillings an acre at least, for it is right land for saintfoyn;[2] and there is 400 acres which will produce clover without any charge more than what the advantage of plowing would defray,—and I think if a right method is taken the improvement will certainly succeed. But these improvements will not be perpetual, for without continual care the land will dwindle into primitive barrenness and part of the charge of improving may be lost, if ever there is a set of bad tenants and an indolent agent upon the estate. By this your Lordship may know how to make the purchase for yourself, or to advise your friend.[3] I am,

Your Lordship's most humble and most faithful servant,

Deen, July 6th, 1727.   DAN: EATON

---

[1] Cardigan's share of hunting expenses at Stroxton. See Appendix 5.
[2] See C. Kirkham, *Two Letters to a Friend*, and Introduction, p. xxxviii.
[3] Cardigan purchased this estate from Mrs. Thorold in 1727: Lincoln R.O., Thorold 2/3, No. 20.

*From July to early October, 1727, Cardigan and his family were at Deene.
Brickmaking was going on steadily: on 28 July the brickmaker Will Newdall
—always referred to as "the poor fellow" or "the poor laborious fellow"— was
paid £8. 8s. 6d. for making 33,700 bricks (ASR 252).*

[149]   [*Tuesday, 3 October, 1727.*]

My Lord,
    Master James and Master Robert Brudenell are very well.   I have
let the close[1] that Philips intends to quit at Lady Day to two men of
Gretton, for one year at the rent. I know them to be very good husbands.
They are to make one new hedge to preserve the young quick, and
Thomas Meadows the other, & they promise to be good tenants as long
as they live, if your Lordship shall think proper.
    I have been at Oakly Woods and have bargained with the labourers
about stubbing the roots in the broadest riding for 2s. 4d. per acre, and
for the narrow padways in proportion. I believe the roots will pay two
thirds of the charge.
    Wee are removing the bricks as fast as possible, and in about seven
days I think they will be all at Little Deen.   I think it will be the best
way to bargain with the joiners to make the stair case by the great. This
indeed is an uncommon way of proceeding, but as I can compute what
the workmanship will come to when the maner of finishing it is laid
down, it will certainly prevent uneasiness in your Lordship, when you
are sure the workmen can't wrong you by being idle. And it will save me
a great deal of trouble in looking after them, for I shall take care to describe the method in which they are to proceed in such a manner in the
contract, if I make one, that they shall want no further instructions till
the work is finish'd.   I think it will be the best way to let the first flight,
that leads to the best chambers, be done by Thomas Nichols, and the
other flight, that goes into the garrets, be done by Hawksby's men seperately. I have spoke to Thomas Nichols about this, and he is willing to go
on after this manner; but begs that it may be by your Lordship's command, for he thinks that Hawksby would take it ill if he knew that he
seperated himself from his men of his own accord. I shall compute upon
the model of the new staircase at Deen, and shall bargain on Munday
next if I have not your Lordships commands to the contrary.
    I sent to the post for the letters on Sunday night, but there being
none, I conclude there wanted no linnen.   I am,
        Your Lordship's most humble and most faithful servant,

Deen, October 3rd, 1727.   DAN: EATON

I sent a packet with two letters for your Lordship by the last post.

[150]   [*Monday, 9 October, 1727.*]

My Lord,
    Master James & Master Robert Brudenell are very well.   Philip
Day & Robert Hibbins are both very ill of the feavour, so that there is

---
[1] Winsal's Close.

nothing done either at the grate in the liberary or dressing room. But Faulkner's men have been here and have put up the two chimney pieces at Little Deen very well. I paid them 20s., and for their board at Hawksby's I put the 20s. at the foot of the bill which Mr. Faulkner will shew your Lordship.

Mr. Lloyd, Mr. Joy's steward, sent to me on Fryday last to desire me to value Mr. Worley's wood that is standing, which I readily agreed to, bycause he told me that Mr. Arney was to be employ'd with me, who I knew had the carracter of a very ingenious man in that way. And I thought that if I got no mony for my trouble, yet my time would not be lost, for hereby my notions of the value of wood wou'd either be im-prov'd or confirm'd. I know I can discover the quantity of wood in a tree as redily as any man, but since I never knew the value of it from any but Lummis & Thomas Bell, I thought more experience might be necessary. And yesterday I had the satisfaction of agreeing so well with Mr. Arney that he consented to set down above 200 of the trees we valued, at the price I first named. I think we shall be about four days more before we have done.

As to Mr. Worley, he is utterly ruined, unless he has some estate or mony that no one hereabout knows of. His person is under an arrest for an action of 475£., and all his goods under seizure for rent. Besides there is a very round ballance of an account due to Mr. Joy, and several bond debts in the country, which all the visible effects will not amount to by a great deal.[1]

I hope I shall bargain with the joiners to morrow about the stair-case, if I don't receive a letter from your Lordship to forbid me. We have remov'd about two thirds of the bricks, but the wether is so wet that the carting has made the way very bad, and I fear we shall be foild to finish them. If I can't get them all carryed, I will cover the rest with straw where they are till frost comes. The pond bank in the park is finish'd very well.

I am your Lordship's
Most humble and most faithful servant,

Deen, October 9th, 1727.   DAN: EATON

[**151**]   [*Wednesday, 11 October, 1727.*]

My Lord,
Master James & Master Robert Brudenell are very well. I have computed the charge of making the first story of the stair-case and finishing the passage at the foot, and likewise that between the two best rooms, and wainscot, window jaums, &c., for the nethermost sash, all which are to be done by Thomas Nichols; but I have not yet actually contracted with him. I have [been[i]] very particular in my computation, and I find that to finish both the carv'd and joiners work of this story will come to 21£., and the other story will come to about 16£. if it is done in the same manner I propose. As soon as the bargain is sign'd I will send your Lordship a copy of it, and likewise of my computation upon which it is to be founded. Thomas Nichols desires to go a way for this week, and then he will stay while he has finish'd his part.

---

[1] See **3, 5,** and **7.**

Your Lordship may think it comes to a great deal of mony, for indeed till I had computed exactly, I thought two thirds of what it amounts to would have been sufficient, but I am convinc'd that it cannot be well done and cheaper. I don't fear but your Lordship will like the method in which it is to be done when you have seen it describ'd in the contracts I shall make.

I am your Lordship's
Most humble and most faithful servant,

Deen, October 11th, 1727.   D: EATON

Here follows a gap of nearly seven weeks.

27 NOVEMBER, 1727 — 30 NOVEMBER, 1727

[**152**]   [*Monday, 27 November, 1727.*]

My Lord,
When I was at Stamford last Munday I bought 20 quarters of very good coak-malt, and we have got ten quarters of it home. I gave 1£. 15s. 9d. [per quarter].[1] I am glad I happend to do so, for our ale-houses give forty shillings a quarter [for all] they brew. I sent to Mr. Whiteing to have had the 20 quarter he profer'd me at 1£. 16s. [. . . per quarter], but it was all sold. I saw him yesterday and he assur'd me he sold most of that at [. . . .] per quarter. Nevertheless he says he will send in two brewings at 1£. 17s. 6d. per quarter if your Lordship pleases. I told him I would let your Lordship know, and he gave me a weeks time to send him an answer. Both his malt and his measure are good, and I would advise your Lordship to have it. He will not part with any more than two brewings at that price. I am sorry I did not buy the first 20 quarter when I might, for barly here is 30s. per quarter. We have empty vessels for 30 hogsheads and there is [just] sixty full ones.

I sent to Weldon for the plow, and tho' when John Peak saw it there was not above an hours work to do at it, yet it was not finish'd; but I shall have it home today.

Mr. Wright of Stanwick (the person I told your Lordship of) is here. The person [he has] 25£. a year of in Stanwick is his cosen, and always told him that whensoever [he] desir'd it, he would cancel his lease, wherein there is five years unexpir'd, but he refuses to be so good as his word. Nevertheless he has some hopes of prevailing upon a young man in that town to take the farm off of his hands. [If so, he will] gladly embrace this oppertunity of making himself easy at Ponton; and in the mean time, he says he will wait upon your Lordship if you desire it, and give you what instructions he is able as to improving the estate.

The children's coat maker has sent a bodice for Master James, that my sister[2] might make marks where it was too big or too little. But he

[1] The edge of this letter is partly torn away, and missing words throughout have, where possible, been supplied conjecturally in square brackets.
[2] Theophila Eaton.

did not send word how to direct to him, so we cannot send it again.
I am going to day to meet Lummis to look over Wards and Pywell's farmes. Mr. Worley's quick stock is to be sold to day, so I have sent Will Wade to buy two or three of the best cows for your Lordship if he can.
I am your Lordship's
Most humble and most faithful servant,

Deen, November 27th, 1727.   DAN: E[ATON]

[**153**]   [*Thursday*, 30 *November*, 1727.]

My Lord,
Master James and Master Robert Brudenell are very well, and as merry as possible.
Thomas Brampton of Stanion was here yesterday morning and told me his case about his fathers and mother's wills, which I believe will ruin him if he cannot agree with his brothers & sisters in a peacable way. For the case is this: his father dyed, and in his will left all the children certain legacy's, and his mother sole executrix with the remainder to herself. This will was in due time put into the hands of Mr. Goode, who was then the nearest surrogate, in order to be registred. His mother dyed soon after, and in her will left all her children legacy's different from what their father had left them, and him sole executor with the remainder to himself. And he took upon himself the executorship of this last will of his mother's, which in my opinion brought the executorship of his fathers will upon him in course, for was his father's will invalid, his mother had no power to make one, and then the personal estate ought to have been equally divided amongst the children. But now he has all his father's legacy's to pay and likewise his mothers, which amount to near 500£., which I believe is full as much as all the effects are worth.
The surrogate may be fin'd in court for the neglect of his duty in not registring the will as he ought to have done, but I don't think that neglect would destroy the will, for if so, every mans effects would be in a surrogates power absolutely. The reason why I have given your Lordship this trouble is bycause I think it concerns you as to the farm, and if you think proper to interfere, it may be a means to keep quietness.
John Peak was with Fletcher, who broke the lock from Priors-Haw gate, at Oundle before Major Creed, who said very little to him, but made him pay about seven shillings. I have survey'd both the plow'd grounds upon the Common. I have been very particular in taking seperate dimentions of the grass ground in those two closes, but have not yet cast them up. The hogs in Bandyslade are all very fatt and I think fit to kill when your Lordship pleases.
We have got the new plow home and it will answer the end when the hills are fitt to cut, but they are so hard now for want of rain that they don't do rightly. Lummis will tell your Lordship our thoughts upon Pywell's & Ward's farms, &c., when he comes to Stroxton. I have nothing else to inform your Lordship of but that Robert Dain and John Risby of Corby starve the hounds they keep. I am,
Your Lordship's most humble and most faithful servant,

Deen, November 30th, 1727.   DAN: EATON

P.S. Will Bell is willing to undertake the carriage of the four hogsheads of wine from London for five guineas, and is endeavouring to get loading thither. So I shall want directions for him, where the wine is.

I have a little pond in my farm which Mr. Joseph Ly[n]wood put some carp into about six years a go and I had a mind to see what was become of them. So I took John Hinks with the little casting net and we caught sixteen brace of little ones, most of which I believe were bred there. I put three brace in again, and brought thirteen brace and put them into the pond in the garden which is stock'd with carp. Some of them were not above two inches long, and I believe there is a great many such small ones in my pond; but the net was so old and torn that they got through it. I hope this pond will be of great service in breeding of carp, for I don't fear but I could make it breed above five hundred brace in a year.

A gap in Dan's letters may usually be presumed to indicate Cardigan's presence at Deene, but from 1st December, 1727 until 15th January, 1729, not a letter has survived. Other correspondence shows that Cardigan was at Cottesmore in late December, 1727, and early January, 1728, and at Stroxton all through February (Bru. MSS. F.iii. 181, 182, 185-8). During April and May, 1728, several attendances at the House of Lords are recorded, and from June to September Mr. Elmsall wrote frequently to the Earl at Deene, unsuccessfully urging him to visit his Yorkshire estates.

15 JANUARY, 1729 — 25 JANUARY, 1729

[**154**]   [*Wednesday, 15 January, 1728/9.*]

My Lord,
    John Taylor of Corby sends me word that he cannot take Wades land in Leicestershire, so I will indeavour to agree with George Taleby about it to morrow.   I have order'd George Nunns to meet me at Slawston to morrow to make things more inteligible in the survey book, which I shall send to London on Sunday next. I have got the books of Weldon Court.[1]   Mr. Walter is discharg'd from being steward and Mr. Norgrave from being bailif to the Duke of Montagu.
    We are going to view Oakly Sale to day. I will not sell one stick of it to any body that ha[-*d*]th not paid [for*i*] the wood last year.   Mr. Eastway tells me that John Bosden of Woethorpe Lodge is so ill that he thinks he cannot live.   I have paid Mr. Orme four guineas for the weather glass; he told my Lady that was what he bargained for. He has mended the old one, but did not ask any thing for doing it.
    I have inclos'd the dogkenell expence. I can not make it regular by cause I don't know certainly when it began, or how much of it is charg'd in the account stated.   Mr. Wright is very willing to accept of

---
[1] The manor court.

fifty shillings a year till Mr. John Lynwoods debt is discharg'd.   I have not seen Robert Jones yet, but David Black came last night to let me know that he will wait upon your Lordship as soon as you return, to sign his bargain.

I am your Lordship's
Most humble and most faithful servant,

Deen, January 15th, 1728.   D: EATON

[*Seal*]

[**155**]   [*Saturday, 18 January, 1728/9.*]

My Lord,
We have view'd Oakly Sale, which comes to 70£. 00. 0. We have appointed Thursday next for the sale day. Thomas Baily and Rice & Meadows, &c., are very uneasy at their being deny'd any part of this sale before they have paid their arrears. They say if your Lordship knew the cause of their being behind you wou'd excuse them, but I have told them what they must trust to. I believe we have order'd the pay day at Corby the same day (viz: 27th instant) that your Lordship has orderd for the receipt of Little Ponton rents; if so, we shou'd order John Clark to appoint another day.

I have been at Slawston and have enquir'd into the several things that wanted explanation in the survey book, so shall send the book to Mr. Brudenell to morrow. I find that we shall not meet with much difficulty to agree with any of the free-holders, except with Widow Newby. They were all with me and seem very well pleasd with the affair. And that poor widow is very willing to comply with anything, but she is only jointur'd in the estate, and the heir her son is a very obstinate fellow. Mr. Elliot had been with all the free holders before me and had explain'd the advantages which every one of them must certainly reap by the enclosure, &c.

There is one Mr. Lee (who bought the Meeting House of Mr. Lummis, who now lives at Corby, and who Mr. Peircy and my Lord Widdrington know very well) wants a farm either of tillage or grazing ground. So I sent Will Dunmore with him to see Orton's and Wades land; and he does not dislike it, but desires time till Munday to consider of it. I believe he intends to marry, for he seem'd very desirous of an house, and was well pleasd when I told him that in a years time at the most there wou'd be a very good one in Glooston for him; for I begin now to think that it is impossible for Mrs. Watts to continue in the farm. I did not see George Taleby, but I hear by several that he says he will not take the land without some rent abated.

I am your Lordship's
Most humble and most faithful servant,

Deen, January 18th, 1728.   D: EATON

[*Direction endorsed:—*]
    To the Right Honble. the Earl of Cardigan.

[*Seal*]

[**156**]   [*Saturday*, 18 *January*, 1728/9.]

My Lord,
     Mr. Janvers, being much out of order, desires me to acquaint your
Lordship that the coach horses are all very well; and Whitefoot, the
horse that was at grass, is rowell'd under the belly, and a wedge put into
Ball's foot according to your Lordship's last orders. Whitefoot will be
purg'd next week, but the farrier is of opinion that Woodcock and the
colt ought not to be purg'd these ten days yet; for while he was at the
Duke of Rutland's they never purg'd such sort of horses till the beginning of February. But that is to be according to the commands which
your Lordship shall be pleasd to send by the return of this messenger.
     Mr. Vane's filly's first rowell runs very well now, but at first it was
nothing but water, so that taking so well, he has thought proper to put
one more into the inside of each thigh. She is better than she was. John
Gooding was yesterday at the Common and brings word that the horses
there are all well. Mr. Janvers has nothing further to say worth your
Lordship's knowledge.
          I your Lordships [*sic*]
               Most faithful servant,

January 18th, 1728.   D: EATON

[*Direction endorsed:*—]
     To the Right Honble. the Earl of Cardigan.

[*Seal*]

[**157**]   [*Monday*, 20 *January*, 1728/9.]

My Lord,
     I receiv'd the honour of your Lordship's letter. I have sent the
survey book.   I have sent to order Harringworth carryer to come to me
to talk with him about the carriage of your Lordship's goods. For admit
that this present carrier was honest, it is very inconvenient his living so
far off, and Harringworth carrier can come thro' Deen with his cart or
wagon instead of going by Bulwick whensoever there is occasion for it,
and it will be easier for him to send hither every Sunday.   I think it
will be better to stop the mony that Kettering carrier has taken more
than his due, than to arrest him for it.
     I know Lee's cercumstances are good, but if he does not agree to
day, I will write to George Taleby and send my servant with it to
morrow.   I have sent by James 52£. 10s. 0d. according to your Lordships order.   There was 29½ brace of jacks came from Burleigh all
alive; they were about 19 inches long, one with the other.   Weldon
Court Day is on Thursday next, so I must send the books to Mr.
Plumpton before that time, but he will deliver them to your Lordship
whensoever you please.   I am,
          Your Lordship's most humble and most faithful servant,

Deen, January 20th, 1728.   D: EATON

My Lord

We have Sold all the Underwood in Oakly Sale and
I have got the mony for it within a very trifle. Wee have view'd
Park hole which comes to £99..00..0. We have besides Stanion Labourers
18 men from Gretton planting Acorns in Corby hill so that will be
finish'd in right time. I did not know of the Carrier Chatteris's coming
to your Lordship or I shou'd have writ by him. I believe your Lordship
will like the terms he proposes to carry the Goods at, he is always
in Summer to carry the Venison from Oundle to London in 24 hours
to Deliver oisters &c at Deen that come from London every Saturday
night; to Send a man here every Sunday, and to come thro' Deen with
his cart whenever requir'd, and Several other conveniencies there will
be by employing him, which I will let your Lordship know to Morrow
he is not to expect the carr of any Considerable Quantity of Goods at a
time, for then I told him your Lordship always employ'd a Jockey
Wagon which Carryed them much Cheaper than 6 pcent. I
have nothing else worth writing.
                    I am Your Lordship's
                              Most humble and
                                  Most faithful
                                      Servant
Deen January 25 1728.   Dan: Eaton

LETTER OF DANIEL EATON TO LORD CARDIGAN.
(¾ original size)

[Facing p. 133]

[**158**]   [*Saturday, 25 January, 1728/9.*]

My Lord,

We have sold all the underwood in Oakly Sale and I have got the mony for it within a very trifle. Wee have view'd Park Hole,[1] which comes to 99£. 00s. 0d. We have, besides Stanion labourers, 18 men from Gretton planting acorns in Corby Hill, so that will be finish'd in right time.

I did not know of the carrier Chatteris's coming to your Lordship or I shou'd have writ by him. I believe your Lordship will like the terms he proposes to carry the goods at: he is always in summer to carry the venison from Oundle to London in 24 hours; to deliver oisters, &c., at Deen that come from London every Saturday night; to send a man here every Sunday; and to come thro' Deen with his cart when'ever requir'd. And several other conveniencies there will be by employing him, which I will let your Lordship know to morrow. He is not to expect the carriage of any considerable quantity of goods at a time, for then I told him your Lordship always employ'd a jockey wagon, which carryed them much cheaper than 6s. per cent. I have nothing else worth writing.

I am your Lordship's

    Most humble and most faithful servant,

Deen, January 25th, 1728.   DAN: EATON

Here comes the longest gap in the whole series of letters—over two years, until 27th April, 1731. Early in 1729 Cardigan was at Deene, as he wrote tartly from there to Hatton about the exchange of woods which had still not been achieved (B.M. Add. MSS. 29,569, fo. 102, 31 Mar. 1729). In April he made several attendances at the House of Lords, but all through that summer he was at Deene, apparently putting off a visit to Yorkshire from month to month. Mr. Elmsall's letters (Bru. MSS. F.iii. 202-209, 211-215) asked with increasing urgency for a visit from the Earl or from some responsible person who would help him to value farms and woods, and in the autumn of 1729, when Cardigan seems to have been at Stroxton, we learn from ASR 253 that it was Dan who eventually visited Yorkshire. On 9 October, 1729, the Earl was at Deene. (B.M. Add. MSS. 29,569, fo. 112.) By the autumn of this year it is evident from the payments for furniture and fittings for Little Deene recorded in the accounts (ASR 253) that the house had at last been completed.

During April and the first half of May, 1730, Cardigan was in London (Journals of the House of Lords, XXIII). On 6th May he and his friends signed an important agreement which regulated their previously informal association for fox hunting over each other's lands in Lincolnshire, Leicestershire, Rutland and Northamptonshire. The parties to the agreement were the Duke of Rutland, the Earl of Gainsborough, the Earl of Cardigan, Lord Gower and Lord Howe. Cardigan was in Northamptonshire "Parliamenteering for Sir Justinian Isham" in (probably) late May. On 7th July Lord Brudenell's wedding took place in London (C.P.) and the Earl apparently stayed on there for the rest of the month (Bru. MSS. F.iii. 219-221). His whereabouts in late summer and autumn are uncertain, but from November 1730 to March 1731 he and his family were at Bath, as we see from their laundry bills there (Bru. MSS. xi.

---

[1] See Index of Places, under Wood Names.

1-9; xvii. 1-5). Dan's marriage took place in February, 1731, while Lord
Cardigan was still at Bath. By mid-March the Earl was back in London (Bru.
MSS. F.iii. 222).

27 APRIL, 1731 — 13 MAY, 1731

[**159**]   [*Tuesday, 27 April,* 1731.]

My Lord,
      I bought a cow and calf yesterday at Brigstock Fare to put the
young cow calf to. The other cows take their calves very well.   I cou'd
not have sold the young bull that I have kept so long for above three
pounds, so I have brought him home again and will have him gelt to
morrow. I think there was not one in the Fare so good by forty shillings;
no body found falt with him but that he was too big for them.   The
cow I have bought will keep the calf very well. She cost me 3£. 18s. 6d.
Her calf is about a fortnight old.
      I thank God I have had no return of the fever since your Lord-
ship left Deen. I took a swet the night before, which I believe did me
good, and which prevented my waiting on your Lordship the morning
your Lordship went away, which I hope your Lordship will pardon.
      We have finish'd the dividing of the Widow Harrisson's ground for
Palmer according to the bargain I made with him, and the labourers are
securing the young quick at the Common.   The weather being very
fine, cattel sold very well at Brigstock.   Some day this week we shall
begin to view the oaks, for the sap runns freely. We shall have but a very
small quantity this year. There are a few trees in Stonton Wood to be
taken down which we shall go and sell next week.
      I have ask'd David Black the reason why he seem'd so indifferent
to your Lordship about the taking of Thomas Meadows's ground[1]; and
he told me that he cou'd not say, but that he thought the grounds both
together were worth the mony, but that Tom was so great a rogue, if he
was to take the grounds willingly, he should expect to suffer some
private mischief by him.
      Tom has made a very great bustle last week, endeavouring to make
his man John Noble eat his words, which he had perswaded him to do,
but honest John having been so very open in declaring that he cou'd
hang him if he pleas'd, Tom found he could not stop the mouths of all
who heard him, he thought proper to let the affair drop. But first he
declar'd he had got a warrant from Major Creed to bring several before
him who had talk'd after that manner; but I have a great deal of reason
to believe that he never apply'd to Major Creed for a warrant.   I do
not think that Tom ever rob'd upon the highway, but I doubt your
Lordship's park has suffer'd by him, for he would not have taken his
man Noble into his bosome again had he not had cause to fear the consequence of his threatnings; for John was never more free with him than
he was to his face before a great many people.
      I have got the young white bull and will keep him as well as I can,

---

[1] Part of Winsal's Close.

and return your Lordship many thank [sic] for the use of him. He wou'd have been admir'd at Brigstock, but I believe no-body wou'd have bought even him.

I am, my Lord,

    Your Lordship's most humble and most faithfull servant,

Deen, April 27th, 1731.   DAN: EATON

[160]   [Sunday, 2 May, 1731.]

My Lord,

    I heard that Lummis was to be at Northampton on Fryday, and I cou'd not tell when I might have an oppertunity of seeing him again. So I beg'd leave to go to meet him; and before I return'd, my Lady had receiv'd your Lordship's letter directed to me from New Market, and had been so good as to send orders to Brightman according to the contents of it by Mr. Eastway.

    I have appointed Tuesday next for viewing at Corby Sale and have order'd Robert Jones to assist us; and we shall view the saplins at Oakly Wood on Wednesday and have the sale day on Saturday, bycause the bark runns very well.   I think we shall go to Stonton either Thursday or Fryday next to sell those trees there, for the sooner they are cut down the better. If any mistakes happen hereafter in the viewing of either timber or underwood, I will be answerable for them my self without leaving any room to blame anybody else, but I think by the method we have always taken there never can happen any mistakes in the value of the timber. But I must confess that in the underwood there might.   I shall do my best to get the Northamptonshire arrears.

I am, my Lord,

    Your Lordship's most humble and most faithful servant,

Deen, May 2d, 1731.   DAN: EATON

[161]   [Thursday, 13 May, 1731.]

My Lord,

    I find that Waterfield, the late miller of Stanion, when he left the wind mill, took out the brass boxes which the gudeons of the wheels run in, and now the present miller wants to make use of it, he cannot. When I went to see that the mill was in repair at his leaving it, I could not discover this fraud bycause the boxes are always conceald. Perhaps when he comes to be examined why he took them away, he may plead that he bought them; but then it must have been in the stead of others that had been there before, and I think he might as well have taken the wheels themselves. In all probability they were worth 3£. 0. 0.

    He likewise holds a cottage which always was rented with the mill and which is much better worth the rent than the mills are. I thought that Waterfield & the present miller had agreed about the holding of the cottage, but find that Waterfield never made him any allowance for it; and it is a great inconveniency to the mill, for without the cottage, the miller has no right to turn an horse into the field. I let your Lordship know this bycause the miller wants relief in this last article very much. But as to the wind mill, I think it wou'd be more for your Lordship's advantage to sell it than to keep it in repair, for it has not gone these two years, & the miller can pay his rent without it, for he wou'd never want water if the dam was but scowered, and I think the mill is worth 50£., and it stands in a bad place for wind.

Nicholas Harrisson's widow prays that she may have either the cottage in Deenthorpe wherein Joseph Starsmore lives or that wherein Widow Starsmore lives, they being both inhabitants in Deen, and that either of them may have the rooms your Lordship design'd for her in Deen. She is willing to pay the rent for Joseph Starsmore's cottage, which is advanc'd to thirty shillings a year, or to pay any rent your Lordship shall be pleas'd to fix upon Widow Starsmores, who never yet paid any. I have not given her any encouragement upon this head bycause I could not tell what reasons your Lordship may have for not complying with her desires. She likewise designs to quit the Riding next Lady Day, but wou'd be glad to leave it at Midsummer next if she could get any body to take it off of her hands; and she desir'd me to speak to David Black about it, but I wou'd not without first acquainting your Lordship about it. She says she has lost three cows and several sheep since she has had it, which makes her afraid to hold it any longer.

Dan Smith has done the wall at Little Deen with slates very well, and I believe when your Lordship has seen it you will have all the rest of the walls done so. Philip Day has done the church porch. We have plow'd the land by the plantation in the park to make it fit for turnips. The gardener return'd on Munday last. The park is now in perfect beauty.

I am, my Lord,
Your Lordship's most humble and most faithful servant,

Deen, May 13th, 1731.   DAN: EATON

During this ten month gap in Dan's letters we learn from other sources that Cardigan was at Deene a good deal between 29 May and 2 August, 1731 (Mont. Corr. I, pp. 113, 115-119). In a long series of letters to him William Elmsall made detailed arrangements for his visit to Yorkshire and expressed his anxiety about his master's deteriorating health (Bru. MSS. Fiii. 224-231). In August Cardigan stayed for about a week at Haigh Hall, one of his Yorkshire seats, and although ill health then forced him home he was well enough to hunt for part of the next winter from Stroxton. On 22 January, 1732 he was back at Deene and it was at about this time that he decided to give up his hunting partnership with the Duke of Rutland, Lord Gainsborough and the others. He had only another few months to live.

[**162**]   [*Sunday, 5 March*, 1731/2.]

My Lord,

I lay at Tuxford on Wednesday night, but could get no further than Wakefield on Thursday, for poor old Bembrook fell lame at Baughtry. He was prick'd and a little graveld, but I got his foot searchd and stuff'd, and he is now very well again.

I was early at Thornhill on Fryday morning, where I found Mr. Elmsall[1] pritty well recover'd but not able to stir out with me, the weather being very cold; so Mr. Ralf[2] & I came hither together, & have been valuing wood in Ardsley closes. I have deliver'd my message to Mrs. Cooper, who says that she will submit to it; and I told her that she must quit the house before I leave the country, which she says she will do, & I will deliver the key to Mr. Elmsall. The weather is now very mild and I hope the latter end of this week Mr. Elmsall will venture along with me.

I met with several violent storms of hail & rain on Thursday, which forc'd me into houses and made me so late at Wakefield. I find there is not above four or five that will or durst contend with your Lordship about tyth hay [in Ardesley*i*], the rest being all your tenants, but before I leave this country I shall know more particularly.

I am, my Lord,

Your Lordship's most humble and most faithful servant,

Haigh Hall, March 5th, 1731.   DAN: EATON

[**163**]   [*Saturday*, 11 *March*, 1731/2.]

My Lord,

I have done very little since my last but value wood in Ardesley. I have been half a day in New Park and one day in Woodchurch. By what I have done, I think I shall find as much in all as will amount to near 700£. But it lies so dispers'd and wide that it will take up a great deal of time to sell it after the rest is view'd, for I have been seven days already, and am sure no man that has a mind to buy can view more in a day than I have done.

I have seen one of the Forge men and him that bought Howley Park wood, and they are both desirous to buy the whole, and a great many of the tenants are desirous to buy what is on their own farms. So that I hope I shall have it in my power to sell it well, but Oats tells me that he will give more for it than any other man can afford, bycause it lies between Howley Park & Wakefield & will spoil his market. So I will take an oppertunity of trying him, but I cannot guess how much time this and other business here will require.

I think it is impossible for me to be at Deen before Lady Day, so I have writ to J. Peak to advise him what to do about Wards cattell; and everything but the sheep at Glooston must be brought to Deen at Lady Day if the hay is all gone. If not, I think Spence will make no unreasonable demands for their staying to finish it. But those sheep

---

[1] William Elmsall, who had been pressing for Dan to come and value farms in Yorkshire.
[2] William Elmsall's son.

must be sold, being most of them ewes & the rest too big for the Common, so that we must buy lesser barren sheep for feeding, & I believe Spence will be a good chap for those sheep. If not, the ewes will sel better when they have lambs than before, & if Spence keeps them a few days after Lady Day and does not buy them, he must be allowd for it what is reasonable. It will be soon enough to settle Grangers Farm in April.

I have seen three of the sub-tenants to Holdgates farm, & by their rent, it will be much the best method to divide that farm; and then I believe it will make more mony than we have valued it at, for there is no such thing as seeing by the face of the land the private conveniences of the people. But now I am here I will not be streightned for time, but will search to the bottom of every thing I can. I must get the numbers of Ardesly wood transcrib'd to day to deliver to Oats & Watts's & the tenants, that they may value it for them selves next week, for I propose to go to Kirstall on Munday, & I hope Mr. Elmsall will be able to go with me, but he mends very slowly. I shall go to Thornhill to night, and if he cannot go with me to Kirstall, shall return hither on Munday, & view the rest of the wood in Woodchurch, New Park, &c., while the chapmen are viewing Ardesley.

I am, my Lord,
Your Lordship's most humble and most faithful servant,

Haigh Hall, March 11th, 1731.   DAN: EATON

[Direction endorsed:—]
To the Right Honble. the Earl of Cardigan at Deen near Rockingham.

[The JB monogram across endorsement as **86**, etc.   Seal.   Date of postmark, 13 [March].]

During March, 1732, Dan's letters from Yorkshire were addressed to Deene, but early in April Lord Cardigan went to Bath, accompanied by his chaplain, Mr. Leaver. Dan wrote to him there in May from Stroxton, where he had gone to value the stock after the dissolution of the hunting partnership. Of the last letters, all sent to Bath, the final two are concerned with the boundary dispute with Lord Hatton. Lord Cardigan's health was now rapidly failing and he did not live to see its outcome.

13 MAY[?], 1732 — 4 JUNE, 1732

[164]   [Saturday, 13[?] May, 1732.][1]

My Lord,
I receiv'd the honour of both your Lordship's letters of the tenth instant. I could not come hither on Thursday for want of an horse, but

---

[1] Date uncertain, but perhaps any day between 12 and 16 May.

with some difficulty I hired a very indifferent one at Weldon to bring me hither yesterday. (My own mare has not entirely recover'd her health. She has the convulsive fits sometimes, but they seem to wear off.)
    I can't give your Lordship any satisfactory account of what I have done today by cause we have not finish'd, but the stears and heffers are in very good order and the sheep seem to be healthful. I have had Jere Richardson, George Wells, & one Mr. Love of this town, who I think is a very ingenious man in his way, to value the stock today, for I thought it would not be proper to have my name made use of in the affair.   We have valued the hay as we go on, and when I send your Lordship the estimate, I will declare my thoughts very particularly upon the whole affair.—The ricks of corn cannot be valued by any of the men I have employd, as they declare; but I shall propose a method in my next to do it.   Tis late at night and I have been fategued all day.
    I am your Lordships
        Most humble and most faithfull servant,

Stroxton, Saturday night.   DAN: EATON

[**165**]   [*Wednesday, 24 May*, 1732.]

My Lord,
    I have inclos'd the plan of the ground platt of Mrs. Coopers house. I drew it by a very large scale bycause I thought that alterations in it might be the more easily & correctly made. I have a rough draught of the chambers, but the rooms being but 7½ foot high below, they must certainly be all alterd, so that by the plan of the walls I think any designs may be made. I have likewise drawn a plan of all the places adjacent by a smaller scale.   There is very good building stone near the house that will be easily dug, and the walls are strong enough to be raisd any height.
    I am, my Lord,
        Your Lordship's most humble and most faithful servant,

Deen, May 24th, 1732.   DAN: EATON

[**166**]   [*Sunday, 28 May*, 1732.]

My Lord,
    It rained here all the day on Wednesday, so I did not go to Cranoe as I proposd, and Thursday was Corby Court. But on Fryday I went, and delivered to Will Worth before his wife, his father, & Robert Brightman notice in writing for him to quit all the land he rents of your Lordship at Lady Day next, or to pay double the rent, & he seem'd very uneasy at it, and so did his wife.
    I heard that Mr. Goode was come home, so I went yesterday to Weldon and found him at his house; and as he was reconcil'd to me before, he desir'd me to alight & come in, which I did. And after some time, he told me that he intended to have waited on your Lordship to have thank'd you for the message you sent him by me, &c. But being

at Grantham some time after, he was assured by a gentleman there that your Lordship had spoke very slightingly of him since that time, which made him think that your intentions were not sincere, which prevented his doing himself that honour.   Upon which I press'd him to tell me who that gentleman was, and at last Mr. Woodward[1] came out; but he told him that it was in company with Mr. Foden & the High Sheriff. I found some difficulty to alter his opinion. I told him the improbability of it, and that he ought not to believe any thing that Mr. Woodward said till he had it from other hands, and after some time I convinc'd him of the groundlessness of that report; or that if there was any truth in it, it was long before you sent me to him.

So then we soon came to the ditch before Priors Haw, and he says that Lantro and Lense and Will Pywell were the fomenters of that affair; that they have labour'd very hard to set my Lord Hatton & him at difference likewise, but that he believes and hopes that it will not be in their power.[2]

And he says that the keeper Peach is frequently disturbing his Lordship with accounts of your killing unwarrantable deer in the Purlees. Then I told him that the reason why your Lordship did so was bycause Peach himself kill'd prickets in Bangroves, which he seem'd glad to hear. And I told him further, to convince him of the truth of this, that when I, about four years since, kill'd a pricket by mistake for a doe, being at a great distance in the wood, your Lordship was very angry, and was pleasd to lay a fine of half a guinea upon me or any body else that should do the like thereafter; and he told me he would tell my Lord Hatton of it.   He seems to have a thoro' dislike to Lantro; he says that he putts my Lord Hatton upon these difficulties that he may have something for him to do.

But at last he concluded to take a journey to London in order to prevail upon Lord Hatton by fair means to level the ground again, which he hopes he shall effect if your Lordship will concurr in this method. And if he cannot do it by fair means, he assur'd me he would not only join with your Lordship in soliciting in a law suit, but will give you his security to bear a tenth of the charge of it; and when he is in London he will apply to Mr. Fesakerly for his advice in the affair.   I was with him four or five hours & this is the substance of what passed between us, which at the conclusion he desir'd I would make your Lordship acquainted with.

I am, my Lord,
Your Lordship's most humble and most faithful servant,

Deen, May 28th, 1732.   DAN: EATON

[**167**]   [*Sunday*, 4 *June*, 1732.]

My Lord,
At my return from Northampton I receiv'd the honour of your Lordship's letter of the 27th of last month. I am extreamly grieved at your account of your own health—God Almighty send you better. Your three sons at Deen are as well, I think, as I ever saw any boys in my

---

[1] A Grantham tradesman.
[2] See Subject Index under Disputes. Lense here is Lensit.

life. Mr. Robert had the ear ach about a fortnight since, I suppose occasion'd by a slight cold, but as it went off in two days without any ill consequences, I though[t] it was not worth while to trouble your Lordship with an account of it.

The meer which Weldon people made in Helcrofts Close is made upon the utmost verge of Weldon Lordship. But Deen people have no meer from that corner of Dibbins next to Deenthorpe Closes at the deer leap in the little close next to Dunstan Leys to the corner of Lammas Close by Cooks [field[i]]. The three times that I have been the perambulation of Deen, we went over the ground where the meer is now dug, but there were no visible mark of the boundery in that place before, but they and we went in the same track. The place whereon Mr. Hawkins stood when he told the perambulators that the park pales stood on Lord Hattons ground was on the spot your Lordship mention's, viz., at the corner of the little close next to Dunstan Leys. And he told them that so many of the pales that stood on the side of that little close to the deer leap were on your Lordships ground, but all those by Dunstan Leys were on Lord Hatton's. John Peak knows that Mr. Good acknowledg'd that your Lordship had 21 foot of freeboard there.

The names of those that dug the ditch before Priors Haw[1] were Joshua Lantro, attorney at law; James Hawkins, gent.; John Lens (alias Lensit), yeoman; William Wells, coppice keeper; Neal Hodgkin, farmer; and William Cave, Henry Noble, Thomas Tea, Robert Tea, Edward Tea, labourers. But I cannot find any body that saw them at work, which is no great matter. Mr. Cuthbert says that as they were all Lord Hattons servants as being personally imploy'd by him, he would advise your Lordship to desire Lord Hatton to wave his priviledge before you proceed against any of them; which if he refuses to do, your Lordship may move the House of Lords against him, and they will take it off. Both Mr. Rose & Mr. Cuthbeard seem to think that your Lordship's cause is a good one, but Mr. Cuthbeard says that in all cases in the trying of titles, the more counsel are imployd, the better.

If it comes to a tryal I think it will be impossible for Lord Hattons agents to prevent our proving it to have been a road time immemorial, and I really believe that Mr. Goode will be sincere in his assistance in trying the cause if Lord Hatton will not level the ditch himself. The last three hours of the time I was at Mr. Goodes house I was never entertaind in a freer and more generous & friendly manner in my life by any one; but your Lordship may be assur'd that in all company and at all times I am very careful of my words.

I hope in God I shall soon hear a better account of your Lordship's health. To morrow is Rowell Fair and I must be there, but on Tuesday I shall go to Stroxton, and hope I shall finish the affair with Mr. Doubleday to your Lordships satisfaction.

I am, my Lord,
Your Lordships most humble & most faithful servant,

Deen, June 4th, 1732.   DAN: EATON

---

[1] This digging of the ditch is described by Cardigan in his letter to John Booth of 22 Jan. - 3 Feb., 1732, in which he says: "When D. Eaton came to them & advised them to forbear, they went no further, but return'd home with their spades." (Mont. Corr. I. 113).   See above, p. xxv.

Lord Cardigan did not recover. He left Bath in the hope of getting back to Deene but only succeeded in reaching Tottenham Court in Wiltshire, the home of his brother-in-law, Lord Ailesbury, where he died on 5th July, 1732.

Sir Justinian Isham has left us an account in his diary of Lord Cardigan's funeral on the 11th of July. The procession had wound slowly along the roads from Wiltshire to Northamptonshire, taking five or six days to accomplish the journey. Sir Justinian, with other neighbours, met the cortège at Weldon and accompanied it on foot to Deene—but let him tell the story in his own words:

> *"Having receiv'd an invitation from John Robinson of Cransley, one of the executors, I met the corps of Lord Cardigan at Weldon from whence it proceeded to Dene Church, and was interr'd in the vault of the family, the pall being supported, besides myself, by Sir John Dolben [of Finedon], Benjamin Allicocke [of Loddington], John Tryon [of Collyweston], George Lynn [of Southwick], and Wheeler Brook [of Great Oakley], Esqs., Mr. Robinson chief mourner."*[1]

---

[1] I(L) 2686, pp. 139, 140. 11 July 1732.

APPENDIXES

*Draft Articles of Agreement between (1) Christopher Dexter and
John Winsall, and (2) Daniel Eaton, on behalf of the Earl of
Cardigan, for alterations to John Lynwood's house, subsequently
named Little Deene. 31 July 1725.*

N.R.O., Bru. MSS. ASR 106b.

ARTICLES of Agreement indented, had, made, concluded and agreed
upon the one and thirtieth day of July in the Year of our Lord 1725 —
between Christopher Dexter of Gretton in the County of Northampton,
carpenter, and John Winsall of Weldon Magna in the said County of Northampton, mason, of the one part and Daniel Eaton of Deen in the said County
of Northampton, for and on the part & behalf of the Right Honble George,
Earl of Cardigan on the other part, in manner following, viz.

Imprimis.   Whereas the Earl of Cardigan has for some time heretofore
been making alterations in that house in Deen aforesaid wherein Mr. John
Lynwood now lives, and the same being at present unfinished, they, the
said Chrisʳ Dexter and John Winsall, (upon consideration of the said Earl's
paying or causing to be paid unto them or either of them the sum of eighty
pounds five shillings at such times as shall be herein after mentioned), do
hereby agree & promise to finish & compleat the same in manner following,
viz:

1.   That they, the said Chrisʳ Dexter & J. Winsall, shall at their own
proper cost & charges procure & provide all manner of materials for finishing
& compleating the said house,—as timber, slate, lead, stone, glass, &c.,
lime & brick only excepted, and shall provide and pay all manner of workmen
as carpenters, masons, stone cutters, plumbers, glassiers & slaters which
they shall employ therein.

2.   And that they, the said Ch.D. & J.W., shall bear, pay & discharge
all manner of expences concerning the premisses except carriage, which the
said Dan: Eaton does agree that the said Earl shall bear & provide.

3.   And that they the said Ch.D. & J.Winsall, shall and will proceed in
compleating the premisses in this manner, viz: That *first* they shall uncover
all that old building at the west end of the present new building.   *Secondly*
they shall raise the walls of that building & likewise of the present new
building to such a convenient heigth [*sic*] that with a double roof the garrets
may be seven foot six inches high from the ceiling to the floor.   *Thirdly* —
they shall procure & provide or make & furnish seven compleat & regular
sashes for the garret windows [and make freestone cases for the same ⁱ]
answerable to those in the rooms below.   *Fourthly* they shall make & glaze
four windows in the north wall that is to be rais'd if so many shall be thought
necessary.   *Fifthly* they shall make two chimny's [in the garrets ⁱ], one in
the east end & the other to be let into the middle tunnells.   *Sixthly* they
shall make a right good & substantial double roof to the whole building &
shall cover the same with slate workmanlike, and the three gutters they shall
lay with lead which shall be run 8 lib. to the foot at least according to the
art of a plumber.   *Seventhly* they shall fix ceiling joice in the ceilings of all
the garrets & thereby make the same ready for the plasterers.   *Eigthly* [*sic*]
they shall make a freestone cornice at the top of the front of the house

according to a mould deliverd in, and shall make the battlements a convenient heigth above it, *ninthly* whereas there are four old sashes in Deen waredrobe, they shall allow to the said Earl eight pounds for the same if Mr Tryon & Dan. Eaton shall hereafter think that they may be made to serve for the garret windows, and *lastly* they shall compleat & finish all & singular the premisses workmanlike & before the seventh day of October next ensuing the date of these presents.

4.   And the said Dan: Eaton for the Earl of Cardigan does promise & agree to & with the said Ch.D. & J.W. that five shillings being paid to them upon the sealing of these presents thirty five pounds more shall be paid upon their finishing that part of the house that is now covered with the old roof & that the other forty five pounds shall be paid immediately after the whole building is finished as aforesaid.

5.   And the said Dan. Eaton for the said Earl, does hereby permit the said Chris. Dexter & John Winsall to remove & take to their own use & uses all such timber both old & new which is either already fram'd or which is to be taken down in the west end of this building, since they are to furnish other timber more fit for the present purpose in its stead, and likewise all the old cornice, and likewise all the windows which were to have been put in the garrets (in the first design) except three that my Lord shall chuse and since they are to find all slate, if there is any old slate left they shall take it for their own use.

APPENDIX II.

Memorandum of a Bargain between (1) Daniel Eaton on behalf of George, Earl of Cardigan and (2) Thomas Nichols of Blatherwick, joiner, for finishing a room and a bedchamber in the house called Little Deene. 14 April 1727.

Bru. MSS. O. xxiv.3.

Memorand. April 14th 1727. That a bargain is made between Daniel Eaton on the part & behalf of the Right Honble. the Earl of Cardigan, and Thomas Nichols of Blatherwick in the County of Northampton, joiner, as followeth: —

That is to say the said T.N. shall before the 1st day of August next ensuing the date hereof, wainscot, floor & compleatly finish the room in the house call'd Little Deen in the Parish of Deen in the County of Northampton which is intended for the dining room, and likewise the room intended for a bedchamber directly over it, in the following manner (viz: —)

First he shall wainscot the said dining room with quarter-round raisd pannells;

Secondly he shall make and hang two pair of well wrought wainscot window shutters to the two sashes of the same room;

Thirdly he shall make and hang a good double wrought wainscot door to the same room;

Fourthly he shall lay the floor of the same room upon sleepers truely plain'd, and shall lay the same exactly level and close;

Fifthly he shall fix the architraves on the door trees;

Sixthly he shall wainscot, floor, & compleatly finish the said chamber after the same modell and manner exactly as he is to do the dining room before describ'd;

And shall make two double wrought doors to the said chamber, one opening upon the staircase the other into the closet, and shall hang the same and fix the architraves;

And shall make and hang two pair of window shutters to the two sashes in the said chamber;

And he shall make all the pannells in both the rooms afore mentioned exactly answerable to a draught shewn him at the making of this bargain;

And shall in every respect, neatly, closely and compleatly finish both the said rooms, — workman like;

And shall at his own charge pay and discharge all the workmen that he shall employ therein;

And shall fur the tracins of the said chamber floor, that the same may be laid exactly levell.

And lastly the said Dan. Eaton for the said Earl does promise that whereas five shillings is paid by him to the said Tho. Nichols upon signing this bargain, twenty pounds and ten shillings more shall be paid to him immediately after the said two rooms are by him compleatly finish'd as afore said.

And further that all necessary materials for finishing the premises shall be provided at the said Earl's charge.

In witness &c.

APPENDIX III.

*Letter from John Elliot to Lord Cardigan
at Bath. 22 October 1726.*

Bru. MSS. F. iii. 268

Welham, Oct^{br} ye 22^d 1726

My Lord,

I had the honour to receive your Lordships by the last post. That letter of Mr. Edwards's you are pleas'd to mention, he gave me to read before he seal'd it: I wish he would act with as much sincerity as he seems to write. The opinion that your Lordship had of him heretofore, he verifies to a tittle, there being no depending upon his ambiguous proceedings.

. . . .

That day after your Lordship set out for the Bath, after evening service he came to my house & seem'd much dissatisfied with the promises he had made your Lordship the Friday before at Welham; he rais'd several scruples, as that your Lordship had heretofore oppos'd him, I believe he meant at the election, & that you had not given him sufficient power to act, because you only did it by word of mouth, when, he says, you should have done it under hand & seal &c. To obviate this, my Lord, I reminded him of the letter of attorney you promised to leave: nevertheless he told me he would make no farther progress in it, unless I would undertake to bring down some of the freeholders to him to court or beg of him to sollicite this affair for them; which accordingly I did the next day, when they gave him their concurrance: but one of them he treated so very unkindly, that I cannot but resent it, as being the occasion of his coming down.

Two days after this, my Lord, he came to me again in a seeming fury, & said that some of Slawston had been with him & complain'd of your Lordships harshness & severity with your tenants & also of the manner of my taking tithe wool, that these things ought to be regulated before he could proceed. After a great many words had pass'd between us, he gave me hints to conjecture that Spence had been with him the night before & infus'd these things.

To vindicate yr Lordships honour, I told him of the great remittances you had made your tenants, that they held upon the old rents, that they always had half a years rent in their hands & that no landlord could use tenants better &c. & as to the way of my tithing wool, that it was in the same method that my predecessors & I had all along done it, & that there never had been any dispute about it amongst the parishioners, but a few days before I had one with Spence. After all, my Lord, he seem'd to adhere to everything that Spence had said & not give credit to my assertions: so that for 2 or 3 days he made it his business to rail against me. But the night before he went to Ireland, I was with him two hours, when we again entred upon the Slawston affair, & then he seem'd to have quite different sentiments to those he had before; for he told me that one of Slawston had been with him & given Spence the character of a hollow dissembling fellow, & that now he believ'd it: in short, he said he would act as he had at first proposed, &

leave my affair of tithes to yr Lordships determination, & so we seemingly parted in a friendly manner, to have all things adjusted upon his return.

. . . .

As to Spences management, my Lord, 'tis as odd as the foregoing: he affirm'd to Mr. Edwards that he never gave your Lordship any promise to agree to an enclosure, but with this proviso, that you would not raise his rent: the very same thing he affirm'd over & over again at Stonton mill with several asseverations, before many of your tenants; & all that Mr. Eaton could say to him to the contrary, could not confront him.

. . . .

As to the freeholders of Slawston, my Lord, 'tis my real opinion, all of 'em will in a little time fall in with this scheme of enclosing, if rightly manag'd, but Mr. Edwards seems to have such strong inclinations to his own interest & advances such odd notions, that some of them are very fearfull to close with him: your Lordship I am sure will be of the same opinion when you come to hear them.

I heartily beg your Lordships excuse for trespassing thus upon your patience, & wish you a speedy return into Northamptonshire in perfect health, which is the sincere desire of

my Lord,
Your Lordships
most dutifull &
obedient servant
J Elliot

The last rent my Lord was paid very well. I intend to wait upon your Lordship the first moment I hear of your arrival at Deen.

APPENDIX IV.

The By-Laws of Great Weldon in 1728

Ordered by the View of Frankpledge with the Court Baron of the Manor of Great Weldon held there on 30 September, 1728, to be enrolled by Joshua Lantrow, steward

N.R.O., F.H.991.

Imprimis
1st   It is ordered that no man shall keep more sheep than he hath commons for, upon pain to fforfeit for every sheep so kept [more than he has comon for ¹] the sum of £0.00*

2d   Item   That no antient cottage shall have commons for more than five cows a ffollower and ten sheep, upon pain to fforfeit for every other cow or bullock the sum of £0.01*

3d   Item   That no man shall keep a team of ffour or more horses within or upon the ffields of the said manor not haveing ten acres of land in each feild, upon pain to fforfeit for every horse so kept the sum of £0.02.6

4th   Item   That no under [tennant in right of his ¹]tenement shall keep any horses, cows or sheep in the ffields of the said manor, upon pain to pay for every horse, cow or sheep so kept the sum of £0.05.0

5th   Item   That no person shall keep more cows or bullocks in the feilds than is allowed by his rate of sheep commons, vizt. for every score of sheep three cows or bullocks, upon pain to forfeit for every offence the sum of £0.03.4

6th   Item   That no person shall plow up any antient baulk or meadow ground, upon pain to forfeit for every offence the sum of £0.03.4

7th   Item   That no person shall admitt any tenant into [his cottage or under tenement within ¹] the said mannor without the consent of the Lord of the said mannor and giving security to the town, upon pain to forfeit for every offence the sum of £5.00.0

8th   Item   That the wheat ffeild hedges and ffences [shall ¹] be made and repaired by the ffeast of St. Andrew, and that every person neglecting his duty in the premisses shall fforfeit the sum of £0.03.4

9th   Item   That no person shall tye any mares haveing [sucking ffoles by their sides ¹] in the fields untill harvest begin, upon pain to fforfeit for every offence the sum of £0.06.8

10th   Item   That no person shall putt upon the common or into the fields any mangie [ffarty (?) or glandred ¹] horses, on pain to fforfeit for every offence the sum of £0.10.0

11th   Item   That no antient cottage shall keep more than two hogs, and undertenements none, upon pain of forfeiting for every hog or pig so kept the sum of £0.00.4

12th   Item   That no person shall tye his horses [except on ¹] his own ground till harvest be done, on pain to forfeit for every offence the sum of £0.03.4

* Edge and last figure torn away.

13th   Item   That the jury shall meet every [year ^i] on All Saints at the usual place at the tolling of the bell, and every jury [man ^i] so neglecting to meet shall forfeit for every offence the sum of £0.01*

14th   Item   That the drains shall be scoured and opened from John Grumbold's to Widdow Gilby's by the persons to whom they belong, the person so neglecting [shall ^i] forfeit [for every offence ^i] the sum of £0.03*

15th   Item   That the whole jury shall meet in the usuall place to take all officers' accounts when notice is given in the church, and that every jury man so neglecting shall fforfeit for every offence the sum of £0.06*

16th   Item   That no person shall keep any cattle but upon his own ground till the herd goes out, and then to be herded together, upon pain to fforfeit for every offence the sum of £0.03.4

17th   Item   That no person shall make or committ any pound breach nor rescue [his cattle ^i] being in lawful custody, on pain to forfeit for every offence the sum of £0.05*

18th   Item   That every person's hoggs shall be ringed and so kept from Michaelmas to Martinmas, on pain to fforfeit for every hogg not ringed the sum of £0.00*

19   Item   That no person shall [keep ^i] any sheep in the fields or upon the plain unbranded, on pain to fforfeit for every offence the sum of £0.03.4

20   Item   That no person shall rent or take any sheep commons in the fields, except for the time of ffolding, upon pain to fforfeit for every offence the sum of £0.10.0

21   Item   That every officer shall make and give up his accounts to the townsmen at the church within forty days after he is off his office, and pay to the succeeding officer what money shall appear to be in his hand on the ballance of his account, on pain to fforfeit for every neglect or default the sum of £0.10.0

22   Item   That no person shall glean any pease or beans till harvest be done, on pain to fforfeit for every offence the sum of £0.05.0

23   Item   That every commoner shall upon notice given go or send one person to help drive the fields and plain, on pain to fforfeit for every neglect the sum of £0.00.6

24   Item   That no person shall put sheep into the late wheat ffeild untill the 15th day of Sep^t, on pain to forfeit for every offence the sum of £0.03.4

25   Item   That every housekeeper shall send a sufficient stone gatherer into the field six days in every year, on pain to fforfeit for every default the sum of £0.02.6

26   Item   That the common fields shall be driven three times in every year, whereof notice shall be given by the headboroughs, on pain of fforfeiting for every offence £0.01.0

27   Item   That no person shall lett any sheep commons upon the plain, upon pain to fforfeit for every offence the sum of £0.10.0

28   Item   That no person shall putt any great cattle into the fallow field without the consent of the whole jury, on pain to fforfeit for every offence the sum of £0.10.0

29   Item   That no person of Great Weldon shall [lett ^i] his commons for beasts to any person of Little Weldon, on pain to forfeit for every offence the sum of £0.10.0

30   Item   That no person shall keep geese (except upon his own ground), on pain to forfeit for every goose so kept the sum of £0.1*

31   Item   That the By Laws shall be read three times in every year,

* Edge of document torn away here.

that is to say at the first parish meeting after Easter day, the ffirst parish meeting after Lamas day, and the first parish meeting after All Saints day, yearly in every year, and that if the fforeman of the jury omitts to tender these laws to be read at any of the times afforesaid, he shall forfeit the sum of £0.02*

Edward Hodgskin
Robt Tebbot
Thomas Bellamy
Adam Bellamey, his mark
Nathanel Wade
Thomas Ayers, junior
Robt Wade, his mark
Anthony Pratt, his mark
John Knight
Tho Smith, his mark
Frank Palmer, his mark
John Chapman
Tho Ayres, sen^r

* Edge of document torn away here.

APPENDIX V.

Hunting Agreement between the Duke of Rutland, the Earl of Cardigan and others. 6 May 1730.

ARTICLES OF AGREEMENT of five parts made this sixth day of May in the third year of the reign of our Sovereign Lord George the Second by the grace of God of Great Britain, France and Ireland, King, Defender of the Faith, etc. Anno Domini 1730, between his grace John, Duke of Rutland of the first part, the Right Honourable George, Earl of Cardigan of the second part, the Right Honorable Baptist, Earl of Gainsborough of the third part, the Right Honorable John, Lord Gower of the fourth part and the Right Honorable Scrope, Lord Howe of the fifth part as follows:—

IMPRIMIS   It is hereby agreed by and between the said partys that the hounds, horses, etc., shall be kept at the joynt charge of the said partys.

Item   that every party obliges himself annually to deposit one hundred pounds on Midsummer Day and fifty pounds on Christmas Day in the hands of Alderman Child at Temple Bar, or in the hands of the said partys steward for the time being, towards defraying the annual expense of the hounds, horses, etc. and all other charges incident to this partnership, the first payment to commence on Midsummer Day next ensuing the date hereof, and if any of the said partys shall neglect to make the said payments on the above-mentioned days, or within six weeks after, then such party so neglecting shall forfeit his share in the hounds, horses, and everything else belonging to the Hunt.

Item   it is mutually covenanted and agreed that the account of the expenses shall be made up once every year, when the overplus of the money, if there should be any, shall be equally divided amongst the said partys, or if the sums agreed upon aforesaid should not be sufficient to defray the expenses, the said partys oblige themselves to make it up share and share alike.

Item   the old hounds, etc. to be kept from the fifteenth of October to the last day of November inclusive at Croxton Park, from the first of December to the last of January inclusive at Cotsmore, from the first of February to the last of March inclusive at Thrawson, from the first of April to the fourteenth of October at such places as shall be determined by the majority of the said partys.

Item   the young hounds, etc. to be kept at such places as shall be determined by the majority of the said partys.

Item   that not any hound shall be hanged, gelt, spayd or parted with, unless by the consent of the majority of the said partys.

Item   that not any hound or hounds shall be added without the consent of the majority of the said partys.

Item   that a list of the bitches to be warded shall be laid before the said partys on the fifth day of December annually, when the major part of such of the partys present shall determine what dogs to put to them.

Item   that none of the said partys shall hunt fox within ten miles of any of those places where the hounds are to be kept, with any hound, hounds, or pack of hounds (excepting with the said partys pack) after the signing and sealing of these Articles, or otherwise destroy or cause foxes to be destroyed, but that every of the said partys shall preserve them as much as in him lyes, on forfeiture of his share in the partys hounds, horses, etc.

Item   that the whelps that shall be bred, shall be equally divided among the said partys and by them put to quarters.

Item   that not any whelps or hounds shall be taken into the pack after the fifteenth of October next ensuing the date of these presents, above twenty one inches high, or under nineteen inches.

Item   that the unnecessary whelps shall be disposed of by the directions of the majority of the said partys.

Item   that a steward, one huntsman, six whippers in and two cooks shall be kept for the use of the old and young hounds, and shall be chose, turned off, paid and disposed of by the directions of the majority of the said partys.

Item   that the majority of the said parties shall resolve on the number of horses necessary to be kept for the use of each pack, and to give orders for the buying or selling of them.

Item   that each of the said partys by turns shall take upon him during the hunting season for the space of one week and no more at a time, the ordering, the stopping of earths, management of the hounds and horses, the appointing the places for hunting, hours of meeting, etc., this to be determined on the first day of meeting at Croxton Park.

Item   on the death of any of the said partys his share in the hounds, horses, or whatever else belongs to the hunt, to devolve to the remaining partys, unless the possessor of the capital seat of the deceased party shall be willing to succeed him in this partnership.

Item   that not any of the said partys shall or may have liberty to resign his share in the hounds, horses, or whatever else belongs to the hunt, except to his son, or to the remaining partys.

Item   that one years notice shall be given by any party that shall be desirous to resign his share in the hounds, horses, etc.

Item   that the said partys reserve to themselves a power of making any new article or articles, or altering any of the aforementioned articles, but not without the consent of all the said partys.

Item   that whenever a day is fixed or appointed by the major part of the said partys for altering these or making any new articles, sufficient notice shall be given to every party to attend or send his proxy, but that to no one, but one of the said partys.

In witness whereof the said partys have hereunto interchangeably sett their hands and seals the day and year first above written.

Signed Sealed and Delivered (being first duly stampt) in the presence of

"Baptist Leveson Gower"	"Rutland"	[Seal]
"John Vernon"	"Cardigan"	[Seal]
? [Tankerv]ille"	"Gainsborough"	[Seal]
"Walpole"	"Gower"	[Seal]
"De Laivan"	"Howe"	[Seal]

Note. "The parties' steward" in 1732 may have been Walter Tankred (see Index of Persons). In Bru. MSS. F. iii. 282-3 we have a letter to him from the Duke of Rutland, regretting that Cardigan and other "confederates" must leave him, and desiring to have the remainder of Cardigan's lease of Stroxton; and one to Cardigan, from Tankred forwarding Rutland's letter. Cf. **164.**

APPENDIX VI.

The Will of Daniel Eaton

In the Name of God Amen. I Daniel Eaton of Deen in the county of Northampton being weak and infirm in body but of sound and perfect mind memory and understanding, do this twelfth day of January in the fifteenth year of the reign of our Soveraign Lord King George the second and so forth, and in the year of our Lord Christ one thousand seven hundred and forty one, make and publish this my last will and testament, in manner and form following:

First, I bequeath my soul into the hand of Almighty God the Author of its being, hoping through the merits of Jesus Christ my Redeemer to obtain everlasting life after death, and my body to the earth, decently to be buried at the discretion of my executors hereinafter named.

Secondly, I give to my dear beloved wife Elizabeth Eaton the sum of one hundred and fifty pounds (besides two hundred and fifty pounds due to her upon bond), and all my household goods and furniture.

Also I give to my mother, Theophila Eaton, the sum of twenty and six pounds a year during her natural life, to be paid to her weekly if she require it.

Also I give to my sisters that are the daughters of my mother, each the sum of ten pounds.

Also I give to Mr. Robert Peach and Mr. Conyers Peach each the sum of twenty and five pounds a year during the time of their executing this my will.

And also to John Webster my servant I give the sum of thirty and one pounds and ten shillings a year, and meat, drink and lodging, and travelling charges and expenses during his executing this my will.

Also I give to the poor of the Parish of Deen the sum of ten pounds and to the poor of the parish of Deenthorp the like sum of ten pounds, the interest of which to be paid to them respectively for ever, in such manner as the interest of money due to them now in the hands of the Right Honourable George, Earl of Cardigan, is paid.

And all the rest and residue of my goods, chattells, effects and personal estate after my debts are paid, and all the proffitts and advantages which in trade shall be made or otherwise out of the said effects by my executors hereinafter named, I give and bequeath to my three sons, Daniel, William and Stephen, equally to be divided amongst them and paid or delivered to them respectively, as they shall attain the age of twenty and one years, and that the charge of maintaining and educating my said sons untill they shall arrive at the age of twenty and one years be deducted out of the proffitts to be made of my said personal effects and my other estates.

And lastly I make and ordain her my said wife, the said Robert Peach, Conyers Peach, and John Webster, joynt executrix and executors of this my last will and testament, and do give them full power to carry on the several businesses of growing woad, matting, ffarming, and grazing, with my above-mentioned stock and effects, or otherwise to act and dispose of the same at their discretion, they applying the proffits thereby and thereof made to the uses and purposes above mentioned.

But in case my said wife should marry again after my decease, from the time of such marriage I exclude her from this executorship, and that neither she nor her husband shall from thenceforward have any part in executing this my will.

In witness whereof I the said Daniel Eaton have to this my last will and testament set my hand and seal the day and year above written. Dan Eaton. Signed, sealed and published and declar'd by the said Daniel Eaton as and for his last will and testament, in the presence of us Thomas Summers, John Ward, John Cordal.

This will was proved at London before the Right Worshipful John Bettesworth, Doctor of Laws, Master Keeper or Commissary of the Prerogative Court of Canterbury lawfully constituted, the eighteenth day of May in the year of our Lord One Thousand Seven Hundred and Forty two, by Elizabeth Eaton, widow, the relict of the deceased, Robert Peach, Conyers Peach, and John Webster, the executors named in the said will, to whom was granted administration of all and singular goods, chattells, and credits of the deceased, being first sworn by Commission duly to administer.

The Tomb of Daniel Eaton in the churchyard at Deene.

APPENDIX VII.

The Postal aspects of The Daniel Eaton Letters

In England during the reign of Edward I posts were established where horses could be had for hire by messengers wearing the royal livery. A regular and organised service is not found until the reign of Edward IV, when because of the war with Scotland he organised a relay of post houses at twenty-mile intervals between the battlefields and the seat of Government. The service ceased at the end of this war, but there is evidence in the Paston Letters that a regular post existed to Norwich at the end of the fourteenth century.

The first Postmaster General, appointed in 1512, was Sir Brian Tuke, but his duties were concerned with the King's posts, private letters being carried as an act of grace, and many of these were not delivered. It was not until 1635, when Thomas Wittering was appointed Postmaster General, that a start to an organised postal service was made.

The six great Post roads of England from London, in the latter part of the seventeenth century, were the Western road to Plymouth, the Bristol, the Chester (continuing to Holyhead), the North (to Edinburgh), the Yarmouth, and the Kent (to Dover). Most of these roads were Roman in origin. There were also many branch posts.

Northamptonshire was served by the Chester road in the west with a branch post to Northampton and Wellingborough from Towcester. Daventry was also a post stage on the Chester road. In the eastern part of the county, Peterborough was served by a branch post from the Great North Road.

In 1691 a new branch post was established from London to Chesterfield and Sheffield. Previously London letters to Sheffield had travelled via Northampton and Derby, but now the route was to be by way of Kettering and Melton Mowbray. This new road branched out from the Chester road at Dunstable, travelling by way of Newport Pagnell and Wellingborough to Kettering and thence to Uppingham. The date when Rockingham became a post stage on this route is uncertain. Letters were carried in 'bags' and there is a reference to a Rockingham 'bag' being lost in 1726 in the correspondence, so this date can be taken as the earliest proof that Rockingham was a post stage.

The previously mentioned rule about post stages being set twenty miles apart was by no means rigid. Many people of influence managed to secure a postal service which was convenient to themselves, and it may be that the establishing of a post stage at Rockingham was for this reason rather than the usual one of the Post Boy having to change horses. The distance between Kettering and Uppingham is only 14 miles, so the former suggestion is more likely.

The other way of determining whether a particular place was a post stage is to discover whether postal markings exist from the place in question.

In England during the seventeenth century the only postal markings were impressed in London. The most usual one was a divided circle which gave the month and day numerals. These markings are known as Bishopmarks, after Henry Bishop who was appointed Postmaster General in 1660. He introduced them in 1661. From the beginning of the eighteenth century town name stamps began to be used on letters, and most of the places known to have been post stages in Northamptonshire were using them by 1730 and some by 1710. The earliest known marking of this type from Rockingham is on a letter dated 1731 from a different correspondence. It appears from this that the suggestion in the Daniel Eaton correspondence for the change of the post route from Kettering to Uppingham to be by way of Weldon instead of Rockingham was not accepted. Another letter from Rockingham to London dated 1721, seen by the writer, does not bear this marking. The covers of most of the Daniel Eaton letters are missing, so unfortunately this means of determining whether Rockingham was a post stage earlier than 1726 is not available.

G. F. OXLEY.

GLOSSARY

The definitions are in many cases restricted to the meaning of the words in the text of the letters.

Architrave. Collective name for the part (lintel, jambs and their mouldings) that surrounds a doorway or window.

Bailiff. Official (under the steward) of a manor court; manager of a home farm.

Ball, ball'd. Description and name of a horse; streaked or marked with white, especially on face. (*cf.* piebald.)

Bead, in the. Of lime: still bubbling or frothing when being slaked.

Beadwork (stucco). A small globular ornament, commonly applied in a row like a string of beads.

Bill. Inventory; statement of accounts; bill of exchange.

Board wages. Special rate of wages given to servants when, in the absence of their employer, they provide their own food.

Boon team. Team used in carting services (part of a tenant's rent for his land).

Bottle. A bundle of sticks for firing (A. E. Baker, *Glossary of Northants Words and Phrases*, 1854).

Brawn. A boar or pig fattened for the table; the flesh of the pig collared (rolled up), boiled and pickled.

Bristol water. Mineral water from the spa at Bristol.

Bucket, 'for carabines'. A leathern socket or rest for a carbine.

Carabine. Carbine, a kind of firearm shorter than a musket.

Centor. A temporary framework upon which an arch is supported while building.

Certificate. A written acknowledgment by the churchwardens and overseers of the poor in a parish that a person has a legal settlement in that parish and a right to poor relief there.

Chair. A small horse-drawn carriage.

Chalder, chaldron. A measure (here used for coal) varying from 32 to 64 bushels.

Chap, chapman, capman. Dealer.

Chap-fallen. With chap or lower jaw hanging down.

Chief rent. A rent paid under a tenure in chief; a rent payable to the owner of a hundred.

Cistiron. Cistern.

Clog'd. Of a hound: fettered or impeded by having a block of wood fastened to neck or leg.

Close. An inclosed field.

Cock-hedge. A trimmed thorn hedge (Wright, *E.D.D.*, 1898-1905).

Coak-malt. Malt dried with a coke fire.

Coller, collar (of brawn). *See* Brawn.

Common, right of. The right of pasturing beasts on land held in common.

Compass sash, compass window. A semi-circular bay window.

Cony-catcher. Rabbit catcher.

Copper. A (copper) vessel used in brewing.

Copyholder. A manorial tenant holding his land by copy of court roll.

Country (sometimes = county). In Dan's usage generally a region or district, as opposed to a town.

Court. A manor court.

Crop, cropt gelding. Having the ears cut to a point.

Cut (a horse). Geld.

Dale. Deal, pine plank or board.

Deer-leap. *See* Introduction, p. xxxvi.

Dilapidation. Legal term for disrepair of parsonages.

Dodderel. Stump of an old tree.

Dog. In this period used for a fox-hound as well as for a spaniel and other kinds of dog.

Eddish. The lattermath or second crop of grass after the first crop has been mown (Baker).

Fleak (scaffolding). A local name for each of the rails passing through holes in the posts of common oaken fencing (Wyatt (Papworth *ed.*), *Dictionary of Architecture*, Architectural Society's Pubs., 1852-92).

Floated (ceiling). Smoothed or levelled.

Flown, overflown. Flooded.

Foundered. Of a horse: collapsed with exhaustion.

Frank, franking. The practice of allowing peers and Members of Parliament to provide that letters should go free through the post by signing their names on the outside.

Freebord. The right of claiming a certain quantity of land outside a fence.

Freeholder. Tenant of freehold land as opposed to copyhold.

Fulling-mill. A mill in which cloth is pressed between rollers and cleansed with soap or fuller's earth.

Glandered, glanders. A contagious disease in horses, characterized by swellings beneath the jaw, and mucous discharge from the nostrils.

Glassier. Glazier.

Great, by the. Piecework: contracts made either with individual labourers or with gangs.

Gudeon, gudgeon. The axle or pivot of a wheel.

Hackney, hack. Saddle-horse for riding and not for hunting.

High, laid. This refers to the ridges in the arable fields which were ploughed high for drainage into the furrows between them.

Hovel. A cattle shed with an open side.

Husband, husbandman. A tenant farmer, here, a careful one.

Impost. The upper course of a pillar, frequently projecting in the form of an ornamental moulding or capital.

Jacks. Small pike.

Jocky wagon. A wagon driven by a postilion.

Joice, joist(s). Timbers on which floor-boards and ceiling laths are nailed.

Jointured. Having property settled as a provision during widowhood.

Joisters. "Agisters": livestock (chiefly cattle) that have been taken in to graze for a money payment.

Kill. Kiln.

Knot (in mare's leg). Probably a splint or a spavin.

Last. Measure for grain or malt (10 quarters or 80 bushels).

Lay-ground (ley). Land temporarily under grass or other green crop.

Legs (thorn). Props.

License and composition, letter of. A document allowing a debtor respite for payment and abatement on his account.

Log (slate). The layer of fissile limestone found at Collyweston, Deene, and the neighbouring area of Northamptonshire, which is quarried and split into roofing slates.

Lordship. *See* Introduction, pp. xxv, xxvi.

Mark. A money of account: 13*s*.4*d*.

Meer. A boundary, boundary mark. *See* Introduction, p. xxviii.

Old. *See* Wold.

Pad. Path.

Pad-mare. An easy-paced horse.

Padded. Trodden down.

Penthouse. A sloping-roofed structure attached to the wall of a building.

Perambulation, perambulator. The ceremony of walking officially round a forest, manor, parish or holding, for the purpose of asserting and recording its boundaries. The person who does this.

Pill'd. Peeled.

Plains. Here, two flat areas of land known as Benefield Lawn and Rockinghamshire (*See* Index of Places and *cf.* F. M. Stenton and A. Mawer, *Place Names of Northants*, p. 107, *under* Stoke Plain).

Plash, *v.* To trim the sides of a hedge and interweave the branches (Baker).

Pluck water. Broth of heart, liver, etc. of beast.

Pollard (deer). A buck which has lost its horns.

Posted. Booked: entered in a book, recorded.

Postilion. Rider of one of a pair or four-in-hand of carriage or wagon horses.

Pour'lles, purlieus. *See* Introduction, pp. xxxi, xxxii and Language liii.

Prick'd. Wounded in the sole of a horse's foot in shoeing.

Pricket (deer). A buck in its second year, having straight unbranched horns.

Proud. On heat.

Quarter. Eight bushels (dry measure).

Quick. Live hawthorn, for hedges.

Quickset, *v.* To plant young hawthorn for making a hedge or repairing gaps.

Rackway(s). A narrow path or track in a wood.

Rag, Weldon. A kind of building stone quarried at Weldon.

Ray-grass. Rye-grass.

Returns. *See* Introduction, p. xlv.

Rick. A stack of corn or hay.

Riding. A green track or lane cut through a wood.

Road. Here often refers to a grass riding or lane.

Role. A garden roller.

Round. The rung of a ladder.

Rowell, rowel. A circular piece of leather with a hole in the centre, inserted between the flesh and skin of a horse to cause discharge of humours.

Run, *v.* Of bark: to peel off easily from a tree.

Sainfoin, saintfoin, saintfoyn. A green crop. *See* Introduction, p. xxxviii.

Sale. A portion of woodland fenced off in preparation for the sale of the wood.

Sash. A sash window.

Scoe. Score.

Scrutore (= escritoire). Writing-desk or bureau.

Sea-coal. Coal brought round by sea from the pits.

Shalloon, shelloon. A closely woven woollen material.

Shire. Here, a piece of land called "the shire", "Rockinghamshire". *See* Index of Places.

Slade. A strip or area of greensward.

Sleeper. A beam supporting a wall, joist, or floor.

Slow. Slough.

Sole (horse's).   The concave plate of horn surrounding the frog of a horse's foot.
Spinney.   A small wood or plantation.
Spring.   Of woods: the young growth.
Springing spaniels.   Springer spaniels (spring: to cause a bird to rise from cover).
State, *v.*   Of accounts: to set down formally the debits and credits.
Stifled.   Of horses or hounds: with dislocation of the stifle bone or hip joint.
Strangles.   A disease of horses, characterized by an inflamed swelling in the throat.
Strike.   A dry measure, usually for corn, varying from a half to four bushels.
Surbase.   A border of moulding immediately above the base or lower panelling of a wainscoted room.
Surrogate.   A diocesan official dealing *inter alia* with wills and marriage licenses.
Swallow-hole, swallet-hole.   A hole in the ground into which a brook disappears to reappear farther on its course.
Sword, sward.   Turf.
Tear'd.   Smeared.
Tithe(s), tithe-hay.   A tenth part of annual produce due to the rector of a parish.
Town.   Commonly used at this period for a village as well as for larger places, e.g. Stamford and London.
Tray, trey.   Hurdle.
Undertaker.   Contractor.
Vert.   Growing wood and timber in a forest.
View, *v.*   To value.
Warrant.   A writ or order to enable an arrest to be made.
Warrantable.   Term applied to a stag of an age to be hunted.
Warren.   A piece of land appropriated to the breeding of rabbits.
Waste.   A piece of uncultivated land used for pasture.
Wheatcase.   From the context, probably a barn or granary.
While.   Till, until (Northamptonshire dialect, *c.* 1900). *See* Language, p. liv.
Wold.   A piece of open uncultivated land.

INDEXES

INDEX OF PLACES

All places are in Northamptonshire, including the Soke of Peterborough, unless otherwise stated. For names of woods, coppices and fields, see end of this Index. Figures in roman type refer to the letters.

A

Aldermaston, Albermaston (Berks.), 141.
Apethorpe, seat of the Earl of Westmorland, 83.
Ardsley, Ardesley (Yorks.), 162, 163.
Ashton Old (near Oundle), 76.

B

Badminton Park (Glos.), seat of the Duke of Beaufort, 47.
Bangroves Riding, 143.
Bath (Som.), 15, 24, 29, 36, 40, 45, 71n., 86, 88, 90, 91, 94, 102, 145, *p. 10, p. 55, pp. 133-4, p. 138, p. 142, p. 148.*
Bawtry, Baughtry (Yorks.), 162.
Beeston, Beeson, perhaps Beeston (Yorks.), near Lord Cardigan's estate, 106, 108.
Benefield, 3-5, 7, 14, 24, 76, 81, 130; *see also* Lawn, The.
Biggin (in Benefield), 3.
Biggleswade (Beds.), 145.
Blatherwick, 90.
Boughton, seat of the Duke of Montagu, 4, 27.
Brampton Ash, 69.
Brigstock, 4, 15, 30, 92, 118, 159.
Bulwick, 9, 16, 24, 28, 31, 85, 102, 130, 157.
Burghley, Burghleigh, Burleigh, seat of the Earl of Exeter, 139, 157.
Burley-on-the-Hill, seat of the Earl of Nottingham, 17.

C

Caldecote (Hunts.), 54n.
Cardigan House, *see* London.
Chatsworth (Derb.), seat of the Duke of Devonshire, 19, 35.
Church Langton, *see* Langton.
Cliff, Cliff Park, *see* Kings Cliffe.
Clifford Street, *see* London.
Collyweston, Colliweston, 43, 47, 77, 139, 140; *p. 142;* Collyweston Park, 76.
Corby, 26, 47, 94n., 155; copyholders (rights of common) at, 54, 55, 134n., 139, 145, 147; hundred rents, 27; labourers of, 98-100, 102, 121; manor, 90; manor court, 58, 86, 87, 90, 166; tenants at, 9, 14, 18, 58, 60, 76, 86, 94, 118, 130, 154; wood money from,

1, 2, 18, 121, 135; woods, management of, 79, 83, 135; woods, viewing, valuation and sale of, 10, 52, 67, 78, 80, 82, 100, 102, 131-133, 135.
Cotterstock, 24, 32, 34, 50, 52, 86, 87.
Cottesmore, Cotchmore (Rut.), Lord Cardigan's hunting box, 49, 65, 66, 68, 86, 94, 100, 101, 105, 127n., *p. 39, p. 130.*
Cottingham, 50.
Cranoe (Leic.), 9, 95, 125, 127, 139, 166.
Church Langton, *see* Langton.
Cransley, *p. 142.*
Croxton, probably Croxton Keryl (Leic.), near Belvoir, 85.

D

Daventry, *p. 157.*
Deene, *passim and see also* Field and Wood Names.
Deene church, 11, 12, 36, 121, 161; Deene Parsonage, Rectory, 12, 36, 121, 122, 123, 126, 128, 129.
Deene, Little, *p. 147;* hay barn at, 101, hounds kept at, 90, 96; reconstruction of, *see* Subject Index *under* Building, alterations and repairs (Little Deene).
Deenthorpe, 2-4, 10, 36, 167; labourers of, 57, 63, 92, 98, 99, 102; poor of, 128; sale; timber in, 94, 98, 106-110, 121, 132, 135; tenants in, 5, 7, 9, 14, 31, 76, 161.
Derby, Darby, 144.
Dingley, Dingly, 69.
Ditchley (Oxon.), seat of the Earl of Lichfield, 99, *p. 55.*
Duddington, 90n., 92.
Dunstanley's Gate (into Deepings, *see* Wood Names), 90.

E

Easton, *see* Great Easton.
Enstone (Oxon.), 99.
Essex, 44.

F

Field names, *see p. 167.*
Finedon, *p. 142.*
Fineshade, seat of the Kirkham family, 92, 148n.
Forest, The (Rockingham), 54, 76, 83.

INDEX OF PERSONS

The numbers in this Index referring to the Letters are printed in ordinary type; those referring to appendixes and to the linking passages between groups of letters are preceded by "p." and are in *italic* type.

A

Abbay, John, ? of Deene, 113.

Abbot, Will, groom or stable helper at Deene, 141.

Ailesbury, Thomas Bruce, 2nd Earl of (1656-1742), *p. 142.*

Albemarle, William Anne Keppel, 2nd Earl of (1702-1754), son-in-law of Lord Cardigan's sister, Anne, Duchess of Richmond, 1, 2.

Alcock, Mr., 102.

Alder, —, of London, 40.

Allam, Mr., prospective tenant in Rutland, 1-3.

Allen, Richard, stone merchant and ? quarry owner; pavior of Deene Church, 76.

Allicock, Benjamin, of Orlingbury and Loddington, friend of Lord Cardigan, 38, *p. 142.*

Arney, Mr., timber valuer, 150.

Ashley, Ashly, James, kennelman to Lord Cardigan at Cottesmore and later at Wothorpe, 7, 25, 64-66, 68, 87, 88, 90, 124, 127, 130, 148.

Ayers, Thomas, jr. and sen., *p. 152.*

Ayre, Ayer, John (also given as Thomas), of Little Oakley; Lord Cardigan's tenant in Stanion, 117-9.

B

Baily, Thomas, of Stanion, wood merchant and collector of wood money, 9, 78, 155.

Baker, Mr., apothecary or physician, 107, 111.

Barnes, Lawrence, ? miller, of Perio Mill, Southwick, 52.

—, Thomas, of Deenthorpe, labourer and fiddler, 57.

—, Will, stable helper, 8, 61.

Barret, Clem, of Bulwick, collector of wood money, 9, 16.

Basset, Christopher, of Slawston, farm tenant, 95, 114, 119.

—, John, Leics. farm tenant, 82.

Bates, William (and son), Leics. farm tenant, 9.

Batt, Thomas, servant of Lord Cardigan, 58.

Bell, Thos., valuer and coppice keeper in Northants.; also assisted in sales of underwood and timber in that county and Leics., 4, 21, 25, 52, 58, 60, 78, 80, 88, 103, 107, 111, 112, 130, 145, 147, 150.

—, Will, ? of Stanion, occasionally employed as carrier, 6, 118, 122, 153.

Bellamey, Adam, *p. 152.*

Bellamy, Mr., ? of Grantham, 65; Thomas, *p. 152.*

Berry, John, of Stonton Wyville, tenant, 95.

Billinges, Billinge, John, 5.

—, Robert, Lord Cardigan's servant with wages of £25 a year; died in 1751 as 'Keeper to the (4th) Earl of Cardigan', 12, 24, 49-52, 54, 82, 88, 131, 145.

Bishop, Henry, *p. 157.*

Black, David, of Deenthorpe, tenant, 154, 159, 161.

—, John, head groom, who managed the hunting stable at Stroxton, 66, 86, 111, 113, 127, 129, 131, 135, 148.

Blyth, Blith, Plythe, Mr., maltster and ? also corn merchant at Stamford, 20, 59, 83, 85, 86, 90, 94, 97, 99, 105.

—, "Young Blythe" (Mr. Blythe's son), 105.

Booth, Mr. John (1684-1783), principal land steward to John, Duke of Montagu from 1720; mapped several of the lordships on the Boughton estate; ancestor of the Booths of Glendon, 3, 4, 86.

Bosden, Thomas and John (jnr.), of Slawston, 60, 95.

—, John, of Wothorpe Lodge, 154.

Bradshaw, Sarah (d.1742), w. of William Bradshaw; housekeeper at Deene Hall, 4, 7, 38, 40, 59, 106-9, 111, 117, 124, 138.

—, William, of Deene, ? husband of above, 40.

—, Mr., of Rockingham, probably park-keeper at Rockingham to Lady Sondes, 49, 50, 55, 61, 107.

Brampton, Thomas, of Stanion, tenant, 153.

Braughton, John, of Deenthorpe, tenant, 4.

Briggs, Rebecca, 9.

Brightman, Robert, Leics. tenant, 9, 60, 109, 125, 160, 166.

Brooke, Brook, Wheeler, of Great Oakley, *p. 142.*

Brooks, Mr., of Duddington, 88.

—, "young Mr.", son of the above, 32-34, 147.

—, Mrs., 28, 38, 99.

Dexter, Christopher (d. May, 1727), of Gretton, carpenter and contractor for work at Little Deene; made canal in the park at Deene, 5-9, 16, 18, 22, 38, 41, 42, 55, 58, 64-66, 94, 132, 141, 142, *pp. 145-6.*

Dolben, Sir John, of Finedon, *p. 142.*

Doubleday, Mr., ? the Duke of Rutland's agent at Stroxton, 167.

Doughty, Mr., 105.

Duchess, *see* Montagu, Duchess of

Dunmore, William, tenant and collector of rents and wood money for Lord Cardigan, 9, 14, 16, 34, 42, 60, 69, 86, 88, 94, 109, 119, 125, 155.

Durham, Mark, tailor, 107.

E

Eastway, the Revd. Richard (b. *c.* 1696), curate of Deene (1726-?1731), 154, 160.

Eaton, Daniel, *passim.*

—, Elizabeth, Dan's half sister "that married the trooper", 9, 130.

—, Stephen, Dan's brother, 58, 88, 139.

—, Theophila, Dan's mother, 15, 65, 77, 117, 124, 130, 138, 139.

—, Theophila, Dan's sister, 18, 117, 135, 152.

Eberill, joiner, 124-6.

Eddins, Mr., ? tanner, 135.

Edwards, Francis, Esq., lord of the manor of Welham, Rutland, and a freeholder at Slawston, 71, 82, 94, 125, 127, 131, 142, 147, *pp. 148-9.*

Elliott, the Revd. John (*c.* 1673-1734), Vicar of Welham and Slawston and ? Rector of Langton, 16, 26, 71, 94, 116, 119, 125, 131, 132, 155, *p. 148.*

Ellis, Mr., tradesman of Grantham, 105.

Ellis, Mary, maid at Deene, 12.

Elmsall, Ralf, son of the following, 162.

—, Mr. William, of Thornhill, Yorks., steward of Lord Cardigan's Yorkshire estates from 1726 in succession to Christopher Hodgson, 162, 163, *p. 55, p. 130, p. 133, p. 136.*

Exeter, Brownlow Cecil, 8th Earl of (1701-1754); owner of Wothorpe, 2, 29, 39, 139.

—, Elizabeth, Countess of, widow of 6th Earl and dau. of Sir John Brownlow, 118n.

F

Falkener, Faulkener, Mr., stone mason, 45, (106), 107, 150.

Fane, *see* Vane.

Fardell, John, ? dog doctor, 76, 105.

Fell, Mr., father in law of John Lummis (*q.v.*), 26, 30, 37, 47, 80, 137.

Fesakerley, Mr., London lawyer, 166.

Fielder, —, owner of a colt, 141, 145.

Fletcher, —, 153.

Foden, Fodern, the Revd. William (d. 1749), Rector of Market Overton, Rutland (1725-40); Rector of Deene (1727-1749), 122, 126, 128, 129, 166.

Freeman, —, of Cranoe, tenant, 9, 14, 60.

French, John, 69.

Fryer, Mr., bone setter, (41), 138.

G

Gach, Mr. John, of Glapthorne, tenant and carrier, 61.

Gaines, Philip, of London, 58, 70.

Gainsborough, Baptist Noel, 4th Earl of (1708-1751), *p. 133, p. 136.*

Gibson, Mr., of London, 69, 70, 105.

Gilby, widow, *p. 151.*

Godfrey, —, of Northants., 9.

Godfrey, Richard, Leics. tenant, 139.

Goode, the Revd. Henry, Rector of Weldon (1684-1727); Rector of Deene (1690-1727), 6, 7, 12, 23, 32-4, 36, 38, 98, 99, 111, 114, 115, 119.

—, the Revd. William, son of the above; Rector of Weldon (1727-61), 23, 99, 122, 123, 141, 153, 166, 167.

—, Mrs., w. of the Revd. Henry, 126.

Gooding, John, 156.

Goodwin, John, 14, 34.

Gower of Stittenham, John Leveson Gower, 2nd Lord (1694-1754), later 1st Earl Gower; an old hunting friend of Lord Cardigan's, 12, 14, 31, 38-9, 60, 65, 97, 103, 105, 127, 131, 132, *p. 10, p. 133.*

Grange, "old", 111.

Granger, Leics. tenant, 163.

Grant, Mr., of Stamford, tradesman, 107.

Grey, Mr. and Mrs., of Benefield, 3.

Griffin of Braybrooke, Edward Griffin, 3rd Lord (1693-1742), lived at Dingley, 69.

Guelder, "old", ? Will, cottage tenant at Deene, 14, 31, 58, 59, 65.

Guilliam, Guiliam, Mr., of Cotterstock, son-in-law and steward to Mrs. Steward (*q.v.*), 32, 34.

H

Haim, Haimes, —, carrier, 37, 43, 107, 123.

Harrisson, Harrison, Elisha, of Deenthorpe, 8, 9.

—, Jenkin, of Deenthorpe, farmer tenant, 4, 90.

—, John, shepherd, 5, 7.

—, Nicholas, Deenthorpe tenant, 31, 161.

—, Richard, shepherd and molecatcher, 5, 7-10.

—, Walter, Deenthorpe labourer, 5, 8, 45.

—, Widow, 112, 159, 161.

INDEX OF SUBJECTS

Figures in roman type refer to the letters. Trades, professions and occupations are grouped together under Trades. A selection of topics from the Introduction is included.